Soviet and Nazi Posters

Soviet and Nazi Posters

Propaganda and Policies

Kees Boterbloem and Lisa Pine

BLOOMSBURY ACADEMIC
LONDON • NEW YORK • OXFORD • NEW DELHI • SYDNEY

BLOOMSBURY ACADEMIC
Bloomsbury Publishing Plc
50 Bedford Square, London, WC1B 3DP, UK
1385 Broadway, New York, NY 10018, USA
29 Earlsfort Terrace, Dublin 2, Ireland

BLOOMSBURY, BLOOMSBURY ACADEMIC and the Diana logo are trademarks of Bloomsbury Publishing Plc

First published in Great Britain 2025

Copyright © Kees Boterbloem and Lisa Pine, 2025

Kees Boterbloem and Lisa Pine have asserted their right under the Copyright, Designs and Patents Act, 1988, to be identified as Authors of this work.

For legal purposes the Acknowledgements on p. xiii constitute an extension of this copyright page.

Cover images: One People, One Nation, One Leader, a Nazi propaganda poster from 1938. Photo by Keystone-France/Gamma-Keystone via Getty Images. Motherland calls for you! Soviet wartime propaganda poster, 1941. Photo by Universal History Archive/Universal Images Group via Getty Images.

All rights reserved. No part of this publication may be reproduced or transmitted in any form or by any means, electronic or mechanical, including photocopying, recording, or any information storage or retrieval system, without prior permission in writing from the publishers.

Bloomsbury Publishing Plc does not have any control over, or responsibility for, any third-party websites referred to or in this book. All internet addresses given in this book were correct at the time of going to press. The author and publisher regret any inconvenience caused if addresses have changed or sites have ceased to exist, but can accept no responsibility for any such changes.

A catalogue record for this book is available from the British Library.

A catalog record for this book is available from the Library of Congress.

ISBN:	HB:	978-1-3503-9945-7
	PB:	978-1-3503-9944-0
	ePDF:	978-1-3503-9946-4
	eBook:	978-1-3503-9947-1

Typeset by Integra Software Services Pvt. Ltd.
Printed and bound in Great Britain

To find out more about our authors and books visit www.bloomsbury.com and sign up for our newsletters.

CONTENTS

List of Figures vi
Acknowledgements xiii
Abbreviations and Glossary xiv

Introduction 1

1 The Soviet Poster 11
2 *Plakate*: The Origins and Role of Posters in Nazi Propaganda 29
3 Soviet Posters in the 1920s and 1930s 47
4 Nazi Posters and the Construction of the *Volksgemeinschaft* ('National Community') 71
5 Nazi Posters, Foreign Policy, Militarism, and the Second World War 95
6 Soviet Posters in the Second World War and Beyond 117

Conclusion 135

Notes 143
Bibliography 164
Index 172

FIGURES

Colour Plates (Soviet)

1 Iraklii Moiseevich Toidze, *'Rodina-Mat' zovyot!'* ('The Motherland Calls', 1941). Source: https://ar.culture.ru/ru/subject/plakat-otchego-vy-ne-v-armii

2 El Lissitzky, 'Beat the Whites with the Red Wedge'. Source: public domain

3 Aleksandr Apsit, 'International'. Source: https://www.posterplakat.com/the-collection/posters/international-arise-ones-who-are-branded-by-the-curse-a-whole-pp-893?src=categories/civil-war

4 'The Growth of Soviet Agriculture after a Decade'. Source: https://www.posterplakat.com/the-collection/posters/the-growth-of-agriculture-in-the-ussr-over-ten-years-pp-1129?src=eras/post-civil-war

5 'In Answer to the Insolent International Popism [A Pope Is a Russian-Orthodox Priest] and Bourgeoisie We Strengthen the Military Preparedness of the USSR and the Military Power of the Red Army'. Source: https://www.posterplakat.com/the-collection/posters/as-an-answer-to-international-papists-and-bourgeoisie-we-will-s-pp-337?src=eras/reconstruction

6 'Greetings to the Opening of the Global Gigant Dneprostroi (DGES [the Dnepropetrovsk Hydro-Electric Station]), Long Live the Shockworkers of the Building of Socialism'. Source: https://www.posterplakat.com/the-collection/posters/greetings-to-the-worlds-largest-dnieprostroi-hydroelectric-st-pp-267?src=eras/reconstruction

7 'Long Live the Brotherly Union and Great Friendship of the USSR Peoples!'. Source: https://www.posterplakat.com/the-collection/posters/long-live-the-brotherly-union-and-great-friendship-of-the-people-pp-891?src=eras/reconstruction

8 'The Endless Steppe Woke Up from Its Dream, and Happiness Is Brought to Us by the Spring of Communism!'. Source: https://www.posterplakat.com/the-collection/posters/the-endless-steppe-has-awakened-from-sleep-spring-brings-to-us-pp-1149?src=eras/post-world-war-2

9 'Kill Him! He Killed Your Loved Ones, Burned Your House Down, Destroyed Your Workplace!'. Source: https://www.posterplakat.com/the-collection/posters/kill-him-he-killed-those-near-to-you-set-fire-to-your-house-an-pp-365?src=eras/world-war-2

10 'What Does a Pig Need Culture and Science For? Its Mind Is After All Tiny: *Mein Kampf* Is the Limit for a Pig Snout, and Its Ideal [Is] the Corporal's Boot!'. Source: https://www.posterplakat.com/the-collection/posters/what-is-a-pig-going-to-do-with-culture-and-science-his-wide-ra-pp-286?src=eras/world-war-2

11 'The Great Patriotic War'. Source: https://www.posterplakat.com/the-collection/posters/great-patriotic-war-poster-newspaper-no-11- proletarians-of-all-pp-941?src=eras/world-war-2

12 'Study the Great Path of the Party of Lenin-Stalin!'. Source: https://www.posterplakat.com/the-collection/posters/learn-the-great-path-of-the-party-of-lenin-and-stalin-pp-875?src=eras/post-world-war-2

Colour Plates (Nazi)

13 Nazi Election Poster 1932 'Our Last Hope: Hitler'. Source: Getty Images #150756466

14 Nazi Election Poster 1932 'National Socialists 1'. Source: Getty Images #113492827

15 'Hitler Is Building Up. Help Out. Buy German Goods'. Source: Getty Images #84358222

16 'Hitler Youth: Germany's Future'. Source: Getty Images #566466271

17 '*Bund Deutscher Mädel in der Hitler Jugend*' ('League of German Girls in the Hitler Youth'). Source: Wikicommons public domain 1214×1702 627900-000013.jpg

18 '*Kraft durch Freude*' Travel Poster. Source: Getty Images #152244789

19 Nazi Family Poster. Source: Getty Images #629452649

20 '*Der ewige Jude*' ('The Eternal Jew'). Source: Getty Images #1354474820

21 Annexation of Austria Poster 1938. Source: Getty Images #587489198

22 *Ein Kampf, Ein Sieg!* ('One Fight, One Victory!'). Source: Getty Images #84358199

23 *Sieg oder Bolschewismus* ('Victory or Bolshevism'). Source: Alamy ID 2G0PBHF

24 *Adolf Hitler ist der Sieg!* ('Adolf Hitler Is Victory!'). Source: Getty Images #84358178

Figures

1.1 'Soviet Radio Earnestly Serves the Cause of Peace!'. Source: https://www.posterplakat.com/the-collection/posters/pp-109   18

1.2 'On the Happy Day of the Liberation from the Yoke of the German Marauders, the Soviet People's First Words of Limitless Gratitude and Love Are for Our Friend and Father Comrade STALIN, the Organizer of Our Fight for Freedom and Independence of Our Motherland'. Source: https://www.posterplakat.com/the-collection/posters/pp-371   26

2.1 Early Nazi Poster 27 February 1925. Source: Getty Images #3135726   37

2.2 Hitler Poster. Source: Wikicommons   41

2.3 Nazi Election Posters on Display 1932. Source: Getty Images #601069774   42

2.4 Posters on Display for Women to Vote Nazi. Source: Getty Images #517431642   44

3.1 'Children Are the Guarantee of the Future and the Joy of the Present!'. Source: https://www.posterplakat.com/the-collection/posters/glory-to-the-mother-heroine-pp-314?src=categories/women 51

3.2 'Female Proletarians toward New Triumphs! For Technology, Culture, for a New Existence!'. Source: https://www.posterplakat.com/the-collection/posters/female-proletarian-to-new-victories-for-technology-culture-f-pp-1116?src=categories/women 52

3.3 'Having All Rights, Soviet Women Vote for a Socialist Motherland, for a Happy Life!'. Source: https://www.posterplakat.com/the-collection/posters/a-soviet-woman-with-full-rights-is-voting-for-a-socialistic-moth-pp-457?src=categories/women 54

3.4 'So That You Know Whose Labour We Honour and Who We Will Sweep Away with a Metal Broom'. Source: https://www.posterplakat.com/the-collection/posters/just-so-you-know-we-will-honor-one-person-by-our-labor-and-anot-pp-354?src=eras/reconstruction 58

3.5 'Long Live the Great, Invincible Banner of Marx, Engels, Lenin and Stalin! Long Live Leninism!'. Source: https://www.posterplakat.com/the-collection/posters/long-live-the-great-unconquerable-flag-of-marx-engels-lenin-pp-224?src=eras/world-war-2 64

4.1 'Youth Serves the Führer'. Source: Getty Images #113491234 78

4.2 *Kraft durch Freude* ('Strength through Joy') Travel Poster. Source: Getty Images #1449445320 83

4.3 Propaganda Poster for the *KdF* Car. Source: Getty Images #959165642 84

4.4 Poster for Radio Listening 'All of Germany Listens to the Leader with the People's Receiver'. Source: Alamy ID KMDM26   86

5.1 *'Populations abandonnées, faites confiance au soldat allemand!'* ('Abandoned Populations, Have Confidence in German Soldiers!'). Source: Wikicommons public domain: Populations abandonnées, faites confiance AU SOLDAT ALLEMAND!.jpg   104

5.2 *SS* recruitment poster in the Netherlands: *'Nederlanders'*. Source: Alamy ID H11K6R   105

5.3 *'Volkssturm'*. Source: Alamy ID GAREC1   110

5.4 *'Der ist Schuld am Kriege!'* ('He is Responsible for the War!'). Source: Alamy ID M23A2J   113

6.1 'It Is Our Sacred Obligation to Extend a Helping Hand to the Fraternal Peoples of Western Ukraine and Western Belarus'. Source: https://www.posterplakat.com/the-collection/posters/give-a-helping-hand-to-our-ukrainian-and-belorussian-brother-nat-pp-003?src=eras/world-war-2   118

6.2 'Nowhere Can the Monster Hide! It Will Receive Its Just Desserts!'. Source: https://www.posterplakat.com/the-collection/posters/there-will-be-no-place-that-a-murderer-and-torturer-can-hide-pp-285?src=eras/world-war-2   122

6.3 'Our Forces Are Countless!'. Source: https://www.posterplakat.com/the-collection/posters/our-forces-are-uncountable-pp-347?src=eras/world-war-2   123

6.4 Andrei Zhdanov and Besieged Leningrad. Source: https://www.posterplakat.com/the-collection/posters/in-leningrad-there-is-no-gap-between-the-front-line-and-the-bac-pp-368?src=eras/world-war-2   125

6.5 'Glory to the Mother Heroine'. Source: https://www.posterplakat.com/the-collection/posters/glory-to-the-mother-heroine-pp-314?src=categories/women 131

6.6 'The New Life'. Source: https://www.posterplakat.com/the-collection/posters/honor-roll-for-the-collective-farm-new-life-we-will-greet-pp-1064?src=categories/women 133

ACKNOWLEDGEMENTS

We would like to thank our editor, Rhodri Mogford, for his enthusiasm for this project and for all his help throughout the publishing process. We are also grateful to the anonymous reviewers of our initial proposal and those who scrutinized the draft manuscript. We are thankful to all who have worked at Bloomsbury Academic on the production of this book. We would like to thank Getty Images, Alamy, and Poster Plakat for permission to reproduce the images that are so important to a book on this subject. Kees would like to express his gratitude to Lisa for approaching him with the idea for this book and for facilitating our utterly smooth collaboration. Additionally, he is thankful to Donald Wright, Paul Robinson, Rudolf Dekker, Erik van Ree, Marc Jansen, the late David Schimmelpenninck van der Oye, Serhy Yekelchyk, Julie Stevens, Klaas-Jan Boterbloem, Nicole van Weringh, Carola Tischler, Murat Tuncali, Martha Gould, Bart van Drunen Littel, Rubin Ootes, Martin Stegeman, Arnoud Jonkhoff, Piet van Steenis, Michiel van Nieuwland, and, most emphatically, to Duncan Mooney and Saskia Mooney (as well as Tundra and Matcha!). Several among them were my mentors and academic 'coaches' and have made me a better scholar. Others have made me (I hope) into a better human being, and some did both (wittingly or not), recently, or much longer ago. Still others have been life-long friends, and have been there when I needed them, exceptionally tolerant of my foibles. Sometimes their mere presence sufficed to inspire me, while at other times profound conversations with them have influenced my writing in this book. Similarly, Lisa would like to express her gratitude to her family, especially her husband Andy Fields and her daughters Gaby Fields and Sasha Fields, who have offered her similar sustenance and support over the years, as well as friends and colleagues for their good advice and helpful conversations. She is grateful to Michael Fields for his careful reading of the manuscript. She would like to thank Kees for his quick agreement to write this book together and for being an exemplary co-author. This book is on a subject we both think is interesting and important and we hope that our readers will concur, and that students will find that it helps them to understand the nature of these regimes and their propaganda.

ABBREVIATIONS AND GLOSSARY

Agit-Plakat	Movement of Soviet artists to innovate Soviet poster-making (after Stalin's death)
agitprop	Agitation and propaganda, necessary according to the Soviet Communists to persuade the population of Communism's truth
AKhRR	*Assotsiatsiia Khudozhnikov Revoliutsionnoi Rossii*: Association of Artists of Revolutionary Russia
Anschluß	Annexation by Nazi Germany of Austria, 13 March 1938
apparatchik	Employee of the Soviet state's or Communist Party's bureaucracy
Art Nouveau	An artistic and architectural movement especially emphasizing round, curved and winding shapes (predominantly French, 1890s–1910s)
l'art pour l'art	'Art for art's sake': A movement of artists who argued that art should exist without concession to public taste
Ballets Russes	A Russian dance ensemble founded in the 1900s by Sergei Diaghilev that introduced new forms of dance, music, and scenery in its performances
BDM	*Bund deutscher Mädel*: League of German Girls
Blut und Boden	'Blood and Soil'
Bolsheviks	Name for followers of Lenin in the Russian Social-Democratic Workers' Party; in 1918

	they adopted the name Communists, but Bolsheviks remained in use as well.
Central Committee	Leading body of the Soviet Communist Party
Collective farm	A farm on which most work is conducted collectively, with most of its production being delivered to the government. The 'means of production' (tools, animals, public buildings such as warehouses) are owned collectively
Committee of Arts Affairs	*Komitet po delam isskustv pri SNK SSSR*: Soviet government committee overseeing the arts (1936–46)
Constructivism	Artists' movement emphasizing the importance of abstract and unadorned architectural shapes in art and architecture (1910s–20s)
Cubism	Artistic movement focused on rendering abstract geometric shapes from different viewpoints in its art (1910s–20s)
Dadaism	European artistic movement emphasizing life's absurdity in its art (1910s)
DAF	*Deutsche Arbeitsfront*: German Labour Front
dekulakization	(*razkulachivanie*): Campaign to eliminate the 'kulaks' from the villages in the Soviet Union from late 1929 to 1933; the alleged kulaks were deported to remote areas and executed if resisting. Their property was handed over to the collective farms organized for (or by) their fellow villagers
Eintopf	One-pot dish
ersatz	Substitute product, originally especially meaning a victual or beverage, distributed in wartime scarcity in Germany in both world wars (as in 'coffee' made from beech nuts)
Expressionism	Primarily German artistic movement in which artist expressed raw emotion and trauma, such as that provoked in the First World War's trenches (1910s–20s)
Five Year Plans	Elaborate plans for the fast-paced economic development of the Soviet Union under strict

	state guidance (First supposedly completed early – 1928–32; Second 1933–7; Third ended by outbreak of war – 1938–41; Fourth 1946–50, etc.)
Formalism	'Bourgeois-type' of artistic deviation condemned in 1930s and 1940s Soviet Union
Freikorps	Paramilitary German units renting out their services after the First World War
Friendship of the Peoples	(*Druzhba Narodov*): Official ideal of ethnic equality among all Soviet nations
Führer	Leader
Futurism	Artistic movement (originally Italian) that tried to render the era of modern, mechanized technology in its art (1900s–10s)
Gau	Region (main territorial division of the NSDAP)
Gauleiter	Regional leader
Gestapo	*Geheime Staatspolizei*: secret state police (in Nazi Germany)
Glavlit	*Glavnoe upravlenie po okhrane gosudarstvennykh tain v pechati pri SNK SSSR*: Main administration for the protection of State Secrets in Print, the main organization of Soviet censorship
Gleichschaltung	'Coordination', the process by which all of German civil society was brought under Nazi control (1933–4)
Golden Age	Period of great artistic flourishing in Russian art and literature (1830s–60s)
gorkom	Contraction of *gorodskii komitet*, Communist Party city committee
GPU	*Gosudarstvennoe Politicheskoe Upravlenie*: State Political Administration, name for Soviet secret police
Great Patriotic War	Soviet name for the Second World War
Great Terror	Time of greatest political reckoning in the Soviet Union, from the spring of 1937 to the late autumn of 1938. More than 690,000

	people executed as political enemies, with and additional million estimated to have been arrested in the USSR and receiving camp or jail sentences
Great Turn	The radical attempt to transform the Soviet Union into a modern industrialized state at breath-taking speed, beginning in earnest in 1929 and involving collectivization, dekulakization, urbanization, and the rapid construction and bringing-into-operation of industrial plant on the basis of Five Year Plans
GULag	*Glavnoe upravlenie lagerei*: State administration of concentration camps (of USSR)
Herrenvolk	'Master race'
HJ	*Hitler Jugend*: Hitler Youth
Holodomor	Ukrainian famine of 1932–3
ideinost'	'Replete with ideas', part of socialist realism
Impressionism	European artistic movement which, instead of exact realist or figurative and still painting (or photographs), produced paintings depicting movement and perception (1870s–80s)
IZOGIZ	*Izdatel'stvo izobrazitel'nogo isskustva*: State Publishing House of (Fine) Art
Jugendstil	Similar to *Art Nouveau*, a German artistic and architectural movement especially emphasizing round, curved, and winding shapes (1890s–1910s)
KdF	*Kraft durch Freude*: Strength through Joy
kinderreich	'Rich in children'
kolkhoz	See collective farm
kolkhoznik (m.)/ *kolkhoznitsa* (f.)	Collective farmers
KPD	German Communist Party
kraikom	Party committee of a large region (*krai*)
kulak	Pejorative term for rich peasant, especially as distinguished by Soviet criteria

KWHW	*Kriegswinterhilfswerk*: War Winter Relief Agency
Lebensraum	'Living space'
LEF	*Levyi front isskustv*: Left Front of the Arts, group of ultraleft pro-Communist artists (1920s)
Lozung	Slogan on a Soviet poster or banner (from the German *Losung*), or shouted during demonstrations
lubki	Russian woodprints
Luftwaffe	Air force
Machtübernahme	Nazi 'seizure of power' in Germany in January 1933
Mensheviks	Moderate wing of the Russian Social-Democratic Workers' Party
MVD	Ministerstvo *Vnutrennykh Del*: Ministry of Internal Affairs (Soviet), secret police's name from March 1946 onwards
Molotov-Ribbentrop Pact	Nazi Soviet pact concluded in August 1939, in which both sides declared not to wage war against each other for ten years. Secretly, they detailed a partitioning of the countries of East Central Europe and the eastern Baltic littoral between each other
montage	Film-editing, sequencing separately made filmshots
Moscow show trials	Widely publicized trials against alleged plotters (all former Communist leaders) trying to destroy the Soviet Union, staged in August–September 1936, January 1937, and March 1938 in Moscow
MOSSKh	*Moskovskii soiuz sovetskikh khudozhnikov*: Moscow Union of Soviet Artists
narodnoe opol'chenie	Soviet Second World War Home Guard
narodnost'	'People's spirit': Part of socialist realism

New Economic Policy (NEP)	Economic policy introduced at Lenin's urging by the Soviet Communist Party's Tenth Congress in March 1921. It allowed for a limited return to market exchanges and private profit (including through small businesses), and abolished grain requisitioning in the countryside, allowing peasants to sell their grain for market prices
NKVD	*Narodnyi Komissariat Vnutrennykh Del*: People's Commissariat of Internal Affairs (Soviet), secret police
NSDAP	German National Socialist Workers' Party (Nazi Party)
Newspeak	Language of dictatorial regimes according to George Orwell in *Nineteen Eighty-Four*
obkom	Contraction of *oblastnyi komitet*, Party committee of a province (*oblast'*)
OGPU	*Ob'edinennoe Gosudarstvennoe Politicheskoe Upravlenie*: United State Political Administration, name for Soviet secret police
ORRP	*Ob'edineniia rabotnikov revoliutsionnogo plakata*: United Cooperative of Workers of the Revolutionary Poster
partiinost'	'Party spirit': Part of socialist realism
People's Commissar	Name for minister of the Soviet government (1917–46)
plakatist	Russian term for poster-maker
Pointillism	Style of painting using points or dots to create flowing or moving images, inspired by Impressionism (1880s–90s)
proletariat	In Marxism, the industrial working class
raikom	District (*raion*) party committee
Red Army	Soviet armed forces
Reds	Communists (the socialist left in Europe had donned Red as its favourite colour)

Reich	Short for *Das dritte Reich* or The Third Reich, Hitler's empire, the third German empire, according to Nazi ideology following the Holy Roman Empire (800–1806) and the Wilhelminian Empire (1871–1918)
Reichstag	Parliament
Rightists	Alleged right-wing Communists opposing Stalin
Rosta	*Rossiiskoe Telegrafnoe Agentstvo*: Soviet-Russian Press Agency (1918–35)
Russian Soviet Federative Socialist Republic (RSFSR)	Official name of the Russian Republic as part of the USSR
SA	*Sturmabteilungen*: stormtroopers
Schönheit der Arbeit	Beauty of Labour
Silver Age	Period of great artistic flourishing in Russian art and literature (late nineteenth century–1917)
socialist realism	Art made according to the true understanding of communist ideology, full of inspiration, and infused with the spirit of the people and the Communist Party
soviets (sovety)	Council of workers', soldiers', peasants' or sailors' deputies, the initially grassroots-elected bodies in whose name the Bolsheviks took power in 1917 a non-capitalized term when used in this sense)
SPD	German Socialist Party
SR	Socialist-Revolutionary Party: Non-Marxist Socialist Party, rival of Bolsheviks in 1917 revolution
SS	*Schutzstaffeln*: Protection Squads
Sturm und Drang	'Storm and Stress': Period of producing art subject to highly volatile moods (originally associated with J. W. Goethe and F. Schiller)
Suprematism	Primarily Russian artistic movement emphasizing geometric forms in art (1910s)

TASS	*Telegrafnoe Agentstvo Sovetskogo Soiuza*: Soviet Press Agency (1925–91)
Typage	Typecasting
Untermenschen	'Subhumans': Racial category used by Nazis for those who were to be ruled as slaves by the 'Master Race' (*Herrenvolk*), particularly used for Slavic peoples
USSR	Union of Socialist Soviet Republics, formal name of Soviet Union (1922–91)
VKhUTEIN	*Vysshii (gosudartsvennyi) khudozhestvenno-tekhnicheskii Institut*: Higher (State) Artistic-Technological Institute (1926–30)
VKhUTEMAS	*Vysshie khudozhestvenno-tekhnicheskie masterskie*: Higher Artistic-Technological Workshops (1920–6)
Volk	Nation
Volksempfänger	'People's receiver' radio set
Volksgemeinschaft	'National community'
Volksgenossen	'National comrades'
Volkssturm	'People's storm'
Volkswagen	'People's car'
Waffen-SS	Military SS
Wanderers	*peredvizhniki*: Russian artistic movement in painting (from 1870s onwards)
Wehrmacht	Armed forces
Weltanschauung	Worldview
Whites	Opponents of the Communists and Red Army in the Russian Civil War
WHW	*Winterhilfswerk*: Winter Relief Agency
Zinovievites	(Alleged) followers of (former) Leningrad Party boss Grigorii Zinoviev

Introduction

Besides the iconic poster of the Cuban Communist Che Guevara, perhaps the most famous twentieth-century poster-image, is the Second World War poster by the Soviet artist Iraklii Toidze (1902–85) on which Mother Russia (literally, the Motherland) calls the viewer to join the struggle against the Hitlerite invaders (see Colour Plate 1). The red-draped 'mother' holds up a declaration of loyalty and promise of good behaviour, a pledge introduced in 1939 for soldiers to make when entering Soviet armed services. Despite its fame, the poster is not a truly original work and it is possible that its fame has been enhanced since its issue, because it is part of a connected series of images that originated with that of British Lord Horatio Kitchener's First World War call to join the ranks (of 1914) and was followed by a poster of Uncle Sam imploring men in the United States to volunteer in 1917. In the Soviet case, Dmitrii Moor (1883–1946)'s 1920 'Did You Sign up as a Volunteer?', a version of the Kitchener/Uncle Sam poster, called Soviet citizens to join the Red Army's ranks against the Poles. Moor's version may have been copied from the Soviets' 'White' opponents in the Russian Civil War (1918–20), who issued a poster 'Why Are You Not in the Army?' ('*Otchego vy ne v armii?*') on behalf of their commander Anton Denikin in 1919. Russians Red and White, one surmises, knew the earlier UK and US versions (and Toidze may have known those originals as well).

Be that as it may, 'The Motherland Calls' conveys perhaps more than any other poster the medium's power. Few can resist its spell, with its protagonist looking the viewer straight in the eye with a commanding, indeed imperious, stare, compelling him (as the target audience was primarily Soviet men) to action. How a poster such as this became such a powerful medium and especially how posters were used by the two most horrific dictatorships, Nazi Germany and the Soviet Union, in their mutual efforts both to create support for their rule and to destroy each other between 1941 and 1945 are the focus of the following pages. We investigate the use of the poster as a crucial means of political propaganda in the middle of the twentieth century. Posters offer us a strong visual point of entry into the regimes.

What do posters yield to the historian? What do they tell us about the regimes and their intentions? The postwar development of communications, media, and advertising, and the rapid expansion of both the media and social media in the twenty-first century as exemplified by someone like Donald J. Trump's use of Twitter, make it harder to ponder the significance of what look like quite old-fashioned means of communication. Indeed, today, we might conceptualize memes, images, or texts (or combinations of the two) copied and spread rapidly on the internet and on social media as the digital equivalent of posters, which no longer predominate our environment in the way they did in the mid-twentieth century. But Stalin's and Hitler's use of posters, as a medium of propaganda and of disseminating their ideologies in a clear visual way that everyone in the streets could easily see, was advanced at the time and far-reaching. Posters were very powerful in terms of the impact on their populations. The use of posters points to how the dictatorships could influence people outside their homes and in public places to support the regimes and their policies. We use specific posters as a point of entry to discuss key policies associated with the regimes. Sometimes very bold and graphic, an analysis of these pictorial sources offers us significant insights into the nature of these governments and the way in which they addressed their populations. Neither the poster nor propaganda more broadly was invented by these regimes, but they employed them in novel, distinctive, and characteristic ways. They utilized posters as part of larger, multi-faceted propaganda arsenals with which to indoctrinate and ideologically sway their populations.

While it is, to be sure, important to examine these posters in their own time and places, it is worth contextualizing this subject with a brief summary of the development of posters, especially in modern history, although, of course, the putting up of hand-drawn public notices dated back to ancient times. An early form of printed advertising originated in the mid-fifteenth century, in the time of William Caxton, who introduced the printing press to Britain. By the nineteenth century, text posters from woodblocks became common; the mid-nineteenth century saw the advent of the colour picture poster, as printing techniques became more advanced. The first colour lithograph posters were produced by the French poster artist Jules Chéret in 1866. Over the next decades, posters became an important aspect of visual culture and eventually of mass culture, as artists experimented further with poster design, incorporating both words and images. They came to form a key part of mass communication during the twentieth century. A new style of propaganda poster originated during the First World War and, subsequently in the 1920s, the Soviet Constructivists revolutionized the poster using photomontage and bold styles. Fascist governments, for example, in Italy and Spain – as well as the Nazi administration in Germany – also produced arresting posters as propaganda. By the 1930s and 1940s (and beyond), posters became a medium of propaganda, utilized by all sorts of governments, not just totalitarian ones, for political communication.

A brief overview of the macro-historical development of poster propaganda from the late-nineteenth century to the mid-twentieth century enables us to see how that of the Soviet and Nazi regimes fitted into this trend. Toby Clark explains that the history of modern propaganda is 'intimately linked with the rise of mass culture' and 'the mass-production of images and messages by industrial techniques'.[1] During both the First World War and the Second World War, the governments of all belligerent nations regarded popular opinion and public morale as issues of great national significance and they addressed their populations through mass-communications media. Modern political propaganda had arrived.[2] Jowett and O'Donnell maintain: 'Propaganda is a form of communication that attempts to achieve a response that furthers the desired intent of the propagandist. Persuasion is interactive and attempts to satisfy the needs of both persuader and persuadee.'[3] Jowett and O'Donnell note that propaganda is monological manipulation, while persuasion is more dialogical, defining propaganda as 'the deliberate, systematic attempt to shape perceptions, manipulate cognitions, and direct behaviour to achieve a response that furthers the desired intent of the propagandist'.[4] They add: 'Persuasion is a reciprocal process in which both parties are dependent on one another. It is a situation of interactive or transactive dependency.'[5] This could be exemplified just as much by a politician seeking votes as by an advertiser promoting a product. For advertising can be defined as 'a series of appeals, symbols, and statements deliberately designed to influence the receiver of the message toward the point of view of the communicator'.[6]

During the course of the late nineteenth and early twentieth centuries, new forms of communication created a mass audience and the emergence of mass society. Before the First World War, the state had played 'a relatively small part in regulating everyday life and made few demands on private individuals'.[7] But from 1914 onwards, mobilizational art on behalf of the state was seen to have a big impact. 'By 1914, advertising had developed into a highly sophisticated form of persuasion.'[8] Alfred Leete's 1914 First World War recruitment poster ('Your Country Needs You') was extremely powerful and made Lord Kitchener instantly recognizable. The intense stare directed straight at the viewer and the pointed index finger are indicative of a 'sudden intensification of the bond between the individual and the state'.[9] In the US Army recruitment poster of 1917, designed by James Montgomery Flagg, Uncle Sam similarly stares out directly at the viewer and points his forefinger, with the words 'I Want You for the US Army' leaving American citizens in no doubt about their duties. The belligerent nations used the mass media that had developed by that point to enable the dissemination of propaganda more expansively than ever before. In order to encourage their populaces to adapt to the necessities of war graphic artists often used 'conventional visual codes already established in mass culture', with recruitment posters, for example, designed to resemble 'advertisements or movie posters'.[10] And, as we mentioned above, they copied successful templates from each other.

In a sort of inversion of the Toidze poster's genealogy, during the Second World War, propaganda techniques associated with autocratic regimes were 'readily borrowed by propagandists in the democratic nations'.[11] 'Insistence on the total dedication and sacrifice of individuals to the national cause temporarily introduced to democratic politics a manner of rhetoric that resembled that of the mass-movement ideologies of communism and fascism'.[12] Furthermore, 'propaganda agencies drew on the expertise of advertising, which in turn had advanced between the wars by applying theories from behavioural psychology and the social sciences'.[13] British wartime posters such as 'Women of Britain Come into the Factories' called women to work. British homefront posters such as 'Dig for Victory' and 'Keep Mum She's Not So Dumb! Careless Talk Costs Lives' directed people to behave in ways which assisted the war effort, as did their American counterparts such as 'Loose Lips [Might] Sink Ships'. After America entered the war, the Office of War Information, established in June 1942, 'distributed its major posters in runs of 1.5 million, and posted messages in subways, streetcars and buses each month'.[14] One crucial distinction between the Nazi and Soviet regimes on the one hand and the democratic nations on the other was that the latter referred to their government propaganda in euphemistic terms, such as 'public information'.[15] Democratic nations avoided the term 'propaganda' because it was not considered to be compatible with their values and it became increasingly associated with totalitarian regimes that openly embraced it as a concept and as a tool.

Nazi and Soviet poster art differed in its aims and intentions from other types of state-sponsored art such as the Works Progress Administration (WPA) Federal Art Project that was part of the New Deal. This was a project directed by Holger Cahill to employ artists during the Great Depression era in the United States, which included graphic art and posters. The Federal Art Project (1935–43) was a relief measure, primarily designed to commission jobless artists to be able to produce and exhibit artistic works.[16] An example of non-state use of posters as a mass medium can be seen in campaigns by the US National Association of Manufacturers (NAM). The NAM utilized large-scale visual propaganda.[17] In particular, 45,000 billboards, designed by the Campbell-Ewald Company, a leading national advertising agency, propagated their free enterprise message during the 1930s and 1940s. It maintained that repeated exposure to emotion-laden messaging could influence the disposition and behaviour of people who saw them. These examples, although also clearly trying to influence and persuade people, were distinctive from those of the Nazi and Soviet regimes because they were produced in a democratic setting, rather than in a totalitarian system. Both the government and private enterprise availed themselves of poster art in the liberal democracies. Whereas business advertising in Nazi Germany might still produce posters that were not vetted by the regime, in the Soviet Union all poster-making was placed under government control. Clark rightly notes that ideologically, the two regimes differed in their views on 'nature, technology, work, warfare, history, and human purpose'.[18] These distinctions were reflected in their poster art. Both the Soviet and Nazi regimes used an entire arsenal of propaganda weaponry, designed not only to influence their populations, but also to indoctrinate them with their ideologies in a didactic manner. As we will see in the following pages, visual propaganda in the form of posters was highly important to both of them.

As the first scholar to investigate in-depth Soviet posters, Stephen White wrote, 'The early Soviet years were ... very rich in their invention or popularisation of symbols and imagery which have had a significant influence upon the graphic art of other countries as well as upon Soviet political art.'[19] Subsequent to the October 1917 coup in Russia, the poster became a prime medium of art and politics in the twentieth century that could be quickly diffused among mass audiences. Perhaps its last upsurge of popularity in the West occurred in the 1960s and 1970s (at least judging from our own recollection), where it was largely depoliticized (despite the popularity of the Che Guevara image), while in the Soviet Union (or in other Communist states such as China or Cuba) the massive production and widespread distribution of political posters hardly ever ceased until 1991, even if its appeal may have withered there, too.[20] Because of its Soviet roots (or the impact of Soviet poster-making), it is appropriate to investigate first how the poster acquired such significance there before we turn to the Nazi use of the poster as a mass medium.

A few words are in order about the manner of selecting the posters for the Soviet side. One encounters an embarrassment of riches, while many posters are readily available in the public domain. Already in 1932, at the first – and only one before 1953 – All-(Soviet) Union poster exhibition in Moscow, no fewer than 206 artists showed their work displaying a total of 410 posters.[21] Subsequently, poster production further increased in terms of print-runs and images, in part because a growing number were produced in the languages of non-Russian Soviet ethnicities. A few examples that seem representative of that latter category are included in our book, but most Soviet posters reproduced here display text in the Russian language. That usually means that their intended audience was Soviet Russians, although it needs to be kept in mind that eventually in the Soviet Union all non-Russians were taught at least a certain amount of Russian as a second language.

While we suggest that an almost unlimited supply of posters from this era can still be found today, in the Soviet case it is evident that the more readily available posters are creations of a not particularly large group of leading lights. Already at the time of their issue widely distributed, such posters stand out in their quality and appeal to this day. In part for that qualitative reason, a number of such posters have been selected. In addition, their makers often were pioneers or trailblazers. But other posters have been chosen for different reasons: sometimes because they illustrate the medium's evolution, sometimes because they underline the appearance of a certain theme or reflect a key Soviet policy.

We have nonetheless left out even some of the most famous Soviet posters. This book is not intended as a gallery of Soviet or Nazi masterpieces in poster art. Indeed, in our analysis of the poster phenomenon we have attempted to pinpoint the political ambiguity of this form of art. In one sense, our purpose is to show how sometimes aesthetically astonishingly beautiful art was wielded towards abject goals such as the humiliation of other human beings, going all the way towards their physical annihilation. Ultimately, perhaps some readers will not be satisfied with the omission of some posters and feel that they have been unjustly left out. We nonetheless suggest that we present here a representative overview of Soviet and Nazi poster art, pertinent to our written analysis of its use as a medium of political propaganda.

Historiographical Survey

There are some older books that deal with comparisons of Nazism and Stalinism, such as Alan Bullock's *Hitler and Stalin: Parallel Lives*, the comparative approach of which has been emulated by Robert Gellately, *Lenin, Stalin, and Hitler*; Richard Overy, *The Dictators: Hitler's Germany, Stalin's Russia*; and Laurence Rees, *Hitler and Stalin*.[22] Comparative approaches as well are presented in the volumes edited by Rousso and by Kershaw and Lewin.[23] An important comparative case study about the concrete impact of both regimes on their subjects is Timothy Snyder's *Bloodlands*.[24] Of interest in this regard, too, is Jan T. Gross, *Revolution from Abroad*.[25] Additionally, there are some older titles on totalitarianism such as the books by Hannah Arendt or Zbigniew Brzezinski and Carl Friedrich, which are soberly assessed by Abbott Gleason.[26]

Totalitarianism is a term, though, that we only use sparingly because it obfuscates more than it illuminates. We suggest that it has some merit when defining it as the effort to achieve total control over people's lives and even minds, a goal impossible to accomplish with the technological means available before 1950 (or even before 2000). While the acquisition of totalitarian control over their populations by the Nazi or Soviet regimes failed, that does not mean that they did not try to achieve such. Stalin succeeded better than Hitler in this effort, for he had more time, and almost any vestige of a civil society (independent from state-controlled organizations) was destroyed after 1928 in the Soviet Union. Even football clubs were under state control. Citizens (which is a misnomer for the inhabitants of the Soviet Union) were not permitted to initiate anything without the regime's permission.

Certainly, then, we are comparing two dictatorial regimes that in some ways show remarkable similarities and at times drew inspiration from each other, but we are leaving it up to readers to draw their conclusions regarding these parallels and compare the two regimes. We will leave it moot in how far the appearance of these dictatorial regimes around 1930 was merely coincidental, a sign of a general sort of watershed in mass politics and political culture, with liberal democracy having lost much of its appeal and seemingly fading. Texts on totalitarianism contain valuable insights, but somewhat simplify ostentatious similarities between both regimes into an overbearing theoretical construct.

No one yet, meanwhile, has undertaken a scholarly comparison of posters and this key visual medium's use during the Nazi-Soviet conflict, the bloodiest military confrontation of the twentieth century.[27] The number of works on Nazi and Soviet propaganda is substantial, but none of them compare, as we do in this book, the significance of posters as a means to spread the ideological message of the two regimes. Most comprehensive as a survey of the Soviet poster is a work by Waschik (Vashik) and Baburina that has, however, remained only available in German (at a prohibitive price) and Russian.[28] The first of two fundamental texts on poster art in English is Victoria Bonnell, *Iconography of Power: Soviet Political Posters under Lenin and Stalin*.[29] Bonnell provided a more incisive analysis and covered a larger time span than the other key text, Stephen White's earlier *Bolshevik Poster*.[30] A number of other treatises, meanwhile, provide key insights into the rise of the Soviet poster.[31] As indicated by Richard Pipes, Bolshevik aesthetics were partially rooted in the Italian Futurist movement (itself responding to *Art Nouveau* and *Jugendstil* posters), while the *fin-de-siècle* ideas of *Mir Isskustva* and the total art of the *Ballets Russes* influenced the artists producing early Soviet posters, for which the works by Engelstein and by Scheijen are illuminating.[32] Further relevant to the early evolution of those posters is Alla Rosenfeld's work, while a particular Russian iteration of visual culture that influenced Soviet poster culture is traced by Stephen Norris.[33] In the literature on Soviet propaganda, general context is provided by Peter Kenez's work and various other scholars, of which Boris Groys' *Total Art of Stalinism* is thought-provoking, as is David Brandenberger's *Propaganda State in Crisis* and Evgeny Dobrenko's *Late Stalinism*.[34] Illustrative for the evolution of the Soviet poster after 1917 are *Windows on the War* and Toland, *Constructing Revolution*.[35] And apart from a number of databases that display Soviet posters with or without much of an elaborate contextualization, extremely helpful is the Russian-language website *Tramvai iskusstv*, which is a work in progress, with new essays continually being added to its section on posters.[36] All of these sources have informed the following pages.

Interesting and important work on Nazi propaganda includes various books and articles, although most are now rather dated, and none of these deal with posters much or specifically.[37] Randall Bytwerk has produced an interesting comparison between Nazi propaganda and that of the German Democratic Republic, but even here there is not much specific treatment of posters.[38] More recently, the literature on the Third *Reich* has developed to include works on related topics like advertising and selling.[39] However, there has been very little published on the poster in the Third *Reich*. Bachrach and Levert's *State of Deception* accompanies an exhibition on this subject and provides some useful context and high-quality colour images.[40] Sylke Wunderlich's recent book, *Propaganda des Terrors*, with text in both German and English, and featuring some 200 images, describes the dangers of Nazi poster art and its manipulation of the German population.[41] Even in German, the topic is not widely covered, and most of the extant literature is very dated, with some limited discussion and examples of Nazi posters appearing alongside those of other political eras: an exception is the recent book by Birgit Witamwas.[42] There are also newer, interesting works on the related theme of posters in the German Democratic Republic, although obviously this regime is outside the remit of this book.[43]

Outline of the Book

Chapter 1 examines the origins, evolution, and role of posters in the Soviet Union, where posters evolved from a means primarily of artistic expression and advertising into a means mainly of mass propaganda. Various traditional and modernist artistic trends drove their making, as this chapter will outline. Some of these were foreign in origin, others domestic (such as through the development of the Russian *lubki*). In addition, technological progress contributed to their mass production. The chapter ponders as well why posters especially found such a ready audience within the ranks of the Communist Party and among the Soviet population. Several pre-revolutionary and early Soviet posters (including those made by Mayakovsky and others for the *Rosta* windows) are analysed in detail to chart their evolution from before 1914 until the end of the civil war and beginning of the New Economic Policy in 1921.

Chapter 2 analyses the origins and role of Nazi posters. Even before the Nazi Party came to power in 1933, Hitler and his propagandists were aware of the benefits of publicity for the party and were determined to use all types of propaganda media, including posters, in order to promote Hitler and the *NSDAP*. In particular, in the election campaigns of 1932, at the peak of the economic crisis in Germany, the *NSDAP* used posters to publicize its cause. In *Mein Kampf*, Hitler had noted, 'The art of the poster lies in the designer's ability to attract the attention of the crowd by form and colour.'[44] This chapter investigates the function of Nazi posters, also placing these within the context of the development of Nazi propaganda as a whole. In particular, it focuses on an analysis of key electoral posters from 1932 including 'Hitler: Our Last Hope' and 'Workers of the Mind, of the Fist: Vote for Front Soldier: Hitler!' It examines the effectiveness of these and other early Nazi posters in terms of their appeal to the emotions and especially in their attempt to attract voters across all sectors of German society to the Nazi Party.

Chapter 3 examines Soviet posters of the 1920s and 1930s. Experimentation and a predilection for abstract art appeared soon after the October coup of 1917 as the hallmarks of the aesthetics of the 'proletarian vanguard'. The Bolshevik leaders' taste in art often jibed with modernism, but they were a rather small group of middle-class intellectuals. Once in power, they needed to strengthen their ties to the rest of the proletariat (and the peasantry), the so-called toiling masses. Posters were well suited as a means to appeal to them and advocate for the Communist programme (and even for more mundane goals such as improving infant healthcare). But as this chapter shows, such an appeal could only cast its message through using recognizable images that in their naturalism seemed the very opposite of the abstract art that had taken the European bourgeoisie by storm after 1880. Soviet poster-makers thus sought the medium between representational and abstract imagery in their work. While by the early 1930s a more traditional aesthetic (usually called Socialist Realism, although that is a term better suited for literature) was imposed on the visual arts by Stalin and his minions, Soviet posters remained a hybrid of abstract and concrete. In this chapter, too, the question is pondered again how popular posters actually were and why that might have been, and in how far Soviet artists deliberately tried to appeal to popular taste in making their posters. In addition, unresolved dilemmas in Soviet discourse between Marxism-Leninism's emphasis on class and gender and ethnicity will be indicated. Work by propagandistic artists such as Moor, Klutsis, Kulagina, Koretsky, Gitsevich, Knoblok, and Deni will be analysed.

Returning to Germany, Chapter 4 offers an analysis of the use of posters as propaganda media in the construction of the *Volksgemeinschaft* or 'national community', especially the poster '*Ein Volk, Ein Reich, Ein Führer*', which emphasized a key Nazi slogan. Here we examine an array of posters designed to appeal to different groups in German society across a range of ideological aims: posters relating to the German youth groups, the Hitler Youth (*HJ*) and the League of German Girls (*BDM*); posters which reified the Nazi Party as the protector of the German family and which promoted large German 'valuable' families; posters which urged German families to take part in the *Eintopf* Sunday or 'one-pot' Sunday charitable drive; posters which encouraged Germans to save for the *Volkswagen* or 'people's car', to listen to the 'people's radio', or to benefit from the holidays, trips, and cultural opportunities offered by the *Kraft durch Freude* (Strength through Joy) organization. The chapter also investigates posters that were used to publicize and indeed to justify the regime's eugenic policies, including sterilization. We use the posters as well in serving as a point of entry for a discussion of key Nazi policies and initiatives.

Chapter 5 moves on to a discussion of Nazi posters in relation to foreign policy and the Second World War, such as the poster for the commemoration of the annexation of Austria, 13 March 1938, and key posters from the period 1939–45. Important Nazi wartime posters included 'Into the Dust with all Enemies of Greater Germany!', depicting a strong fist smashing the French, the British, and the Jews, and the 1943 poster '*Adolf Hitler ist der Sieg!*' ('Adolf Hitler is Victory!'). Posters were used to emphasize the important struggle of the Nazi war effort, to excoriate and vilify 'enemies' and to encourage mobilization on the home front. Nazi wartime posters captured a variety of themes including the evacuation of the cities, enrolment for the 'people's army' towards the end of the war, discouragement of women from 'hamstering', making trips to the countryside to barter non-perishable items for food from the farmers. Anti-Semitic posters are also considered in this chapter, including '*Der Ewige Jude*' ('The Eternal Jew'). Once again in this chapter, key Nazi posters are analysed and then utilized to investigate important Nazi policies and aims.

The final chapter, Chapter 6, turns back to the USSR to examine Soviet posters of the 'Great Patriotic War' and beyond. Soviet posters may have reached an all-time height of popularity in the Second World War. This was in part because they proved best suited among all mass media to buttress the home front's morale, as they were cheap, easily distributed, and simple to understand. The existential struggle with the Nazi empire allowed for a deluge of depictions of the enemy in the ugliest way possible. And because of the highly developed Soviet poster culture of the previous quarter century, after 22 June 1941 poster-makers could mine the plethora of ideas and images tried out prior to the invasion. Thus, the *Rosta* windows were reborn as the *TASS* windows. In this vein, for example, we already saw how Toidze's poster of the Motherland's call to arms was a version of the First World War era and civil war posters. By then, it was evident what worked and Soviet posters may have reached a maturity and quality that was matched neither before nor after the war. Posters, nonetheless, became such a staple of Soviet life that they remained a highly popular means of mass communication until 1991. A discussion of their descent into formulaic blandness will be the topic of the last poster analyses in this chapter.

1

The Soviet Poster

The historical context of the production of Soviet posters is complex, with art history, cultural history, technology and politics intersecting.[1] Before charting its chronological evolution in a more detailed fashion, this chapter first explores its ideological and technological sides. It then ponders its aesthetic side, in terms of both its history within the evolution of designing and manufacturing of posters and its place among other visual-art (and to some extent, literary) genres. In addition, we will investigate why posters were considered effective means of mass communication, whether or not Soviet authorities attempted to measure this efficacy, and how Soviet audiences received the posters, as much as those three things can be gauged. Then we will briefly proceed to chart the development of Soviet posters with particular reference to the Second World War, comparing and contrasting them with posters released in the Nazi *Reich*. But the main analysis of the period from the late 1910s to the mid-1950s and beyond will be conducted in the two subsequent chapters on Soviet posters.

Ideology

Agitation and propaganda were key components of Bolshevik (Communist[2]) ideology since Lenin's definition of their essence in the early 1900s. This was so even if, in his foundational treatise *What Is to Be Done?*, Lenin defined debating political issues in small circles as agitation, while especially *writing* for larger crowds amounted to propaganda, with both activities soon combined in the *Newspeak*ian word *agitprop*.[3] As a young revolutionary in 1890s St Petersburg Lenin himself had engaged in both activities, but *agitprop*'s theoretical significance went back to Karl Marx's argument that the working class (that is, factory workers and miners, wage labourers in an urban environment) needed to be made aware of the injustice of capitalist exploitation that made them suffer.[4] The emergence of such class consciousness (fundamental to which was the idea that the workers of the world had 'nothing to lose but their chains', as the 1848 *Communist Manifesto* had announced) was to be ideally mediated by emancipated workers who had seen the light of the radiant communist future and had read and understood the laws of history as outlined by historical materialism. In reality, however, it was overwhelmingly middle-class intellectuals who (convinced themselves to have) grasped the essence of the Marxist message and appointed themselves as the enlightened guides to the proletarian paradise. The entire leadership of both branches of the Russian Marxist party (the Russian Social-Democratic Labour or Workers' Party), the Mensheviks and Bolsheviks, therefore, consisted of men (and a few women) who were far more educated and in tune with the artistic renewal and experimentation that was sweeping through Europe around 1900 than those in whose name they led their movement. Such sophistication exuded an influence on the appreciation of poster art among Communist Party leaders. It is not as if they were converts to the European artistic vanguard, but they were relatively open to much of its innovation and experimentation away from representative or figurative art.

Despite their different cultural sensibility from the masses they aspired to lead, during the revolution of 1917 the Bolsheviks nonetheless managed to strike a genuine chord not just with factory workers and miners (who still formed a small minority in a country of agriculturalists), but even with many of the 'peasants-in-uniform' who were serving in the Russian armed forces. The support the Bolsheviks received from workers and soldiers in the autumn of 1917 was sufficiently large to dare Lenin and his comrades to take power in October. This backing sustained Lenin's regime at least until the March 1918 peace treaty of Brest-Litovsk, which ended the First World War in north-eastern Europe.

At that moment, however, a new problem arose for Lenin and his comrades: How could they continue to appeal to a population now mainly interested in returning to the prewar – mainly rural – life they had led before August 1914? In their own minds, the Bolsheviks (or Communists, as Lenin's followers began to call themselves ever more assertively) were legitimate rulers of the empire of the former tsar, upon whom History had called to begin the inexorable march to global communism, ushering in a worldwide society of human equality, freedom, and economic affluence. They were obliged to do their utmost to stay in power and make Soviet Russia the platform from which to launch working-class revolutions in other countries.

Formally a party of and for the working class, it was somewhat unfortunate that the Communists had taken power in a country that was far from fully industrialized, indeed, one that was largely composed of peasants living in villages rather than urban-based factory workers and miners. Ideological sophistry (in which especially their key leader Lev Trotsky [1879–1940] was proficient) was used to explain that Russia was 'capitalism's weakest link'. This chain, once broken, would lead to the collapse of capitalism in the more industrialized countries such as Germany, the UK, or the United States. And similar dodgy reasoning held that a communist party could take power in a country in which the productive forces of modern capitalism had not yet been fully developed and full-fledged industrialization had yet to happen: Massaging Marx's analysis of the historical process, the Bolshevik leaders suggested that in the former tsarist empire the 'bourgeois stage' in which this industrialization was to unfold could be bypassed by a nascent working class, if it struck an alliance with the realm's exploited and impoverished peasantry.

Such explanations of their cause's righteousness convinced at least the Bolshevik leaders themselves from October 1917 onwards, but they faced a problem in having to persuade the mass of the population over whom they now lorded it of its validity. In a very cynical reading of the Bolshevik regime, Richard Pipes has argued that Lenin deliberately pushed towards a civil war in 1918.[5] Such a violent conflict would force the Russian masses to choose the side that had most to offer to them and oppose those who seemed to want (or, indeed, were depicted as wanting) to take away their land and reintroduce capitalist exploitation. Pipes may make Lenin, Trotsky, and their fellow Bolsheviks into overly lugubrious characters, but there is no doubt that they wanted and needed to shore up their shaky legitimacy in 1918. It is in this existential crisis (for in 1918 and 1919 there were a number of occasions when the Communist regime seemed on the verge of collapse) that the Soviet political poster was born.

Images are of course powerful. If presented well, they summarize tropes and messages more directly and profoundly than mere words, particularly when embedded in a cultural tradition using a semiotics (consciously or not) familiar to their audience (and Soviet posters tended to combine a few memorable words or catchy slogans with an image). Posters exert a powerful attraction to viewers, as long as they are sympathetic to either their subject matter or artistic quality, or both. And once the poster was found to be an ideal propaganda means, the Soviet regime continued to deploy it: for decades after the civil war, it felt a compelling need to rally its subjects behind a cause which brought few tangible benefits to them (and sometimes even considerably worsened their lives). The themes of Soviet political posters changed over time, but their contents and their widespread distribution consistently betray a sense of insecurity about the justice of the dictatorship's cause among the very dictators themselves.[6] Of course, it was easier to vilify actual foes, like during the civil war and the Second World War, as the mortal enemies of the people's happiness. It should not be forgotten, however, that even in those military conflicts the amount of desertion in the Red Army's forces was staggering and was met with brutal counter measures: it proved difficult to convince people of communism's merits or have even some of its true believers stay faithful to the cause for a long period, especially when confronted with some of its less wholesome aspects.[7]

Manfred Hildermeier and others justifiably argue that the posters' message changed from being aggressive and agitational to more appeasing during the timespan that we are investigating.[8] The initial bellicose quality of the posters' contents was based on developments in art history as such during the modernist period that combined with the specific Russian circumstances of the orgy of violence of world and civil wars. This belligerent quality may have been blunted in the brief intermezzo of the New Economic Policy (1921–9) but was rekindled during the epochal changes unleashed in 1929, after which it was sustained all the way until 1945. Only with the end of the Second World War does the *Sturm-und-Drang* period of the Soviet poster come to a close. To a degree, then, poster images do reflect the historical context of the time of their making.

The representation of abject violence had always been a standard element in Bolshevik imagery, and it was therefore, after 22 June 1941, not difficult to replace domestic foes with degenerate or demonic foreign enemies.[9] Of course, this extreme demonization was hyperbole at times, but Bolshevism had triumphed after October 1917 in a brutal civil war, in which both sides routinely committed what the Nuremberg Trials in 1945–6 defined as crimes against humanity. Almost all inhabitants of the former Russian empire were therefore confronted with baffling atrocities in one form or another. The 'Russian' Civil War had many battlefields, with Kyiv, for instance, changing hands eight times between March 1918 and early 1921, each time witnessing some sort of bloody reckoning. The Red Army occupied Azerbaijan, Armenia, Georgia, and eastern Siberia and Central Asia between 1920 and 1924, with military conflict there too being followed by the bloodshed of settling scores with alleged counterrevolutionaries.

In European Russia, civil war violence (including a reckoning with anti-Bolshevik peasants in 1921) gave way to a devastating famine in 1921 and 1922, killing millions who resided along the Volga, from Nizhnii Novgorod in the north to Astrakhan in the south.[10] After a lull of a few years, violence returned in 1929 with the imposition of the collectivization of agriculture, the victims of which were the first inmates of the burgeoning penal system of special settlements and labour camps, often called the *Gulag Archipelago* following Aleksandr Solzhenitsyn's lead. Strictly speaking, *GULag* stood for *Glavnoe Upravlenie Lagerei*, that is merely (the administration tasked with running) the labour camps, but the special settlements of exiled rich peasants (*kulak*s) and their families as well as their alleged sympathizers (often priests and mullahs) were part of the same coercive system that fell under the auspices of the state-security organs.[11]

The famine that affected Ukraine, Kazakstan, and southern Russia in 1932–3 and the Great Terror of 1937–8 desensitized or inured Soviet people to feelings of empathy. State-organized violence following world war and civil war made it such that few Soviet people did not know profound human suffering first-hand, unlike many of their German counterparts (that is, if the latter had managed to avoid serving in the armed forces during the First World War). The depiction of Nazi demons preying on Soviet citizens on posters therefore often easily struck a chord, for countless demons had preyed on the inhabitants of the Russian empire and the Soviet Union since at least 1914.

Indeed, between some prewar and wartime posters a clear likeness can be detected between caricatures of the Jew Trotsky and the German Hitler, a preposterous transposition. Such an abomination, however, had been (perhaps) persuasively linked in official Soviet public discourse. At the three Moscow show trials held between August 1936 and March 1938, Lev Trotsky, the key organizer of both the October 1917 coup and the Red victory in the civil war, was singled out as a pivotal figure trying to destroy the Soviet Union. He was depicted as the demon plotter who had connected his underground anti-Soviet network with foreign allies, of whom Nazi Germany was most prominent (the *Gestapo* was likewise depicted as crucial in egging on a military plot by senior Red Army commanders that was 'discovered' in the spring of 1937). This conspiracy was trumpeted in the major Soviet newspapers and depicted in their cartoons.[12] That Trotsky was Jewish was ignored, at least formally, even if some depictions of him subtly seemed to hint at anti-Semitic tropes, which were formally alien to Bolshevism.

Posters tell in their own way the nuances in the Soviet story from 1917 to 1953, the year of Stalin's death, but their production and contents can never be separated from the constant context of violent coercion. It is difficult to assess their exact efficacy, that is, how they were received by their audience. Paying lip-service to the cause and applauding the poster were a safe way to sidestep any awkward questions about one's allegiance. In other words, we ourselves may be captivated by the aesthetic beauty or artistic vision and skill of Soviet posters (as may have been Stalin and his friends), but that does not mean that their target audience was likewise impressed. Indeed, the endless tinkering with posters' proper form in the endeavour to reach the masses suggests that their effect did not meet the expectations of their producers, and especially of those Soviet bosses ordering their production. Ultimately, one particular truism may have made it impossible to design the perfect poster: There is no accounting for taste. Stalin and his circle might have appreciated a poster and believed it to be ideal as a means of *agitprop*, but their subjects might not have agreed with them. As a result of Stalin's autocracy, indeed, poster-makers moved away from trying to appeal to the masses: what counted was that the posters appealed to Stalin and his cronies.[13] This may to a considerable degree explain the milquetoast quality of postwar posters, when the old and tired dictator ever more strongly wanted to think of himself as the leader of a country in which serene and harmonious happiness reigned and still better things were to come.

Technology

When the Bolsheviks came to power in October 1917, their desire to rally the country behind their cause found a key tool in visual imagery, not least because the 'land of the soviets'[14] was populated by a great number of people who were at best half-literate.[15] The propagandistic power of images was channelled into such media as motion pictures (films), photographs or in posters. Film was considered the best-suited (and quintessentially modern) means to spread the Communist gospel and the Bolsheviks' favourite, beginning with Lenin. Eventually, among Stalin's subordinates even a minister for cinematography, I. G. Bol'shakov (1902–80), was found.[16] But filmmaking's complicated and expensive production process and the difficulty of showing movies to everyone living in a vast country hindered the goal of blanket coverage.[17] So, while Sergei Eisenstein (1898–1948) might be compared to Leni Riefenstahl (1902–2003) in harnessing great art to evil purposes, Riefenstahl and her counterparts' films could easily be watched by almost any of the *Reich*'s inhabitants, whereas Eisenstein's, Vsevolod Pudovkin (1893–1953)'s and their colleagues' movies were accessible to a far smaller proportion of the Soviet population.[18] In addition, Soviet film was mainly a *Russian* artistic enterprise, not just linguistically – which only became a problem once talking movies became the norm after 1930 – but also in terms of its subject matter.[19] Prince Alexander Nevsky or Tsar Ivan the Terrible, the focus of Eisenstein's last films, were historical figures who did not easily appeal to Uzbeks, Azeris, or Tatars, even if Muslims might have agreed with the negative depiction of Christianity in Eisenstein's *oeuvre*. Such linguistic and cultural challenges were of no concern to Nazi filmmakers, at least not until the outbreak of war in 1939 and the annexation or occupation of large non-German-speaking regions.

Photographs as such were not especially useful for Soviet *agitprop*, unless accompanied by a caption explaining who or what was depicted (and their rough quality when reproduced in mass newspapers left much to be desired).[20] It was difficult to stage a photograph credibly for propagandistic purposes. The exact effect of a photographic rendition of Lenin or Stalin differed per viewer (and was famously lampooned by Orwell in *Nineteen Eighty-Four*), but might acquire religious overtones, as in the 'beautiful' or 'Red' corner of the peasant hut, where a framed photograph of the beloved leader replaced the traditional Orthodox icon, in front of which a candle might be burned.[21] But beyond satisfying such religious cravings photographs as such did not convey much of a message. Staging and retouching became the habit if photos were used for *agitprop*, and as such began to blend with photomontage used in posters by the middle of the 1920s.[22] While towards 1930 certain films disappeared from circulation because their directors or artists had fallen foul of the regime or their protagonists antagonized it, photographs were retouched, wholly deleting fallen heroes, from Lev Trotsky and Grigorii Zinoviev to their persecutor Nikolai Ezhov.[23] Posters were in this sense, too, better suited as a means of propaganda, as their existence was short-lived, falling apart and tearing after a short while. Former people thus easily vanished.

A short-lived popularity of the 'photo-story' was enjoyed during the 1930s, which was a series of images presented as a story, somewhat akin to today's graphic novel but with photographs instead of drawings, although its narrative was – officially – non-fiction.[24] But after an initial splash, the 'photo-story' appears to have been abandoned, as its narratives seemed inauthentic and boring, even when some of its champions engaged in a spirited defence of its allegedly superior qualities.[25] In addition, photograph magazines were quite expensive; one such periodical was primarily produced for the Soviet elite's and foreign consumption, and initially was financed by the Soviet central bank.[26] Nevertheless, the sequential presentation of photographs did influence the photomontage technique in the production of posters.

Photographs often did indeed provide the raw material used for posters (and the Soviets may have pioneered the use of photographs in posters – photomontage – during the 1920s),[27] and they were stylized, enlarged and retouched and printed, sown, or engraved on banners and flags carried around in parades, or decorated the walls of public buildings and offices.[28] It was likely Aleksandr Rodchenko (1891–1956) who introduced photomontage to Soviet art, while the German poster artist John Heartfield, who spent some time in the Soviet Union in the early 1930s, served as a key inspiration. Its best-known Soviet pioneering practitioner was the Latvian Gustav Gustavovich Klutsis (Gustavs Klucis, 1895–1938), whose heyday came in the 1930s but who fell victim to the Great Terror that reigned in the second half of that same decade.[29] Posters using photomontage nonetheless remained in fashion afterwards.[30]

Soviet radio broadcasts originated during the Russian Civil War, but until well after the Second World War, radio signals did not reach everywhere across the country, nor did many people own a radio receiver.[31] Privately owned radios only became a common feature in postwar Soviet elite *urban* households, while televisions only appeared on a massive scale in the 1970s. Propaganda distributed by radio-waves, therefore, did not reach the volume and level of diffusion desired by Stalin's regime.

Figure 1.1 shows a late Stalinist poster by Viktor S. Ivanov (1909–68) heralding Soviet radio.[32] The text at its bottom reads, 'Soviet Radio Earnestly Serves the Cause of Peace!' The Moscow Kremlin forms its background, while red banners wave that say 'Hail to the Great Stalin!'; 'Forward toward Communism!'; and 'For Peace in the Entire World!' The man at the microphone appears reading from the front pages of the largest Soviet newspaper, the daily *Pravda*, which has as a headline something about the Communist Party's Central Committee's appeals. He is dressed in a manner often favoured in the postwar years, when workers in coveralls with hammers and women in dresses with head-scarfs wielding scythes fell out of fashion in Soviet imagery. Instead, the suit-and-tie look became the sartorial ideal for the successful Soviet man (who was expected to be *kul'turnyi*, or 'cultured') who had left the workbench behind and had moved on to the

FIGURE 1.1 *'Soviet Radio Earnestly Serves the Cause of Peace!'*.

office or, in this case, the broadcasting studio. The image and its protagonist radiate a confidence that the future was bright for a country that had overcome the hardship of the first three decades or so of Communist rule. Its aesthetic quality is formulaic and less dramatic than Ivanov's Second World War work, of which an example is displayed later in this book.

Gramophones, while another new medium, were poorly suited as a means to spread propaganda. They were expensive, too, as were gramophone records, which were, in any event, hard to find.

Technological challenges, therefore, may be a key component in understanding the long-lasting popularity of the poster in the Soviet Union, although force of habit and a sophisticated and appealing tradition of poster-making explain its survival into the very last days of the regime. It is perhaps difficult to grasp in our computerized, or digitized, age, but a century ago, posters seemed to be not just a stopgap means, an *ersatz* medium for lack of radio or film projector, but presented a relatively new, modern medium, and therefore all the more appropriate to the new revolutionary age. As Maria Gough summarizes, it was one of 'those arts that shared with modern industrial production its primary condition of technological reproducibility, such as graphic design, photomontage, photography, and cinema'.[33]

Furthermore, posters were cheap, visually appealing, easily distributed and could be hung anywhere: on blind walls and in glass-covered display cases next to pinned-up newspapers along the walkways in city parks, in libraries, at bus-stops, railway and metro stations, and in the countryside along the walls of the collective farms' cultural clubs.

Like photography, cinematography or radio broadcasting, the technology to mass-produce posters was relatively recent, originating in a sophistication of the lithographic production process that occurred around 1880.[34] The poster may have truly arrived as an artistic medium through Henri de Toulouse-Lautrec (1864–1901)'s work, not least his advertising posters for the Moulin Rouge cabaret in Paris in the early 1890s. At first an artistic means of advertising, the poster's role as a means of state propaganda emerged in the early months of the First World War.[35] As we saw, the Soviets appear subsequently to have been among the pioneers in using photographs (instead of, or together with, illustrations) in producing posters, further accentuating their modern look.

Graphic design became a cherished form of artistic expression, especially for the artists known as Constructivists whose heyday coincided with the early Soviet years. Their original or professed intention had been to realize their designs as three-dimensional structures.[36] Lacking funds and know-how to execute their projects, they channelled their ideas instead into their two-dimensional works, including posters. They competed, however, with those who used more traditional images for their posters. Although by the early 1930s the wildest forms of abstraction (Suprematist, Constructivist, Dadaist, Cubist, etc.) were banished by the regime's artistic code, both naturalistic (or figurative) and abstract traits remain visible in Soviet posters afterwards. And despite a greater rigidity of aesthetic conventions, increased technological possibilities also pushed the envelope and piecemeal changed posters' make-up. Finally, to return to the technological perspective, poster-making resembled a sort of factory production, with artists in the role of industrial designers or inventors, designing factory-made commodities, and in that respect as well stood for modernity.[37]

Aesthetics

The aesthetics of early Soviet posters frequently echoed the newest trends in modern art, although they were equally influenced by the long tradition of satirical caricatures dating back to William Hogarth (1697–1764).[38]

Political cartoons (such as the lithographed prints by the Frenchman Honoré Daumier [1808–79]) had become a regular accompaniment of political commentary during the nineteenth century, albeit less so in tsarist Russia, where censorship was harshly enforced before 1905. Of course, political posters do not need to be critical per definition, and, indeed, were more often than not used by the powers-that-be to convey a message in support of the government. Meanwhile, Toulouse-Lautrec's posters were commercial, and Russian-made posters before 1914 were overwhelmingly commercial as well.[39] After 1917, too, a steady stream of non-political posters continued to be produced in the Soviet Union, with some advertising commodities, exhibitions, plays, or films, while others were mainly instructional in nature. For example, posters were made to instruct women on infant care, including breast-feeding. Despite the highly touted end the Bolsheviks had brought to the free-market economy (especially after 1929), Soviet 'trade posters' continued to engage in advertising, even if it was for products made by state-owned enterprises that did not have competitors.[40] Their main purpose seems to have been to acquaint Soviet consumers with new products that had become available rather than to outdo the competition producing the same commodities.[41] Such a comradely aim may not always have worked, as differently tasting sweets or cigarettes might rival each other for the customers' favour.

Most of the peculiarly Russian woodprints called *lubki*, which began to be diffused on a wide scale in the early nineteenth century in response to the war with Napoleonic France, traditionally conveyed pro-government messages. These *lubki* are a peculiarly early iteration of visual propaganda in Russia. Stephen M. Norris convincingly links this pre-revolutionary form of graphic expression with the subsequent Soviet poster culture.[42] They resembled the illustrated pamphlets, chap books, and broadsheets of early-modern Western Europe, although their satire was much more circumscribed in comparison, reserved for government-approved foreign enemies in a country where in the nineteenth-century censorship was much more strictly enforced than in eighteenth-century Western Europe. As Norris shows, at the outbreak of each war involving Russia after 1815, a veritable avalanche of *lubki* was released in support of the Russian war effort.[43] During the Russian Silver Age, *lubki* production coincided with an outpouring of modernist print matter and political cartoons.[44] After the outbreak of war in 1914 the *lubki* figurative satirical appearance, somewhat surprisingly, began to merge in the work of some artists previously exploring abstract art, such as Kazimir Malevich (1878–1935), in making patriotic posters.[45] The young Vladimir Mayakovsky (1893–1930) likewise produced anti-German and anti-Ottoman art in the early months of the war.[46] *Lubki* eventually were adopted in Soviet iconography, their revolutionary iteration being produced by famous artists such as Mayakovsky and Dmitrii Moor.[47] The *lubki* strongly influenced the first mass-produced Soviet posters that were displayed in the *Rosta* press agency's wall windows.[48]

Besides a long-standing tradition of icon painting and the more recent popularity of the *lubki*, Russian visual art had not been especially original either before or during the epoch of the Golden Age in literature and remained parochial long beyond the 1840s. One of the first truly interesting visual artists was Karl Briullov (1799–1852), although his work and that of the Wanderers (*peredvizhniki*) of the 1870s and 1880s still appear as derivative of contemporary European (naturalist or figurative) academic art, perhaps at their best matching rather than transcending it.[49] A real pioneer was Mikhail Vrubel (1856–1910), who by the 1890s created on his canvases an increasingly haunting concoction of religious, classical, and folkloristic imagery anchored in Russian iconography. Eventually, Vrubel lost his mind. Although Vrubel had few acolytes, he influenced those who really transformed Russian art around 1900 (not least Marc Chagall, 1887–1985), when it merged with and responded to the other rapidly succeeding European schools of art, from Impressionism and Pointillism onwards.[50] Eventually, truly original Russian artists acquired global fame and influence, but Vasilii Kandinsky (1866–1944), Nicholas Roerich (Rerikh; 1874–1947) or Marc Chagall at most only fleetingly made posters, while they all preferred residing outside the Soviet Union after brief flirtations with the new regime.

By 1900 a seemingly endless stream of young artists emerged in the Russian empire, who often for a spell were connected with the journal *Mir Isskustva* (Roerich was among them), behind which especially the impresario and art visionary Sergei Diaghilev was a driving force.[51] Many of these artists (Léon Bakst, Ivan Bilibin and Alexander Benois) used a form of lithographic printing as a medium of their artistic expression.[52] Subsequently, as Alla Rosenfeld writes, 'World War I, the Bolshevik revolution of 1917, and Civil War ... shifted emphasis to the social and political poster which greatly differed from the goals and aesthetics of the Style Moderne period.'[53]

The First World War, the first global war in history in which tens of millions of soldiers and civilians participated, provoked a desire to create art that reached those masses who did the fighting and kept the war machine going. Overly 'decadent' art appealing to the tastes of the happy few made way for populist art (or at a minimum sought to do so) that could be massively distributed: hence the reinvigorated production of *lubki* produced by Malevich and others. Posters were commissioned in the First World War by the tsarist authorities, but in Russia the heyday of the *afisha* or *plakat* (poster) was to come after the February 1917 revolution.

Given their diverse roots, early Bolshevik posters therefore lack a uniform aesthetic. They veered between contemporary artistic experimentation (affiliated with any of the movements such as Cubism, German Expressionism, *Art Nouveau*, *Jugendstil*, Futurism, Suprematism, Constructivism, etc.), the naturalistic essence of the European political caricature and the satire of Russian *lubki*, and often moved between the abstract and the concrete. Photomontage, which appeared in Soviet posters from the middle of the 1920s onwards, found its roots in the collage technique which had been particularly practised by Dada artists in the 1910s and early 1920s, but may have appealed as well because its composition evoked *lubki* and had the figurative quality easily understood by its audience.[54] Again, the Soviet style of poster-making borrowed heavily from elsewhere, but likewise drew on Russian artists' work such as that by Leon Bakst (1866–1924, who was a Russian pioneer in making artistic *affiches* in the style pioneered by Toulouse-Lautrec), Vladimir Tatlin (1885–1953), Kazimir Malevich, El Lissitzky (1890–1941), Liubov Popova (1889–1924), Olga Rozanova (1886–1918), Mayakovsky, Natalia Goncharova (1881–1962), or her colleague, the *decor*-maker of the *Ballets Russes*, Alexander Benois (1870–1960).[55]

Colour Plate 2 shows a famous poster made by El Lissitzky, called 'Beat the Whites with the Red Wedge'. It is from 1919 or 1920, and was made on behalf of the political direction (the *agitprop* department) of the Red Army's western front in the civil war against the White armies. Art critics and historians have been awed by this poster. Its contemporary resonance, however, is unclear (we do not even know whether it was printed and distributed in any sort of print-run). It will have elicited a response among El Lissitzky's fellow Suprematists, Constructivists, and other experimental artists, but did it strike a chord with the Red soldiers or the civilians under Bolshevik rule? Even an erudite Bolshevik such as Trotsky needed to ask Mayakovsky in the early 1920s what Futurism actually stood for. With neither Soviet leaders nor their subjects understanding abstract art very well, poster-makers eventually turned to more realistic depictions, discarding much of the experimentation of the early Soviet period.

Colour played an important role in Soviet posters, and, for a long time, printing in colour set posters apart from both moving and still black-and-white photography. Soviet film only began to be shot in colour after the Second World War, while the availability of any mass-produced colour photographs was an equally late development (which is, in its timeline, not that different from the rest of the world). Still, the colour palette that could be used in poster-making was limited, as colouring in everything might add to its production cost and complication. For a considerable while, the advantage of making posters using photomontage was that they tended to leave most of the photographs used in a monochromatic black-and-white. But even those posters hardly ever seem to have escaped a good dose of the colour red, beloved both in traditional Russian culture and in the international revolutionary movement since the French Revolution. Red colour in Soviet posters almost invariably signified something good or important, sometimes emphasizing its written message, sometimes identifying the good, that is, Soviet side in politics. Tellingly, some of the wartime anti-Hitler or anti-Nazi posters lacked any red in them, and sported a rather unusual amount of black, a colour that had few positive connotations in Soviet discourse. That the Nazis favoured the colour red as well did not apparently trouble the Soviet artists and their overseers, meanwhile. After the war, in keeping with the growing emphasis on harmony and the radiant future, soft pastel colours began to be used more, which may have been, unconsciously or not, soothing to the eyes of people who had witnessed and undergone so much suffering. Possibly, even the increased use of gold and to a lesser degree silver (which also came into vogue on book coverings) indicated the newfound riches that now began to be accumulated in the much less threatening postwar world. Despite the Cold War's beginning, the Soviet Union was far less embattled than before 1941, as it was by 1950 surrounded by countries in which friendly, communist-type regimes had been installed, whether in North Korea, China, or in East-Central Europe (and Outer Mongolia had been a Soviet satellite state since the civil war). The job of making the world communist was far from being done, but some enjoyment of the spoils of all the hard work seemed to be in the offing for the long-suffering Soviet population.

Finally, it needs to be pointed out that Soviet political posters almost invariably were accompanied by text. As Robert Bird suggests, 'posters frequently focus on the mediation between concept and action, which in Soviet discourse meant providing a slogan (*lozung*)'.[56] *Lozung*, ironically, was a word borrowed from German (in which it is spelled with an s); it also means the sort of battle cry shouted by demonstrators during street protests, or, indeed, the slogan written on the banners they carried. A punchy text was required, in other words, sometimes consisting of a mere line or two by the Marxist founders or their best pupils Lenin and Stalin, but sometimes consisting of a somewhat lengthier poem or forceful statement. Mayakovsky and his colleagues had in some ways provided the model for this manner of presentation in the *Rosta* years. The image, then, graphically illustrated the meaning of the words, although often enough the words rather explained the image. In this sense, Lenin's emphasis on propaganda as a *written* component of *agitprop* still fitted the poster as a means to spread the message.

The Bolsheviks and Soviet Posters

It is a matter of debate whether the Bolshevik leaders admired the plethora of new artistic styles that emerged during the first two decades of the twentieth century, or whether they were primarily enchanted by the effectiveness of some of these movements' artistic products in spreading a message.[57] Laura Engelstein has detailed the *fin-de-siècle* fascination with newness and experimentation among the Russian intelligentsia, while Richard Pipes has made a pitch for Italian Futurism having more than just an aesthetic influence on Bolshevism as a political movement, likening Bolshevism's response to Futurism to that of Italian fascism.[58] The earlier-mentioned Bolshevik fondness for recently invented mass media at least attests to their fascination with such novel means. Political avantgardism for a while went hand-in-hand with artistic avantgardism. As Boris Groys writes, 'because it was associated with backwardness and a feeling of inferiority, [a] purely aesthetic distaste for the old accounts for the fact that Russia was more receptive than the West itself to new aesthetic forms'.[59]

Initially, the production of posters and their aesthetic evolution aligned with the tremendous Soviet emphasis on agitation and propaganda. Having captured the state's commanding heights, the Bolsheviks expended far more effort expounding the truth of their cause than any other regime before theirs. Their original emphasis on *agitprop* was heavily reinforced by the civil war that developed in the course of 1918, in which the allegiance of the soldiers and civilians to either side was shaky. The need became manifest of consistently having to convince the population of the Bolshevik cause's merit in order to mobilize people behind its red flag.

Despite being the single uncontested political party in the Soviet Union monopolizing all levels of political power, the expenditure and effort that went into *agitprop* hardly diminished once, by late 1920, the civil war was won by the Reds. Even the colour red itself was a visual symbol of left-wing political movements and of international socialism and thus adopted by the Communists, who saw themselves as the definitive incarnation of left-wing revolutionaries.

The importance of mass media in manipulating the collective mindset was unquestioned among them. Even those who may have harboured some scepticism about Lenin's advocacy of *agitprop* could not deny the evidence of the power of the printing press, as had been amply displayed just before 1900 through W. R. Hearst's and Joseph Pulitzer's mass-circulating newspapers' success in whipping up chauvinistic support in the 1898 Spanish-American War. In 1915, the American director D. W. Griffith had effectively shown how film, too, might be harnessed to political cause in *The Birth of a Nation*. In the mid-1920s Soviet film directors such as Sergei Eisenstein followed suit with the silent movies *Strike*, *Battleship Potemkin* and *October*. Soviet newspapers, both countrywide and local, were innumerable, and many printed political cartoons following the style of posters, while cartoons in their turn influenced posters. Starting as a newspaper supplement in 1922 (and co-founded by Mikhail Cheremnykh [1890–1962] of *Rosta* fame), the satirical weekly *Krokodil* was replete with illustrations lampooning foreign capitalist exploiters and domestic bureaucratic loafers.[60]

But far from all Soviet residents subscribed to newspapers, either because they could not afford the subscription costs or because they lacked the required reading skills. To compensate, though, wall newspapers were displayed behind glass in windows at the workplace or on the streets, before which people gathered to acquire information. It allowed *agitprop* workers or voluntary interpreters to relay the news to these spectators/readers (some of whom might be half-literate), framing it in its proper political context (or so it was hoped). Of course, arresting images were far more likely to draw in the curious than even the printed headlines of a newspaper: images were juxtaposed on posters to the printed word for that reason as well.[61] And indeed, many posters were produced that had a sheer educative function, going as far as explaining how tomatoes could be cultivated and canned.[62] Somewhere at the border between propaganda and education during the 1920s stood the posters advocating literacy programmes (*likvidatsiia bezgramotnosti* or *likbez*).[63] More straightforwardly was posters' anti-religious propaganda, atheism being a core part of the Bolshevik programme and already strongly advocated on some early Soviet posters.[64]

The heyday of the Soviet poster coincides with Stalin's autocracy (1929–53) and perhaps especially the years 1930–45.[65] The Second World War may have been its climax, for then film showings became patchy, radio signals intermittent, newspapers scarce and smaller, and few had much time available to spend reading beyond their army service or incessant labour in the Soviet hinterland to keep the war machine going.[66] The poster substituted for the absence of those media as an easily distributed powerful means boosting morale. But did posters truly spur on an optimistic spirit?

By far the most famous poster of the Second World War became Irakli Moisevich Toidze's *Rodina-Mat' zovyot* ('The Motherland Calls'), itself based on a Russian Civil War template, which was copied from the West (see Colour Plate 1).[67] While its image even now stirs up the emotions of its viewers, it is nonetheless hard to establish the exact impression it, or posters like it, made on its Soviet audience during their 'Great Patriotic War'. For example, one might suggest that it generated a sense of panic among some as it may have indicated desperation, at a time when during the early months of warfare one calamity after the next befell the Soviet defenders.

The question then is whether the poster boom of the Second World War actually did what it was supposed to do, or whether massive amounts of posters were produced to soothe the conscience of Soviet *agitprop* officials and their bosses, who had very few other means at their disposal to bolster morale. Despite reservations, we suggest that posters were largely positively received and sometimes left an indelible impression on contemporary Soviet viewers, for they still elicit an emotional response from many viewers today, who live in a completely different world. Certainly, the Soviet leaders did not show any qualms about the efficacy of posters in mobilizing the masses behind their cause. The outlay on poster production in wartime would surely have been less if posters' effect was in serious doubt.

Audience reception of writing, public speeches or visual art is obviously difficult, perhaps even impossible, to gauge. While Hitler's speeches could stir his listeners during Nazi rallies or even when speaking on the radio, we know that Stalin's listeners were much less captivated by his oratory, but they ritualistically applauded his words when attending Party meetings at which he spoke. Stalin's written words were possibly more convincing than his oral presentations, as he wrote in a straightforward style, without rhetorical flourish, repeating his main points lucidly, which resounded with his readers.[68] Indeed, a *silent* Stalin, as author or even as an image, may have been a more powerful rallying point than Stalin as a public speaker. The innumerable pictures of him in the Soviet empire made his image omnipresent, as Orwell so aptly portrays in *Nineteen Eighty-Four*. Perhaps 'Big Brother' was not 'Watching You', but 'you' were watching the leader everywhere. Posters were replete with portraits of Stalin after 1929. And at least for some, his image became literally iconic, like an Eastern-Orthodox icon (and might like it be superstitiously associated with supernatural powers), which may explain why even today some Russians like to look at it (see Figure 1.2).

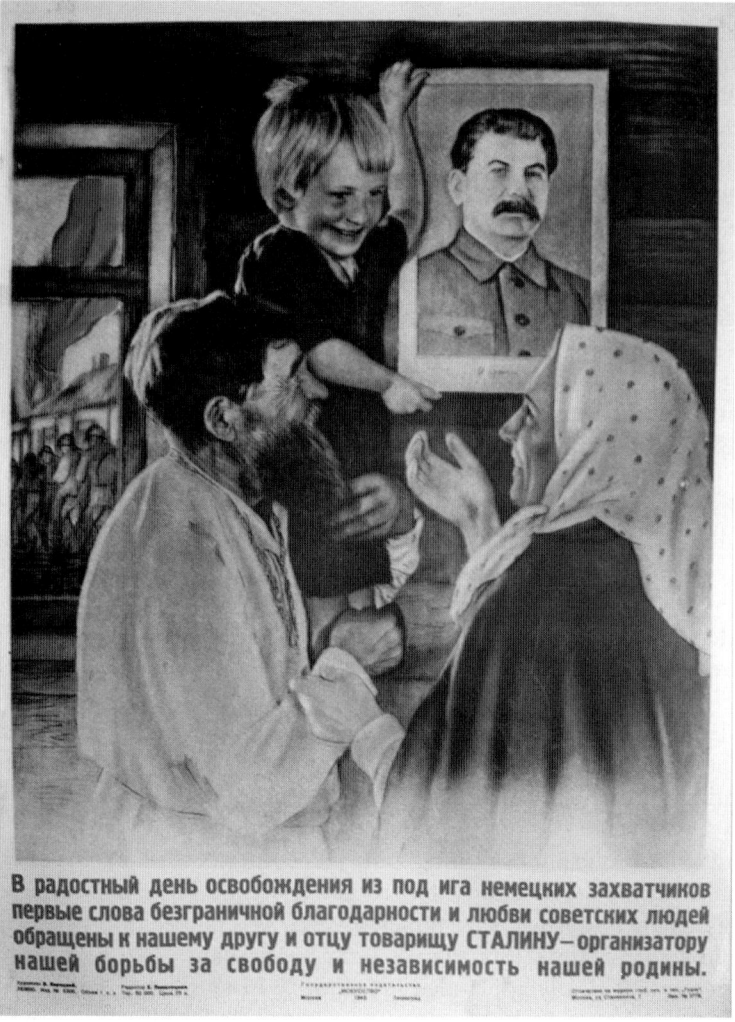

FIGURE 1.2 '*On the Happy Day of the Liberation from the Yoke of the German Marauders, the Soviet People's First Words of Limitless Gratitude and Love Are for Our Friend and Father Comrade STALIN, the Organizer of Our Fight for Freedom and Independence of Our Motherland*'.

The poster's text reads, 'On the happy day of the liberation from the yoke of the German marauders, the Soviet people's first words of limitless gratitude and love are for our friend and father comrade STALIN, the organiser of our fight for freedom and independence of our motherland.'[69] This 1943 poster, of which 50,000 copies were printed, was made by Viktor Borisovich Koretskii. It is an iteration of the popular technique of photomontage. Koretskii was inspired by both Heartfield and Klutsis, pioneers of photomontage posters, but fell foul of the authorities in the early 1950s because of this 'formalism' and probably because he was Jewish. Stalin's death may have prevented his arrest. He was to create no fewer than 700 posters during his life. At the time this poster was released, the Soviet chances of prevailing in the Second World War were much better than in the previous years, but the victory was far from certain yet. Koretskii refers to the tradition of icon veneration common among Orthodox peasants, with Stalin's poster replacing the religious icon.

2

Plakate: The Origins and Role of Posters in Nazi Propaganda

This chapter investigates the origins, role, and development of Nazi *Plakate* (posters), as well as placing these within the context of Nazi propaganda as a whole. Even before the National Socialist German Workers' Party (*NSDAP*) or Nazi Party came to power in 1933, Hitler and his propagandists were already aware of the benefits of publicity and determined to use all types of propaganda media, including posters, in order to promote themselves. In *Mein Kampf* (1925), Hitler had noted: 'The art of the poster lies in the designer's ability to attract the attention of the crowd by form and colour.'[1] In particular, in the election campaigns in 1932, at the peak of the economic crisis in Germany, the *NSDAP* used posters to publicize its cause and to attract voters. The first part of this chapter discusses Nazi propaganda more conceptually and places this subject in its historical and historiographical context. The second section of the chapter moves on to examine the effectiveness of early Nazi posters in terms of their emotional and psychological appeal, and especially in their role of attracting voters across all sectors of German society for the Nazi Party in the years leading up to the Nazi *Machtergreifung* ('seizure of power'). The display of posters and placards formed a significant part of the propaganda and presentation work of the *NSDAP* from the early years of the movement.

Nazi Propaganda: History and Historiography

Nicholas O'Shaughnessy contends that Nazi propaganda, together with marketing and a 'mastery of persuasion', formed 'the essential core of government'.[2] He describes the 'choreography' of Nazi politics through a range of 'methods of sensory assault', with mass meetings, street processions, leaflet distribution and posters working together to convey the Nazi message.[3] Robert Wistrich notes how Hitler could see with great clarity 'the similarity between selling a commercial product and marketing a politician to the people'.[4] The Nazis had a strong sense of reading the popular mindset and connecting to this. O'Shaughnessy argues that 'Germans began to live life in imitation of their propaganda'.[5] And that while the Nazis were 'expert at mood control', the German 'people were also willing co-conspirators in their own self-deceit'.[6] Before we examine posters, it is worthwhile discussing the nature of Nazi propaganda as a whole, in order to see how posters fitted into the overall schema. The Nazis, from a very early date, comprehended the power of persuasion of the masses. They applied propaganda techniques designed to ideologically sway the German populace. They constructed and manufactured the idealized image of Hitler, the Party and the nation, on the one hand, and pitted these against the hated enemies of the nation, on the other. The Nazi Party realized from its earliest years the impact of symbols, words, and slogans. While Hitler came down on the side of repetitive messages until every last German understood his ideology, Goebbels was determined to use all means available to 'bring to the masses the new way of thinking in a modern, up-to-date, interesting and appealing manner'.[7] Goebbels's method was less direct, aiming to disseminate Nazi ideology among the population without them even realizing it. He constantly innovated and updated Nazi propaganda, gauging public opinion and making alterations when he considered this to be necessary. The power of suggestion and the predation upon the capacity for human persuasion were key aspects of Nazi propaganda work. Goebbels believed that just by holding up a 'dazzling campaign poster' he could move the people. This was easy enough when things were going well, but even when times were more challenging, he maintained that all he needed to do was persist and overcome adversity. But repetition was also important. Nazi propaganda succeeded most, argues David Welch, when it reinforced existing ideas or beliefs.[8] Hence, for example, it was easy to exploit anti-Weimar sentiments when people were disgruntled and exasperated with the Weimar system; or feelings of hurt national pride when people were humiliated not only by the loss of the First World War, but also by the Versailles settlement.

Goebbels understood well how to utilize propaganda effectively:

> [P]ropaganda will reach the broad masses of the people only if at every stage it is uniform. Nothing confuses the people more than lack of clarity ... The goal is not to present the common man with as many varied and contradictory theories as possible. The essence of propaganda is not in variety, but rather the forcefulness and persistence with which one selects ideas from the larger pool and hammers them into the masses using the most varied methods.[9]

In order to achieve this aim, and to saturate the population with its messages, the Nazi Party indeed employed various methods and their combined impact was vast. In this propaganda arsenal, the use of public space was crucial, and loudspeakers set up in town squares for people to hear Hitler speak were a key instance of this. Posters were another crucial aspect of the use of public space to influence people – a good example of this was in the construction of 'the Jew' as an enemy. Anti-Semitic posters and slogans in town squares, streets, walls, and billboards could not fail to have an impact on people walking past them. Repetitively and pervasively, such propaganda material drip-fed anti-Semitism to the population, bit by bit, especially because it was also reinforced by all the other propaganda media available to the regime. Where existing anti-Semitism was already latent, this was easy, but even where it was not, anti-Semitic sentiment was introduced and fuelled in this way, because the posters were impossible to ignore on the simplest errand or stroll, when people left their homes and went into the streets. Within the Nazi *Reichskulturkammer* (RKK or National Chamber of Culture), the Chamber for Visual Arts had a subdivision for graphic design, employing some 6,000 designers.[10] The aim of the RKK was to 'merge together the creative elements from all fields for carrying out, under the leadership of the state, a single will'.[11] And so, the graphic artists and designers had their part to play in this.

Furthermore, the Nazis were able to see the similarities between advertising and political propaganda, and to apply techniques that were known to be successful in commercial advertising to their political campaigns.[12] Sylke Wunderlich notes how '[t]he *NSDAP*'s propaganda strategists cleverly managed to blend the sophisticated methods of brand advertising with political agitation' in their posters.[13] Their aim was to systematically win over support for their ideology in a similar way to that in which an advertiser repeatedly hammers home the product until the consumer caves in and makes the purchase. This power, through the use of posters and billboards, was very strong, because people were susceptible to the messages and slogans as they went about their daily activities and errands outside the home, in public spaces. The French sociologist and post-modernist writer Jean Baudrillard (1929–2007) commented on the dangers of this phenomenon of a 'saturation' of images and slogans, as it developed throughout the twentieth century, but we can see its evolution in the first half of the twentieth century and Nazi posters provide a good example of this.[14]

We can conceptualize Nazi propaganda as 'political advertising'.[15] The Nazis sought a lasting impact and executed their aims through appealing to the emotions of the masses. They exploited the styles, forms, and techniques of new media both to their own advantage and to the detriment of their opponents. For Goebbels, quite simply, the dissemination of the Party ideology was central, and he maintained that any means that helped him to do that was useful. He aimed to utterly transform the way of thinking of the German nation and would settle for nothing less than complete absorption and acceptance of Nazi ideology by the whole population. This was no small task. In addition, the creation and the rejection of the 'other' not only identitifed and vilified enemies, but also engendered uniformity or homogeneity of the faithful or those who belonged to the *Volk*. In the field of psychology were not lost on Nazi propagandists. In particular in this regard, the French psychologist Gustave Le Bon's *The Crowd: A Study of the Popular Mind* (1895), a work on the psychology of the collective mind, was highly significant and influential. The Nazis knew that their propaganda could work to change the nature and thinking of the German populace. The crowds that lined the streets or the Nazi formations that filled the vast parade grounds of the Nuremberg Rallies each year signified the loss of individuality. Submerged in crowds, or as part of particular groups and leagues, individuals behaved differently. They reacted more strongly to emotional appeals and were swayed by the power of suggestion. The application of reason, which might have been present in them individually, left them once they were in the crowd.

Furthermore, as noted by Jacques Ellul, 'the propagandee is by no means just an innocent victim'.[16] Ellul argues that propaganda 'could not spread' without the 'implicit consent' of the propagandee. Persuasion was also a gradual process.[17] As Robert Gellately maintains, 'far from forcing unwanted or repellent messages down the throats of the population, the Nazis carefully tailored what they said, wrote, and especially what they did, in order to win and hold the support of the people'.[18] Hitler created and disseminated not only a political party and system, but also a *Weltanschauung* (worldview), which, as Randall Bytwerk notes, 'claimed authority over every area of life'.[19] It was a worldview that 'encompassed familiar aspects of German history, German thinking, and German culture'.[20] And in this respect, the intentions of the Nazi administration and its propagandists were sweeping: to transform every aspect of life and to infuse all spaces with their ideology.

Goebbels's stated aim at a press conference on 15 March 1933 was: 'It is not enough for people to be more or less reconciled to our regime, to be persuaded to adopt a neutral attitude towards us, rather we want to work on people until they have capitulated to us.'[21] Although the Party knew, in reality, that it would have to make do with quiescence rather than active support among the entire population, this propaganda work nevertheless took a huge amount of effort and manpower. Goebbels's ministry, which began with 350 employees in 1933, had expanded to encompass over 1,900 employees by 1942. Furthermore, forty-two regional propaganda offices employed a further 1,400 people. But in addition to these, the Nazi Party Central Propaganda Office (*Reichspropagandaleitung*, or *RPL*), located in Munich, also under Goebbels's aegis, carried out a large range of propaganda activities. The 'active propaganda' section was charged with 'carrying out propaganda actions at every level', including 'the production and distribution of appropriate posters and leaflets'.[22] A labyrinthine bureaucratic process, therefore, employing thousands of people in offices at the national and the local level, under both state government and party leadership, undertook a vast propaganda campaign. These offices outlined the content of the propaganda and aimed to deliver the ideology of the *NSDAP* to each and every German citizen. Moreover, dissent was discouraged by the very suggestion that the level of public support for the regime was great. At a certain point, it became too dangerous to express serious criticism of the Nazi government or its policies. As Bytwerk notes, there was 'enormous pressure on people to avoid behaviour that undermined the public façade of unanimity'.[23] Ultimately, the need to conform 'led citizens gradually to shift their internal opinions to be consistent with their public behaviour'.[24]

Much of Nazi propaganda, presenting a utopian vision for the future, was based on the propagation of myths, most significantly perhaps the legend surrounding the infallible *Führer* himself. Then there was the myth of the classless society, the *Volksgemeinschaft*, in which all Germans were supposed to be living in parity, enjoying the same advantages of living in the Third *Reich* during its economic recovery and making the same sacrifices during harder times and especially during the war. To be sure, this too was a fallacy, but at face value, perhaps, the German masses could believe it, for some of the time at least. The fabrication of 'enemies' was an especially powerful form of garnering mass support for the *NSDAP*. Putting together 'Communists' and 'Jews' as the eternal enemies of National Socialism and of the nation, the regime made it very clear who belonged to the *Volksgemeinschaft* and who did not. The crude demonization of enemies was crucial to Nazi propaganda and was amply evident on the posters of the era. Simple and direct messages, that were ubiquitous and difficult to avoid, could reach the broad masses through this medium. Posters used in this way fit with Ellul's observation about propaganda that it aims 'to surround man by all possible routes ... through his conscious and his unconscious, assailing him in both his private and his public life'.[25]

The Nazis also hated Weimar democracy and everything that the Weimar Republic stood for, especially its progressiveness. Their early posters focused on 'defaming parliamentarianism and democratic politicians'.[26] They mythologized the Weimar Republic into a hateful and decadent system that only they could redress. Its 'villains' had signed the Treaty of Versailles. The Weimar Republic represented everything the Nazis opposed and so, by contrast, the new National Socialist system would replace the corrupt Weimar system and bring about a national renewal or 'palingenesis'. Roger Griffin has conceptualized Nazi (and fascist) ideology as 'a palingenetic form of populist ultra-nationalism'.[27] Returning to its German essence and a *völkisch* tradition, the Nazis maintained, the nation would be saved from the perils of metropolitan and cosmopolitan life, the Jews and other bad influences, under the banner of the swastika. The new *Volksgemeinschaft* would bring all Germans together towards a common goal and eradicate competing loyalties to class, church, or region. It would be pure, untainted by impure blood or by 'inferior' people, including the 'hereditarily ill'. This 'national community' which was simultaneously inclusive (of *Volksgenossen* or 'national comrades') and exclusive (of Jews and others regarded as 'inferior') clearly found popular appeal. Those that fitted in could relax and enjoy the 'benefits' offered to them by the Nazi administration, but those that did not were vilified (and ultimately annihilated).

The Nazi regime was characterized by many inherent contradictions, often displaying a mismatch between ideology and policy, such as the concern to appear new and modern (while at the same time excoriating the modernist elements of the Weimar Republic) on the one hand yet a return to the past, harking back to the origins of the German *Volk*, *Blut und Boden* (Blood and Soil) and the glorification of rural idylls on the other.[28] The posters of the era showcase these discrepancies – some concerned with technology, motorization, and travel, others focused on the simple life of the German farmer. As O'Shaughnessy notes,

> The posters transferred Germans to a magical realm away from the everyday. They melded the medieval and the modern, heroes and autobahns and ancient high-gabled townhouses, knights in armour, statistics and pictograms, futurism combined with the sham archaic.[29]

And the contradictions inherent in this media output, as in other types of Nazi propaganda, were unimportant and went mainly unchallenged, because they appealed to the emotions, not to reason. Indeed, the dream and the promise offered by Nazi propaganda enabled ordinary people 'to choose to overlook evil and see illusions of good'.[30]

The utilization of symbols was highly significant to the Nazi propaganda machine. The Nazis employed symbols to appeal to people's emotions too, especially because they were easy to imbibe and absorb. As O'Shaughnessy notes, they were 'fresh, sanitised, ostensibly not evil at all'.[31] Symbols both captured and created the public mood – in daily life, and in rituals and activities. Wherever people looked, they were confronted with symbols of the Third *Reich*. The swastika, of course, was the most prevailing of these. Most symbols were deliberately derived from German history and traditions.[32] The colours of the Nazi Party and its flag formed a crucial part of symbolization. O'Shaughnessy describes how the 'violent red of poster and banner tore into consciousness'.[33] The brightness of the colours used was also important, with 'whole batches of posters being rejected after printing because the colours were thought to be too pallid'.[34] The slanting of symbols to create a sense of motion and action became an important poster technique. The eagle was a much-used Nazi symbol – representative of the old German empire, and therefore familiar, yet associated at the same time with the *NSDAP*, and thus contemporaneous. The Nazi propagandists understood that such representations were extremely useful for creating identity. As Wunderlich notes, the swastika, *SS* rune and eagle were 'all inextricably associated with the Third *Reich*'.[35] The ubiquity of posters meant that people were confronted with these symbols constantly.

To be sure, the words that accompanied the symbols on Nazi posters were equally important. Persuasive language and slogans, expressions of National-Socialist rhetoric and ideology, made it clear to those viewing the posters how they should feel. Together, the symbols and words seemed to close out independent thought or critical faculty. The German masses could latch on to the images and words easily – there was no requirement to think hard or to think at all. This worked to engender homogeneity and uniformity, like the process of *Gleichschaltung* and the creation of the *Volksgemeinschaft* more generally. In terms of language use and control under National Socialism, and its impact on the mind, O'Shaughnessy notes 'the speed with which this new lingua franca took hold'.[36] The slogans were always powerful and dynamic.

Typography on Nazi posters was also of great importance in their overall presentation. Fraktur (or Gothic or blackletter), characterized by angular broken lines, had been the official typescript style of the German Empire after its establishment in 1871. During the Weimar Republic, either these broken scripts or antiqua scripts were employed 'more or less equally in books and newspapers until the end of the 1920s'.[37] The Nazis moved to almost all printed matter (newspapers, pamphlets, magazines, and posters) being produced in Fraktur, which was associated with nationalism. Once Hitler was in power, Fraktur became the mandatory script for all official printed materials. New broken fonts were developed and designed including Deutschland, Element, and Tannenberg, which became known as 'jackboot gothic', indicative of 'discipline and conformity'.[38] The Tannenberg typescript became one of the most popular during the Third *Reich*. It is worth noting that in 1941, however, Hitler suddenly 'issued a circular prohibiting the further use of fraktur'.[39] Having successfully invaded Poland, France, Holland, and Belgium, he realized that only 'normal fonts' or antiqua fonts should be employed, so that people in Nazi-occupied territories, who were unaccustomed to the fraktur-type fonts, would be able to read them.[40]

The language of contempt was strong and insistent too. For example, the 'Judeo-Bolshevik enemy' was portrayed as a threat to the existence of the nation, and it was also one that had to be dealt with swiftly before it destroyed the German *Volk*. The Nazi anti-Semitic slogans, together with the extreme and crude caricatures, appealed to the mentality of the crowd, which, as Le Bon had explained, turned it into an absolute truth, with no real questioning of its veracity. This constructed foe was a simple one, eliminating any complexity, easy for all to comprehend and resonating with people's sentiments and biases, whether these were tacit or overt, conscious or unconscious. The Jews were characterized as 'inferior', parasitic, deceitful, duplicitous, diabolical, and associated with disease and pestilence. In contrast, the German 'race' was 'superior' and pure, associated with honour, decency, cleanliness, and good health. These contrasts were amply evident in the visual language of Nazi posters. The so-called racial purity of the *Herrenvolk* ('master race') was pitted against 'racial inferiority' of Jews, Sinti and Roma, Slavs and other 'enemies'. Indeed, the existence or manufacture of the 'other' reinforced the sense of self-belief of the nation and those who belonged. We shall return to this in more detail in Chapter 4. Now, in the following section, we shall examine Nazi poster propaganda in the early years of the movement and up to the *Machtergreifung* in January 1933.

Nazi Posters before 1933

This early *NSDAP* poster advertising a meeting addressed by Hitler in Munich, on 27 February 1925, with the title 'Germany's Future and Our Movement', is quite basic and essentially factual (see Figure 2.1). It uses no images. It is simply used to publicize this political event, giving details of the date, time, and location, in addition to the title of Hitler's speech. It is one of many posters put up by the *NSDAP* – as well as by other political parties – to advertise their meetings. As the years progressed, however, the Nazi Party utilized posters to attract German voters, to good effect, by employing colourful images, as well as words and slogans. The Party recognized the importance of posters and spent considerable funds on getting its posters designed and put up. The posters evolved over the course of these years. Indeed, they needed to be skilful and effective, because the German political landscape was complex indeed, and other political parties – in particular, the German Communist Party (*KPD*) and the German Socialist Party (*SPD*) – used posters too, not only to publicize their own cause, but also to vilify the *NSDAP*. Moreover, the Nazis carefully and deliberately analysed the publicity materials produced by their political adversaries, especially the Communists. They closely observed and openly copied poster styles from the *KPD* with 'large mono-coloured areas and the use of catchy symbols and large formats', as well as the technique of photomontage.

It is important to note that while posters were just one form within a wide array of propaganda media and techniques – including marches, flags and uniforms, mass rallies, and meetings – employed by the Nazi Party, they have been largely neglected in the historical literature of the period in comparison with other aspects of Nazi propaganda. In conjunction with the Nazi press, the *Völkischer Beobachter* (*People's Observer*) and the meetings where Hitler's speeches influenced his audience and drew attention to the Nazi cause, posters conveyed messages and slogans devised and honed to appeal to the German population. From the late 1920s, Gregor Strasser, in charge of the Party's Propaganda Directorate, put into place active recruitment and propaganda campaigns, creating grassroots support through his effective organization of the Party, both vertically and horizontally. Local Nazi organizations were instructed about how to target different audiences and about how and where to put up posters. A considerable amount of effort and attention went into how to attract public attention, including 'when to

ORIGINS AND ROLE OF POSTERS IN NAZI PROPAGANDA 37

FIGURE 2.1 *Early Nazi Poster 27 February 1925.*

stack several versions of the same poster on a kiosk or when to use different posters'.[41] It was necessary to create eye-catching posters with strong images and memorable slogans. This entailed a sophisticated message of persuasion that is perhaps belied by the seeming simplicity of posters as a medium for the widespread dissemination of ideology. Nazi posters were inspired by examples from existing models and examples, not only posters from the First World War and from Mussolini's fascist regime in Italy, which had already been in power since October 1922, but also from the USSR. The Soviet Union was a less likely source of inspiration ideologically, to be sure, but the Nazis could see how Stalin had already utilized this type of propaganda to consolidate his rule.

The figure of Hitler himself was, of course, a crucial point of focus in the Nazi poster campaigns. Across all propaganda media, Hitler was portrayed as a messianic leader destined to restore Germany to greatness. He attracted a very broad cross-section of German society with his promises, and Nazism became alluring for a whole variety of reasons, including self-interest. Hitler's charismatic image and the leadership cult that surrounded him led to increasing electoral success. The Party's way of presenting itself was a very significant factor. It was a party committed to the revival of the fortunes of Germany. Nazi posters had an important role here in the appeal to the German populace. Hitler and his propagandists articulated the fears and concerns, expectations, and hopes of the German people, creating a mass movement. The appeal of the Nazi Party lay in its capacity to tailor specific – but not necessarily compatible – messages to different sections of the German population. The *NSDAP* portrayed itself as a party of universal appeal, and in this way attracted significant and broad electoral success. Hitler maintained that the most successful and effective propaganda should be directed at 'the emotions of the masses' and that the function of propaganda lay in 'calling the masses' attention to certain facts, processes, necessities etc., whose significance is thus for the first time placed within their field of vision'.[42] For this, posters were, to be sure, an ideal form. We can observe how posters were utilized by the Nazi Party during the final years of the Weimar Republic to generate popular support. Hitler had noted in *Mein Kampf*: 'All advertising, whether in the field of business or politics, achieves success only through the continuity and sustained uniformity of its application.'[43] And he was determined to achieve this advertising success for the *NSDAP* throughout his electoral campaigns. The different parties in Germany, across the political spectrum, utilized posters and placards, especially between 1930 and 1933 and, therefore, it was especially important for the *NSDAP* to make them as striking and effective as possible – using bold colours, satire, and effective artistry. The Nazi posters portrayed Hitler's political adversaries as evil. Enemies were attacked and vilified. The posters were put up on the windows of Party offices, the windows of Hitler's supporters, as well as kiosks and walls. They had stark and simple themes, which aided in their appeal and effectiveness. By this point, the *NSDAP* was not concerned about being ignored any longer – its presence was clearly felt. Powerful but simple slogans were repeated again and again, accompanied by striking and strident images.

In 1928, the Nazi Party had attracted just 2.8 per cent of the national vote and held only twelve seats in the *Reichstag*. After the Wall Street Crash (October 1929), unemployment rates in Germany soared. By the winter of 1930–1, there were already over 5 million unemployed, with this figure rising to 6 million a year later. Unemployment took a serious toll on life in Germany – it destroyed people's self-respect and undermined their status. Ever-growing numbers of homeless young men lived on the streets of Germany's towns and cities, becoming increasingly despondent. As young men aimlessly wandered the streets or sat doing nothing at home, Richard Evans notes: 'German society seemed to be descending into a morass of misery and criminality ..., people began to grasp at political straws: anything, however extreme, seemed better than the hopeless mess they appeared to be in now.'[44] The ability of the NSDAP to attract millions of voters after 1929 ensured that the Party became the decisive factor in German politics during the political, social, and economic crises of the early 1930s. The Nazi Party capitalized upon the atmosphere of hopelessness and desperation to appeal to a substantial percentage of the German population. Between 1929 and 1932, the success of the NSDAP at the polls made it a party to be taken seriously. Once the economic crisis had hit Germany, the Nazi Party was able to make enormous electoral gains. In the elections of July 1932, the NSDAP attracted 13.75 million votes (37.3 per cent of the vote), making it the largest parliamentary party. Nazi election posters impacted the complex political terrain, especially in 1932, at the height of the political morass and economic depression in Germany.

The Nazis put out a number of different posters that were intended to appeal to the working class. One national election poster from November 1932 shows a darkened and gloomy image of idle German factories under communism and socialism; contrasted directly adjacent to this is the colourful, bright, orange picture of well-lit and industrious German factories, with smoking chimneys indicating their activity, under National Socialism. This artful juxtaposition made the appeal of Hitler and National Socialism look very strong indeed. Designed by Hans Wittig-Friesen, this poster associated the wording '*Elend u. Hunger*' ('Misery and Hunger') with the symbols of the Communists and the Socialists, and '*Arbeit und Brot*' ('Work and Bread') with the swastika, the symbol of National Socialism. Urging the people to vote for Hitler, this poster was plainly directed at the working-class electorate. The poster used symbols representing powerful ideologies – not only that, but the message conveyed about which ideology people should choose was amply clear. Moreover, this was also particularly appealing to wider sections of the German populace, at a time when middle-class Germans, as well as German industrialists, felt threatened by the political left, with a pervasive fear of the 'red threat' or 'red menace' posed by Communism. The Nazi Party, as its name National Socialist German Workers' Party intimated, had always tried to secure electoral support from German workers, initially with very little success. It had failed to recruit workers as members and voters during the 1920s, up until 1928. Indeed, this is a large part of the reason for which it shifted its electoral emphasis to the middle class after that. Yet the NSDAP did attract some workers, particularly from small manufacturing sectors, rural areas, and small towns. In fact, as Dick Geary has shown, 'one worker in every four voted for Hitler in July 1932', and it is from these sectors of German workers that Nazi support came. Nazism appealed much less to the organized working classes in the large cities and industrial areas, closely linked to trade unions and strongly affiliated to either the Socialist

Party (*SPD*) or the Communist Party (*KPD*). While the Nazi Party clearly won many workers' votes at the height of its popularity in July 1932, the social profile of its working-class electorate was very different from that of the *SPD* and the *KPD*, whose support came from the industrialized working class. Thus, for example, if the *NSDAP* attracted the votes of fitters, mechanics and metalworkers, it was those who worked in small garages, repair shops, and small-scale workshops and enterprises, rather than those in large factories and engineering plants. The *NSDAP* appealed to non-unionized workers, to rural labourers, those in domestic service, as well as workers in transport, the utility companies and the postal service. In this way, the Nazis split the blue-collar electorate and attracted working-class votes towards them.

The poster entitled '*Arbeiter der Stirn der Faust Wählt den Frontsoldaten Hitler!*' ('Workers of the Mind, of the Fist: Vote for Front Soldier: Hitler!') was also intended to appeal to all types of workers, both blue-collar and white-collar. It is all in block capitals, with red and black lettering, and with the word 'Hitler' in the largest font size. Designed to attract the vote of all German workers, there is also the clear message here that Hitler, as a front-line soldier in the First World War, could be trusted in his intention and determination to save and to serve the German nation.

The Nazi poster, '*Gegen Hunger und Verzweiflung! Wählt Hitler!*' ('Against Hunger and Despair! Vote Hitler!'), from the March 1932 presidential election campaign, designed by Hans Schweitzer, was also very powerful. With simple words (again with the word 'Hitler' in a larger size than the rest of the text) and graphically depicting a miserable and dejected German family, the message was clear. Ordinary German families could strongly identify with this image, and they could envisage hope in the event of Hitler's electoral success.

Another poster that ably depicted the misery of the times was '*Unsere letzte Hoffnung: Hitler*' ('Our Last Hope: Hitler'), designed by Mjölnir (Hans Schweitzer) for the March 1932 presidential election campaign (see Colour Plate 13). Here, a miserable and wretched image of mainly German men, but also a woman carrying a small child, shows them looking ahead for a way out of economic despair. The clear message portrayed at this point was that all other options had been tried and had failed, and quite literally that Hitler – in very large block letters at the bottom of the poster – was the 'last hope' for the German people.

The Hitler poster from 1932 printed by Heinz Franke in Munich from a photograph taken by Heinrich Hoffmann, the official photographer of Hitler, who was also based in Munich, is powerful in its simplicity (see Figure 2.2). Hitler looks straight ahead, strong, serious, and decisive. The simplicity of this poster was key to its effectiveness – just one headshot of Hitler and just one word, 'Hitler', in large, white lettering against a black backdrop. This

FIGURE 2.2 *Hitler Poster.*

poster was used in the March 1932 presidential election campaign, in which Hitler stood against Hindenburg.

Another Nazi poster from the 1932 presidential election campaign, designed by Hans Schweitzer, depicted a strong, muscular, Nordic man breaking free from chains, with the caption at the top '*Schluss jetzt!*' ('Enough is enough!') and at the bottom *Wählt Hitler* ('Vote Hitler'). The word 'Hitler' was in a significantly larger font size than the other words. This red and white poster, with broad brushstrokes and simplicity of style, both followed Communist-type propaganda and vividly signified the identity of the *NSDAP*, with a swastika belt buckle at the man's waist. It was time for Germans to break free from the failure and misery of the Weimar Republic by supporting and voting for National Socialism.

The 1932 poster, '*Arbeit Freiheit und Brot!*' ('Work, Freedom and Bread!'), designed by Felix Albrecht, urged people to vote for the National Socialists. Using strong red lettering on a creamy yellow background, the image of a strong German farmer, in harvesting mode and looking towards

FIGURE 2.3 *Nazi Election Posters on Display 1932.*

the future, had particular appeal to those living in the countryside. The Nazis employed posters artfully to appeal to different sectors of the population.

During the March and July 1932 election campaigns, the Nazi Party used 'both figurative posters and austere designs in black, white and red', which 'appeared side by side on advertising columns'.[45] (see Figure 2.3) Large depictions of Nazi symbols, especially the swastika, accompanied by distinctive lettering created powerful visual propaganda that could be effective from a distance. Wunderlich notes how they 'created a dynamic impression by means of motifs aligned to the diagonal, such as a flag or a cross, usually oriented towards the top left'.[46] Thus, nothing was left to chance – even when the posters gave the impression of simplicity, they had been crafted and created very carefully to achieve maximum impact.

PLATE 1 *Iraklii Moiseevich Toidze*, 'Rodina-Mat' zovyot!' *('The Motherland Calls', 1941).*

PLATE 2 *El Lissitzky, 'Beat the Whites with the Red Wedge'.*

PLATE 3 *Aleksandr Apsit, 'International'.*

PLATE 4 *'The Growth of Soviet Agriculture after a Decade'*.

PLATE 5 *'In Answer to the Insolent International Popism [A Pope Is a Russian-Orthodox Priest] and Bourgeoisie We Strengthen the Military Preparedness of the USSR and the Military Power of the Red Army'.*

PLATE 6 *'Greetings to the Opening of the Global Gigant Dneprostroi (DGES [the Dnepropetrovsk Hydro-Electric Station]), Long Live the Shockworkers of the Building of Socialism'.*

PLATE 7 'Long Live the Brotherly Union and Great Friendship of the USSR Peoples!'.

PLATE 8 'The Endless Steppe Woke Up from Its Dream, and Happiness Is Brought to Us by the Spring of Communism!'.

PLATE 9 *'Kill Him! He Killed Your Loved Ones, Burned Your House Down, Destroyed Your Workplace!'*.

PLATE 10 *'What Does a Pig Need Culture and Science For? Its Mind Is After All Tiny:* Mein Kampf *Is the Limit for a Pig Snout, and Its Ideal [Is] the Corporal's Boot!'*.

PLATE 11 'The Great Patriotic War'.

PLATE 12 *'Study the Great Path of the Party of Lenin-Stalin!'*.

The election posters by Wilhelm Jakob Engelhard from November 1932 and March 1933, respectively, show very bold, three-dimensional swastika images, both using just red, black, and white. The November 1932 poster states: '*Das Volk wählt Liste 1 – Nationalsozialisten*' ('The People Vote for List 1 – National Socialists') (see Colour Plate 14). A large red number one rises from a large red swastika, with crowds depicted as being drawn towards it, as if to a magnet. The March 1933 poster claims: '*Hitler baut auf – Wählt Liste 1*' ('Hitler is making progress – Vote for List 1'). Here, the image is of a three-dimensional swastika shaped into a tall, red edifice. This is clear and powerful iconography. In the March and November 1933 posters, Hitler is shown alongside Hindenburg, indicating that the Nazi Party had support from the President and creating legitimacy for Hitler.

The National Socialists also aimed some of their posters directly towards women: '*Deutsche Frauen Denkt an Eure Kinder*' ('German Women, Think of Your Children'), with the suggestion that voting for Hitler was the best way to secure their children's future (see Figure 2.4). One such poster shows an anxious woman with her two children – clambering and hanging on to her for solace. Another poster depicts a young family, with a dejected father (unemployed) and a serious and worried-looking mother accompanied by a message to 'save the German family' by voting for Hitler.

Additionally, the *NSDAP* appealed considerably to youth, as a new party and a party of dynamism and activism. A poster from 1930 by Ludwig Hohlwein called upon students to be propagandists for Hitler: '*Studenten: Seid Propagandisten des Führers*' ('Students: Be Propagandists for the Leader'). Thus, we can understand that the Nazi Party covered all possible bases – directing their propaganda at particular groups within the population and simultaneously appealing to the nation as a whole, as was the case with one particular poster, showing Hitler in an active pose, looking towards the future, with the arresting caption: 'We take the future of the nation in hand'. This poster showed that Hitler meant business. Here was a man of action and a party that would make a difference. The message on this poster conveyed decisive action, not only to take Germany out of its economic misery and political chaos, but also to lead it to a glorious forthcoming destiny.

There were some anti-Semitic posters put up by the *NSDAP* during the Weimar years. For instance, in 1924, posters showed a fat Jew in a top hat (representing capitalist greed) sitting on the shoulders of a German worker. In addition, the poster '*Der Schlag muss sitzen!*' ('The Blow must Hit Home!'), by Philipp Rupprecht, signed Fips, from 1928, showed hostility and violence towards Jews. However, often the anti-Semitic rhetoric was toned down, in order to make the Nazi Party appear respectable, although in some areas, for example, Nuremberg, where Julius Streicher, *Gauleiter* (regional leader) of Franconia, regularly put out anti-Semitic propaganda in his weekly *Der Stürmer*, this seemed to be less of a concern. Once the Nazis came to power, of course, their anti-Semitic rhetoric and policies became increasingly radical, as we shall see in later chapters.

FIGURE 2.4 *Posters on Display for Women to Vote Nazi.*

The Nazis used a combination of violence and propaganda in their campaigning during the last years of the Weimar Republic. Street brawls between the Nazi stormtroopers (*SA*) and the Communists paid off as the *NSDAP* was seen, particularly by the middle-class and business interests, as the party acting against the 'red' (Communist) threat. In addition, widespread campaigns in the presidential election of spring 1932 made Hitler more visible. Joseph Goebbels stated, 'Our placards have become wonderful .... [t]he whole country has to pay attention'.[47] The Nazi Party chartered aeroplanes to fly Hitler across Germany. This was a new technique that took Hitler across the country to both urban and rural areas to address public rallies. Hitler was instantly recognizable and although he lost the presidential election (Hindenburg won with 53 per cent of the votes), this had an impact going forward.

Its use of modern methods and mass communication meant that when Hitler came to power in January 1933, he had a party with significant and broad grassroots support. His party had a skilful propaganda directorate. Goebbels did not have one of the original three Nazi cabinet positions in the new coalition government, which was initially disappointing for him, but through his persistence and his propaganda acumen, as well as his loyalty, it was only a matter of weeks before he was given the position of Minister of Popular Enlightenment and Propaganda on 13 March 1933. His earlier propaganda campaigns as *Gauleiter* (regional leader) of Berlin had won him the admiration of Hitler who was ready to reward him. The position of Minister of Popular Enlightenment and Propaganda was established by special decree and with it came a cabinet position. From there, Goebbels conducted for the next twelve years, in peacetime and at war, a carefully orchestrated propaganda campaign to sway the German populace. In this propaganda arsenal, the posters were an important weapon – if perhaps somewhat overlooked in the secondary literature, in comparison with others such as film, press and radio. As noted by Hans Bohrmann, 'the poster played a special role' in Nazi propaganda, because 'everyone was confronted with it' directly.[48]

3

Soviet Posters in the 1920s and 1930s

Both Russian-Imperial and international artistic developments influenced the genesis of the Soviet poster, as we suggested earlier. In her standard work, Victoria Bonnell emphasized the Russian tradition of icon painting as a key source of inspiration for the poster artists, something which we have not yet pondered.[1] Before 1917, icons were ubiquitous in Eastern-Slavic homes in the tsar's empire and Soviet posters occasionally referred explicitly to religious themes with which their viewers were familiar. But religious imagery influenced other contemporary European visual arts as well, of course, and it is not that easy to tease out a deliberate play on a specific Orthodox tradition in Soviet posters. Vice versa, it would be wrong to propose an aesthetics for Soviet posters that is wholly derivative of 'Western' artistic tradition. Stephen Norris's thorough exploration of the survival *lubki* tradition irrefutably shows this.[2]

What mattered most, as Bonnell notes as well, was that the display of powerful images was possibly the most effective means of propaganda in a country whose population was far from fully literate, and in which most individuals had no ready access to the means of communication that became omnipresent during the twentieth century.[3] Even telephones were a rarity in 1917, at least outside of the larger Soviet cities. Lithographic presses allowed for a quick, comparatively cheap, and abundant reproduction of images. In other words, in the absence of radios, televisions, or computers and given the paucity of cinema theatres (or even of time to see a film), and the much more time-consuming process of producing newspapers intended for a select audience, the poster suddenly burst on to the scene.

The Birth of the Soviet Poster

The poster's time had come in the Russian Civil War that broke out in the spring of 1918. This was all the more so on the Bolshevik side, for the Communists throughout the conflict maintained control over most major railways in much more populated European Russia. This allowed for swift transport of the poster (metal) templates to the printers located in the region's population centres. While posters were thus most visible in Moscow and Petrograd, they also hung in Smolensk, Tver', Ryazan, Nizhnii Novgorod, Novgorod, Vologda, Iaroslavl', Voronezh, or Kazan. And even when two decades later in the Second World War radio receivers had become more common and literacy rates were far higher, posters still proved one of the most effective communication means that the Soviet regime had at its disposal.

By that time, though, many years of testing various poster designs had additionally appeared to make their message highly effective, which was another part of their sustained popularity (at least among those who were responsible for their production and distribution). Irrespective of the exact degree of positive audience reception, a quest to make the most effective political poster can be detected from 1918 until at least the mid-1930s. Though perhaps the fail-safe formula for the ideal poster was never found, by 1941 enough had been learned to produce posters whose images were profoundly gripping. Initially, in the civil war years, though, artists and *agitprop* officials were sometimes at a loss in their search for the optimal poster to enthuse their audience, leading to some awkward results. Only gradually did creative originality mesh with popular penchants and tastes, as well as with the expectations of Communist Party officials.

Elena Barkhatova has written that '[f]rom the very first days of the Soviet state's existence, the poster, which before the 1917 revolution had been little more than the stepchild of Russian graphics, became its favorite'.[4] Barkhatova's chronology might not be quite accurate, as the first officially sponsored political poster seems to have been released in August 1918 rather than in late 1917, but her overall point seems correct.[5] The arrival of the poster as a mass means of Bolshevik (Communist) propaganda occurred during the Russian Civil War, which began in the late spring of 1918 and concluded in the early months of 1921.[6] The political poster was not an entirely new phenomenon, however: at the beginning of the First World War, Kazimir Malevich and Vladimir Mayakovsky had made patriotic posters in the *lubki* style, as we have seen.[7] They gained thereby experience in terms of the mechanics of making posters as well as some insight into selling political messages by way of such *plakaty*.

After the October 1917 coup, the Bolshevik regime ever more assertively engaged in a process that resembles the *Gleichschaltung* in Nazi Germany in 1933 and 1934. It entailed bringing politics, cultural expression and (which was different from the *Reich*) even economic endeavour under control of the regime. In this vein, the Communists actively directed the production and distribution of posters, determining their contents while ensuring their widest distribution.[8] By the early summer of 1918, when the civil war heated up and people needed to be mobilized behind the Communist cause, posters began to be diffused across Communist-held territory through the Soviet press agency *Rosta*. This organization's employees usually hung politically charged 'captioned cartoons' in glassed-in display cases attached to walls or in empty shop windows, because of which they are usually known in English as wall windows.[9] In the absence of newspapers due to the lack of paper, ink, printers, or sophisticated (letter) printing presses, this was one effective means of preaching the Bolshevik gospel.[10]

Rosta was led in 1919 and 1920 by Platon Kerzhentsev (1881–1940), who left a considerable imprint on Soviet art as a Communist Party *agitprop* official in the late 1920s and head of the government's Committee of Arts Affairs during the 1930s.[11] Kerzhentsev was the son of a medical doctor. We recognize in him therefore how another scion of the Russian empire's upper tiers imposed his sophisticated cultural taste on the proletarian masses. Nonetheless, he endeavoured to meet less refined predilections halfway, as in his 1936 criticism of the Shostakovich opera *Lady Macbeth of Mtsensk*, a piece of music that flirted with atonal and discordant elements that had become the fashion in Western-European composition. At the same time, Kerzhentsev's criticism about the opera's alleged cacophony had been triggered by Stalin, who had been aghast at a performance he attended of this work in Moscow's Bolshoi Theatre. In other words, Kerzhentsev knew whom Soviet art should particularly please: the leaders, not the people. Conveniently for Kerzhentsev, as we will further explore below, the 1930s leaders' taste was not that different from the people.

During the civil war, the premier pioneering Soviet poster-makers were Aleksandrs Apsitis (Aleksandr Apsit, 1880–1944), the multi-talented Vladimir Mayakovsky (already by 1917 famous as a futurist poet), his girlfriend, the artist Lilya Brik (1891–1978), Mikhail Cheremnykh and Ivan Maliutin (1891–1932).[12] They churned out hundreds of posters (in which the *lubki* tradition markedly surfaced), displaying the captioned cartoons noted earlier, which were distributed to dozens of towns across Communist-controlled territory through the *Rosta* agency.

But while a civil war raged in the former tsarist empire, less violent clashes erupted between all sorts of artistic schools, not least among the poster-makers. Literal or figurative artists were condemned by modernists who revelled in abstraction and symbolism.[13] The camps were only loosely divided, however, since all were united in seeking a way to effectively sell the communist message. A futurist or 'absurdist' such as Mayakovsky, who wrote difficult to comprehend poetry, operated in a highly eclectic manner. He had no qualms about drawing on the old-fashioned *lubki* tradition in order to get the message across to his audience: after all, his quest and that of many of his fellow artists in the early Soviet years were to counter '*l'art pour l'art*' sentiments, the elitist decadence of aesthetes like the Symbolist poets Zinaida Gippius (1869–1945) and Dmitrii Merezhkovskii (1866–1941) who made art for the true connoisseur, and condemned the October coup as a manifestation of the 'people-beast' (*narod-zver*').[14] Instead, Mayakovsky sought to create art that was truly of the people (*narodnyi*), a somewhat opaque concept.

Despite the incessant trumpeting of the cause of human emancipation and the announced imminent arrival of a world of equal human beings, the poster-makers could not quite escape the prejudices of their time. A work by Cheremnykh from 1919 displays vile racism, with a nasty depiction of what presumably are meant to be nude – albeit armed – Africans being dispatched as part of the Entente forces to Russia.[15] Undoubtedly, this was par for the course in Western 'bourgeois' or 'capitalist' publications, as may be seen from *Tintin au Congo*, Hergé's first *bande dessinée*, published in Brussels in 1931.[16] Belgium was of course the colonial power ruling Congo, and Hergé had introduced his protagonist in a serialized strip in 1929, which had Tintin visit a heavily caricaturized Soviet Union.[17] But Cheremnykh's Africans were no less dehumanized than Hergé's, belying the cause of human equality for which communism stood, an ideal that was not shared by the conservative publishers of Hergé's *oeuvre*.

Likewise, misogyny can be detected, defying the professed quality of the sexes in Soviet Russia in these early posters. Apsit's 1918 or 1919 officially commissioned poster *Internatsional*, captioned by the eponymous socialist hymn, shows a sort of tentacled beast representing capitalism, which is under heavy assault from uniformly male proletarians[18] (see Colour Plate 3). This nightmarish poster was published under the direct authority of the soviets' central executive committee – the official legislature – of the Russian Socialist Federative Socialist Republic (RSFSR) in Moscow.[19] The text of the *International*, the revolutionary anthem, is rendered beneath a macabre depiction of the class struggle between monstrous capital and heroic proletariat. The female monster is being slain (as Marxist ideology mandated), its pedestal of capital and gold torn down by male revolutionaries, but at great sacrifice. The gender binary opposition seems evident to us: Was Apsit, though, fully conscious of his misogyny? Religious overtones are evident, with the beast echoing the Book of Revelation's Whore of Babylon. She is crowned by Orthodox Church's cupolas. Whether Apsit's poster is intended as an assault on religion is less obvious: he may have used the reference to the Biblical Book of Revelation either because of his own religious (Lutheran) upbringing, or since he suspected that the salacious tale about the Whore was familiar to his audience. Likely more because of its overt use of religious symbolism than for its misogyny, this was not a metaphor that was re-used in Soviet poster art. Intriguing is the Mata Hari-esque winged woman sitting, unperturbed, before the monster. Dmitrii Moor and others would subsequently chastise Apsit for his confusing compositions, and one can here easily see why.

Apsit left the Soviet republic soon after the civil war's end (and was to die in Nazi Germany in 1944!) and abandoned the typically radical ideological convictions of Soviet poster artists, but Soviet posters' artistic propaganda was never quite able to escape its reflection of discriminatory genderization: the best-known example is the standard juxtaposition of the male factory worker and the female collective farmer during the 1930s and 1940s.[20]

Experimentation with Form: The 1920s

A good illustration of the persistence of traditional gender roles in the Soviet Union is the odd early poster of 1923 by the female artist Aleksandra S. Soborova (1882–1935) (see Figure 3.1).[21] At the top, its text reads, 'Children Are the Guarantee of the Future and the Joy of the Present!' Its lower text advertises 'The Week of the Protection of Motherhood and Youth, of the Orphaned and Ill Child', which apparently stretched out from 30 April to 8 May. The style is quite traditional and a bit sugary, reminiscent of Victorian illustrations in children's books (Soborova indeed illustrated such texts). It also displays vaguely religious overtones of the *Bogoroditsa* (Mother of God) of the Russian-Orthodox iconic tradition. It shows the unease with

FIGURE 3.1 '*Children Are the Guarantee of the Future and the Joy of the Present!*' (Soborova).

the official gender equality that was one of the key Soviet principles. Women continued to be seen as the prime caretakers of children (why, indeed, is there no adult man in this image?), and, as it is implied on Soborova's poster, were commonly the teachers of pre-pubescent children. Men only began to teach children in the grades (forms) equivalent to secondary school. At the same time, even in the first years after the civil war, most women worked, as such was the obligation of every adult Soviet citizen (and thought to aid their self-actualization that was part of socialism's ontology), while few households could make ends meet without their women being employed. But the result was that, for much of Soviet history, women faced a threefold task: child-rearing, keeping house, and working, while they were at most token members of both the Communist party and the government without any meaningful political influence. Soborova made other posters advocating better childcare, including on the advantages of breast-feeding. That a woman made this poster shows that not just men adhered to this idea of women in a sort of auxiliary role to men; women saw themselves in a subordinate role long after 1917. Meanwhile, the civil war and famine (1917–22) had caused an enormous growth in the number of orphans and children that were left to fend for themselves, a challenge that was difficult to solve for the impoverished Soviet government: the poster and the campaign that it advertises reflect this stark reality as well.

FIGURE 3.2 *'Female Proletarians toward New Triumphs! For Technoлogy, Culture, for a New Existence!'*.

In contrast, a January 1933 poster (see Figure 3.2) breaks the traditional mould of men being associated with industrial work.[22] It shows Ukrainian women who are lauded for their contribution towards the radiant future of communism. It reads, 'Female Proletarians toward New Triumphs! For Technology, Culture, For a New Existence!' Made by the female artist Mariia Isaevna Volkova (1905–79), it was printed in Kharkiv, then the capital of the Ukrainian soviet republic. Ukrainians traditionally were farmers while most of the labourers in its industries and mines were Russian, or people from other non-Ukrainian ethnicities (such as Tatars, Jews, or Poles) before 1929. But collectivization in Ukraine, too, aimed to reduce the number of workhands needed in agriculture, with those freed up joining the urban workforce. It is noteworthy here that women are imagined to work in all sorts of jobs: as welders, miners, soldiers, or teachers, while their role as mothers is depicted as well. But there is a sad irony to this image: while this poster rolled off the printing presses, Ukraine was undergoing a devastating famine (nowadays known as the *Holodomor*) that killed up to 4 million of its people. The famine was a direct consequence of the havoc in the countryside wrought by collectivization. Collective farmers were deprived of the necessary means to produce the bountiful harvest Soviet authorities believed would ensue. Rather than admitting their error, Soviet requisition squads appeared in the countryside during the late summer and autumn of 1932 that forcibly confiscated the grain the state needed to feed the urban population. Ukrainian peasants were accused of hoarding grain to drive up prices, and even most seed grain was requisitioned, if necessary, at gunpoint. Ukrainian cities were cordoned off to ensure that no refugees from the countryside could flee to them to seek solace. The poster, in other words, papers over a human tragedy. Volkova was born in Simferopol on the Crimean peninsula, but although she had studied in Kharkiv, she appears to have lived in Moscow by the time she designed this poster. She may not have been aware of the devastation of the Ukrainian countryside (which was a tight-kept secret). Later, during the Second World War, she collaborated on the wartime *TASS* poster windows.

Figure 3.3 shows a 1938 poster by Pyotr Ia. Karanchentsov (1907–98) underlining the Soviet regime's ill-thought-out concept of gender equality, intersecting here with its hazy concept of ethnic equality.[23] It was issued when the worst of the chaos caused by collectivization had abated, although its echoes lingered in the Great Terror of 1937 and 1938, when a renewed hunt for *kulak*s (exploitative peasants who had been expropriated and deported to remote areas in 1929 and 1930) was launched. Karanchentsov's poster encourages women to participate in elections for the Soviet republics' official parliament staged in that year, proclaiming 'Having All Rights, Soviet Women Vote for a Socialist Motherland, for a Happy Life!' Behind the woman and child, who may supposed to be (generic?) non-Slavic, given especially the boy's dress and hat (which hints at a Muslim type of headgear), we see a

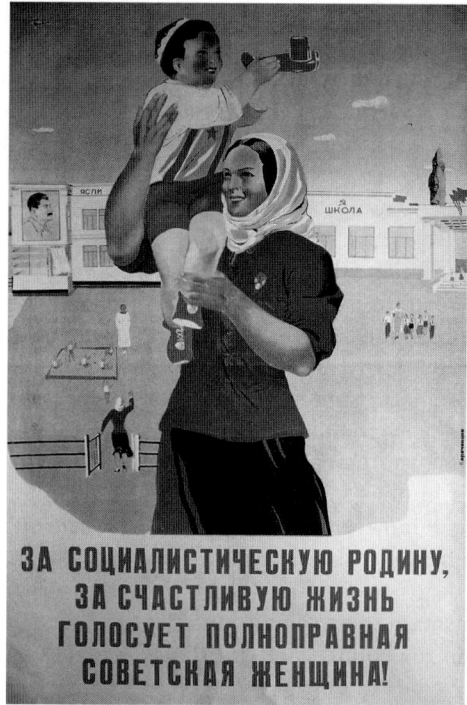

FIGURE 3.3 'Having All Rights, Soviet Women Vote for a Socialist Motherland, for a Happy Life!'.

day care (indicated also with the word *iasli*) and school. Hanging from the kindergarten's edifice, Stalin's image is disproportionally large compared to the building size. His depiction in this manner is not only a consequence of his growing cult, but he usefully serves as the benevolent father figure carefully watching over his children, too. During the 1930s, Karachentsov, who had studied with Dmitri Moor, specialized on depicting women and the feminized household, the private space which was considered women's domain despite the professions of gender equality in the Soviet Union. A real communist hack as an artist, Karachentsov's work is markedly sycophantic and rather crude, but he did distinguish himself fighting in the Second World War, including at the battle of Stalingrad.

Despite formal declarations of equality, the predominantly female *kolkhoz* farmers were second-class citizens in the Soviet Union, who after 1932 were tied to their farms as they were deprived of the internal passports that permitted one to travel within the country (a prohibition that remained in force until 1977).[24] And even in the cities, women tended to be employed in jobs that were less well remunerated and respected. Miners and factory workers in heavy industry (metallurgy and so on) were largely men and received better wages than women employed in textile mills. Such male factory workers might even earn as much as female teachers or medical doctors. The senior positions within the Communist Party itself were dominated by men, not just in its central departments in Moscow, but everywhere.

Rosenfeld suggests that after the civil war ended in 1921 the subject matter to which posters were dedicated switched. Foremost among the new themes was public health, including the call to aid the devastating famine laying waste to the population residing along the Volga shores in 1921 and 1922.[25] Subsequently, posters often sported topics such as education and the fight against illiteracy.[26] Mayakovsky and Rodchenko even turned to advertising in the liberal environment that prevailed after the NEP had been introduced in the spring of 1921.[27] And artists designed posters for the experimental films by Eisenstein and others as well as the theatre or opera during the 1920s.[28]

Nonetheless, as Rosenfeld writes, 'the traditions which developed in the poster art of the civil war period were not interrupted or forgotten in later years'.[29] This goes both for its themes and for the manner of its distribution through *Rosta*: The satirical or caricatural depiction of various enemies remained a standard and made a strong come-back in the 1930s. Posters then justified the back-breaking efforts necessary to modernize the country at warp speed in the face of the hostile bourgeois world preying on it, and even more so when after on 22 June 1941 the struggle with enemies trying to destroy the Soviet Union became all-encompassing. After the Nazi invasion, too, the wall-window display of *Rosta* (by then named *TASS*) was resurrected to distribute propaganda as expeditiously as possible on the homefront.

Colour Plate 4 shows an anonymous 1927 poster called 'The Growth of Soviet Agriculture after a Decade'.[30] Produced in 13,500 copies under the auspices of the Moscow-based Artists' Association of Revolutionary Russia (*AKhRR*), it was issued on the cusp of Stalin's Great Turn that would transform the Soviet countryside and cities. Rather than truthfully representing farming in 1927 Russia, the poster hints at its hoped-for future. Tractors, for instance, were rare during the 1920s. Nonetheless, some of the statistics regarding the growth of farm animals or sown area in the NEP rendered on it reflected an undeniable agricultural recovery that had set in after 1922. But such an idyllic depiction of the Soviet countryside belied its stark reality once collectivization was unleashed in 1929 and omitted the return of armed grain-requisitioning detachments to the villages in that very year of 1927. The artistic quality of the poster is middling at most. Its aim may have been primarily intended to advertise agitation meetings conducted in village soviets' cultural-technological centre ('agronomical corner') depicted at its top-right-hand side. The poster resembles a classroom alphabet-board or history display that was in use across much of the Western world in the middle of the twentieth century. Of note as well is its depiction of the farmer, whose dress, short beard, worker's cap and decently cut hair show the desired influence of 'urban civilization' on a male peasantry that still commonly sported unkempt beards and bowl-haircuts.

By the mid-1920s, posters were produced in a plethora of styles, as Colour Plate 4 indicates. Eisenstein's *typage* and *montage* in film were matched by the photomontage's increasing presence on posters.[31] But not everyone was pleased with all this experimentation.[32] In response, to which the poster on Soviet agriculture's progress attests, a shift became palpable towards 'the image and the re-introduction of naturalistic modes of representation'.[33] The rapidly growing popularity of the photomontage poster may have been another symptom of this shift towards realism. Most emphatically was the return to figurative depictions on posters expressed by the rise in popularity of a 'Soviet lubok', which determinedly reintroduced a realistic style and rejected the photomontage technique.[34] Traditionalists, organized in *AKhRR*, quarrelled with those associated with the *VKhUTEMAS* (Higher Artistic-Technological Workshop), founded in 1920 and its 1926 successor, *VKhUTEIN* (Higher Artistic-Technological Institute), which were hotbeds of the teaching of avant-garde art in poster-making, printing, and other fields of art.[35]

Posters after the Great Turn

Meanwhile, artists such as Rodchenko and Mayakovsky were increasingly criticized for the apolitical nature of some of their work, which included Rodchenko's posters (Mayakovsky had ceased making posters by then).[36] But Klutsis's more politically engaged work, which superseded Rodchenko's in terms of its diffusion and apparent popularity, was destined for no more than a brief heyday. Whether this was solely due to a conventional public taste is moot. Public taste (or audience reception) is an especially hazy concept in the Soviet context. No doubt artists fought each other over what appropriate proletarian, communist, or Soviet art constituted, but the arbitrator in such matters was neither the artistic world nor the Soviet masses: it was the highest leadership of the Communist Party. In comparing the Nazi propaganda machine to the Soviet *agitprop apparatchik*s who ever more strongly placed their imprint on artistic production, Leonid Maksimenkov suggests how 'Stalinism in power (and without power Stalinism did not exist) is an openly terrorist dictatorship of the most reactionary and chauvinist elements of the Russian *déclassé petit-bourgeoisie* and *lumpenproletariat*'.[37]

This philistine taste was to determine the contents of Soviet art after 1930, even if loftily abstracted in the indeterminate triad of *ideinost'*, *narodnost'*, and *partiinost'* of 'socialist realism' as defined by a then rising star in the Soviet firmament, Andrei Zhdanov (1896–1948), at the first Soviet Writers' Congress of 1934.[38] Literally, the three terms may be translated as 'being replete with ideas', 'being in tune with the people' and 'being infused with the

Party's spirit', but what concretely each of these concepts meant remained open to wide interpretation, even if a corollary mandate was developed about the necessity of a plotline with positive heroes and a depiction of sundry enemies in the most negative sense. To return to Maksimenkov's remarks, this was an aesthetic that was popular among the prerevolutionary *Spießbürger*, the petty bourgeois, and the outcasts, and, indeed, was popular as well among the Nazi leaders and many of their followers during the 1930s.

Matthew Lenoe has suggested:

> Between 1925 and 1930, Soviet newspapermen, under pressure from party leaders to mobilize society for the huge task of industrialization, molded a new master narrative for Soviet history and a new Bolshevik identity for millions of novice Communists. They began to present everyday labor as an epic battle to industrialize the USSR, a battle fought against shirkers and saboteurs within and imperialist enemies without ...
>
> [N]ewspapers, the education commissariat, artists, psychologists, and others pursued with great seriousness the job of reshaping the language, culture and thinking processes of 'the masses' and turning them into politically conscious citizens of the new socialist state.[39]

Although this may give the impression of a better organized campaign than actually unfolded, Lenoe is correct in arguing that already towards the end of NEP in 1927 and 1928, Soviet mass media found a new tone that was reflected on Soviet posters, even if it was not hegemonic yet. A muscular, bellicose imagery gradually revealed itself, representing somewhat of a comeback of the aggressive civil war style (see Figure 3.4).[40] It reproduces a 1929 poster of which the theme is the importance of labour discipline for the economic transformation of the Soviet Union. Its main text reads, 'So that you know whose labour we honour and who we will sweep away with a metal broom.' Aiming to improve labour discipline, it addressed a key issue in a country in which suddenly millions of former peasants had to become accustomed to the regular, unforgiving hands of the factory clock and the incessant motion of the conveyor belt. The poster compares slacking at work to army desertion in its text and right-side images. Traits of the posters imploring to aid the hungry of 1921 and 1922, and of the preceding civil war era can both be recognized in it, with truant enemies made into caricatures. The 'sweeper' with the grab-instrument already resembles the ideal square-jawed and muscular Soviet blue-collar worker, but he is still stylized, not yet acquiring the life-like depiction that he was to don soon after, on most posters of the 1930s.

This hard-line trend in poster imagery was reinforced once Stalin's attempt at the 'socialist transformation' of his country took on concrete form in 1929. All means of mass communication were now mobilized behind the effort of break-neck speed industrialization and agriculture's

FIGURE 3.4 *'So That You Know Whose Labour We Honour and Who We Will Sweep Away with a Metal Broom'*.

collectivization, which was to end private farming and, indeed, working for private profit altogether.

In Stalin's Great Turn, a new assault on all forms of religion was concomitantly unleashed, as the Marxist base (material conditions) and superstructure (society and culture) were to make a quantum leap towards the radiant future of communism, a future of fully equal and enlightened human beings who no longer felt the need, or had a need, for private property.

The Great Turn initiated by Stalin in 1929 did not cause any change to the Soviet regime's great appreciation of visual means of propaganda. This was reflected in its continued subsidizing of poster production. That being said, after 1917 money had never been especially plentiful to pay artists for their efforts.[41] The enormous outlay required for fast-paced industrialization and the more basic demands of the 'cultural revolution' (such as an increase in the amount of years of compulsory schooling which required more classroom space or the attempt to definitively liquidate illiteracy) after 1929 might have reduced the means available for the production of posters. But it seems that the expenses may have been bundled, with fewer people and printers producing posters, while the print-run of posters issued may have increased.[42]

It is noteworthy that at least before 1930, posters were not always distributed free of charge, but their purchasing price of a few kopecks was doubtlessly considered a trifle by their purchasers. It is meanwhile not entirely obvious how they were distributed: Did the Party's *agitprop* workers offer them to provincial and city councils (*kraikomy, obkomy, gorkomy*), rural soviets, institutions, or factories? Were their bosses allowed to decline such offerings, or was their purchase required? The nominal price (which even then may have been paid by the Communist Party) shows how the Soviet Union had peculiar budget priorities, such as expending vast sums on its security-police apparatus, or spending considerable funds on propaganda. The largest all-Union newspaper, *Pravda*, had an enormous circulation as well, reaching 3 million even in a war year like 1944.[43]

Not only was funding remarkably high, but oversight could be intense as well: the highest leadership kept a close eye on artistic output, from Stalin's meeting with Maxim Gorky (Maksim Gor'kii, 1868–1936) in October 1932 to the 1934 Congress of Soviet Writers, the scrutiny of film scripts and so on. The dawn of Stalin's autocracy around 1930 did affect the contents and presentation of Soviet posters, even if Stalin himself was far less interested in the visual arts than he was in film, theatre, literature, architecture, or even music.[44] The first sign of interference from above was a resolution of the Communist Party's Central Committee of 11 March 1931, which complained about posters' poor quality and 'anti-Soviet' contents.[45] Klutsis's photomontaged work was in subsequent months criticized for its artificiality and 'banality'.[46]

The switch to a fully planned economy with a strong emphasis on heavy industry (producing machinery, mining and armaments) of the Five Year Plans that began in 1929 was informed by a great fear for an imminent invasion of the country by communism's mortal enemy, capitalism. The 1931 poster by Vladimir I. Kozlinskii (1881–1967) and Boris G. Klinch (alias of Garri Petrushanskii, 1892–1946) reflects this reading of a hostile world (and its agents) firmly being faced down by a militarily prepared Soviet Union (see Colour Plate 5).[47] Its text reads, 'In Answer to the Insolent International Popism [a *pope* is a Russian-Orthodox priest] and Bourgeoisie We Strengthen the Military Preparedness of the USSR and the Military Power of the Red Army.' A key purpose of the Five Year Plans was to build up the military strength of the Soviet Union. A capitalist attack was continually said to be imminent throughout the 1920s and 1930s. Marxism-Leninism held that the Soviet Union was 'encircled' by 'capitalists', who could not tolerate the existence of the world's first socialist country, in which exploitation of fellow human beings had ended and everyone was (or would be) equal. Thus, the poster depicts how capitalist countries, at the urging of the captains of industry, with the connivance of organized religion (in this case, the Catholic Pope) and with the aid of what appear to be German Nazis (the swastika – here incorrectly depicted – was already fairly well known as a Nazi symbol by 1930, while the helmeted brute may be based on a German *Freikorps* soldier who had marauded in the Baltic region and Ukraine after the First World War), as well as gas-masked French soldiers, were poised to invade. The new industrial might of the USSR, however, allowed well-fed and well-armed strapping soldiers to defend their country. These guards were immune to attempts by priests, propped up by *kulak*s and white officers in league through the use of the telephone with the capitalists, to convince them, 'To Love Thy Neighbour as Thyself', as the book held up by the cleric reads. It should be noted that the caricatures of the various Soviet foes on this poster appear to refer to racist tropes that were formally outlawed in the Soviet Union: The top-hatted capitalist draws from anti-Semitic images of allegedly Jewish capitalists, while, oddly, the German character appears a sort of crudely distorted depiction of an African, perhaps signifying a 'savage'.

Certainly, the image of the boss (*vozhd'*) himself was ever more frequently represented on Soviet posters.[48] During the early 1930s, Klutsis enthusiastically contributed to Stalin's leadership cult and was probably the most acclaimed poster artist.[49] An example of his work is the 1932 poster rendered on Colour Plate 6, which reflects the heyday of photomontage posters during the first two Five Year Plans.[50] Its text reads, 'Greetings to the Opening of the Global Gigant *Dneprostroi* (DGES [the Dnepropetrovsk Hydro-Electric Station]), Long Live the Shockworkers of the Building of Socialism.' It shows how some of the artistic styles with which poster artists had worked in the 1920s became the standard of the 1930s. Klutsis' composition here is compelling, although the actual dam fades somewhat into the background. The worker facing the public is nicely typecast, very much in the style of other exemplary workers depicted on 1930s posters. The hydroelectric dam celebrated by the poster became literally a 'poster-child' of Soviet economic accomplishments as trumpeted loudly by Soviet propaganda. In reality, such projects were only completed through the extreme allocation of resources and labour to them and came at the expense of the outlay on other, less prestigious, projects that remained unfinished for much longer. In the First Five Year Plan, which formally was fulfilled by 13 December 1932 (and thus had allegedly been completed in a little more than *four* years rather than five), very few of the grandiose projects came online at the time planned for their completion. Dneprostroi was thus an exception. The dam was destroyed in the Second World War, but after its postwar reconstruction remained a source of Soviet pride.

After 1930, a dispute festered between Klutsis and his supporters, who championed photomontage posters, and those agitating for 'hand-drawn' designs, including Deni and Moor (with the latter eventually switching sides after Klutsis had been killed).[51] Initially, both schools continued to receive the state's support. The photomontage school lost popularity, but was never entirely banished, even if Klutsis was executed by Soviet authorities in the Great Terror in 1938. Deni's images became ever more unsettling during the 1930s, when his aggressive style developed in the civil war returned to fashion during the cauldron of Five Year Plans, collectivization and Great Terror.[52] But the artist himself increasingly succumbed to the stress of these years, drowning himself in drink. Rodchenko, having learned his lesson, tried to pivot into a more conformist direction, but then overdid his sycophancy, or, at least, did not quite grasp how the blossoming leadership cult was supposed to limit itself to one figure. Designing a folio-sized cover for a commemorative publication regarding the storied Red Cavalry, his team overly praised its commander K. E. Voroshilov (by then People's Commissar of Defence) and cavalry commander S. M. Budyonny.[53] Stalin personally took offence at the epithets awarded to his comrades. Rodchenko saved his skin and proceeded dutifully in the heyday of the Great Terror to blacken out the faces of fallen leaders on photographs that were in his possession.[54]

By 1932, the indulgence in artistic experimentation suddenly ended. A sort of return to nineteenth-century aesthetics (called socialist realism in pictorial art as well) emerged, although some of the highlights of early Soviet art were never quite rejected.[55] A Communist Party Central Committee decree of 11 March 1931 handed the monopoly on poster production to the State Publishing House of Art (*IZOGIZ*), which stood under the direct supervision of this highest Party body.[56] Poster-makers tried to pre-empt being organized from above by founding in response to this decree a 'united cooperative of workers of the revolutionary poster' (*Ob'edineniia rabotnikov revoliutsionnogo plakata* or ORRP), a sort of labour union.[57] Chaired by Dmitrii Moor, it was placed under the authority of the Russian (rather than Soviet) people's commissariat of enlightenment's art department. Among its members were Deni, Mikhail Dlugach, Boris Efimov (1900–2008), Klutsis, Nikolai Dolgorukov (1902–80), Viktor Koretskii and Cheremnykh, that is, virtually all of the leading Soviet-Russian *plakatisti*.[58] But already by June 1932 it was dissolved, although a separate section of poster-makers was retained in *MOSSKh*, Moscow's artist union that became part of the Union of USSR Artists, following a Central-Committee decree of 23 April 1932.[59] As Rueschemeyer, Golomshtok, and Kennedy write, '[This second decree] eliminated all previously existing art associations, trends, groups ... and along with them the last vestiges of creative freedom.'[60]

Henceforth, unauthorized experimentation was rejected and ideological content carefully scrutinized. The decree was sharpened in the following months by various promulgations emanating from the Communist Academy, the ideologically driven rival that had been set up by the Communist regime to challenge the traditional Academy of Sciences that had been founded in 1725.[61] Accusations of sympathies for the illegal opposition groups that had been banished from the Party in the later 1920s were now hurled at each other by various leading artists. The dire consequences of slinging such invectives at each other would only become visible after Sergei Kirov's murder in Leningrad on 1 December 1934.

While the ideological reins were tightened, the high esteem in which posters were held as a legitimate form of Soviet artistic expression was further underlined. In early April 1932, the first all-Union poster exhibition was staged in Moscow's Tretyakov Gallery.[62] Its formal title, 'The Poster in the Service of the Five Year Plan', conveyed its theme; Klutsis's poster of Dneprostroi is a good example. No fewer than 206 artists showed their work, including all leading lights of *ORPP*. Its catalogue contained several essays, among which was one by Moor. The volume was to be published by *Izogiz*, the state art publishing house that was then under the auspices of the short-lived *ORPP*, but, for unknown reasons, was never published.[63] One suspects that the authorities' desire for closer oversight of artistic efforts and the curtailment of artistic independence, indeed of any organizing initiative from below, was linked to the project's shelving.

ORPP was disbanded soon after the exhibition, and careful control over poster production was established, as Alla Rosenfeld suggests:

> Initially, annual thematic plans for poster production were developed by the publishing houses based on the 'recommendations' (which were in reality demands) of the Propaganda Department of the Central Committee of the Communist Party. These topics had to be approved by the senior editor, senior artistic director, and director of a publishing house. After that, all topics for the posters had to be submitted for final approval to the Central Committee of the Communist Party. Designs had to undergo a similar process: they were reviewed by the *Khudsovet* (Artistic Advisory Board), followed by their evaluation by *Glavlit* [the main organisation of Soviet censorship].[64]

No other all-Union poster exhibition was staged again until after Stalin's death.

An ill wind began to blow now: the chaos especially caused by collectivization, disrupting time-honoured agricultural traditions, caused a devastating famine in Ukraine, southern Russia and Kazakstan that developed in the course of the summer of 1932. The worst of the famine was overcome by the next summer, but the sense of relief was brief if anything. For in January 1933, the international situation deteriorated sharply from the Soviet point of view. The Nazi take-over in Germany added greater urgency to Soviet industrialization plans, especially with regards to arms production: Nazism was the ideological opposite, the self-declared archenemy of communism. It was true that Soviet communists had consistently maintained that all of the surrounding capitalist world was hostile to the Soviet Union, but it was equally known that Nazism was especially inimical. Within weeks of the

Machtübernahme, the prohibition of the German Communist Party (*KPD*) – for which the *Reichstag* fire was a convenient pretext – and the persecution of German communists confirmed this hostility.

Posters in the Great Terror

Domestically, a maniacal fear of espionage and treason burst into the open when Party boss Sergei Kirov was shot and killed in his Leningrad headquarters on 1 December 1934. The sense that the Bolshevik fortress was besieged returned as if it was 1919 all over again, but it was now accompanied by a loud campaign that announced the infiltration of foreign agents throughout Soviet society who were linked to resentful one-time rivals of Stalin. The conspiracy was alleged to have been using any means to destroy the Soviet Union according to the narrative from the 1936–8 Moscow trials, the proceedings of which were reported in great detail by Soviet newspapers. The exiled (and Jewish) 'Judas-Trotsky' – desperately jealous of the USSR's great economic transformation – was now said to be in league with the Nazis, Poles, and British. The paranoid atmosphere was reflected by posters' imagery, and the optimistic ebullience or braggadocio of the First Five Year Plan's poster images vanished.

Around the time of Kirov's murder, Klutsis's championing of photomontage started to be condemned.[65] It was never entirely banished, but it was apparently not life-like or naturalist enough to the taste of the Soviet bosses and said to fail in striking a chord with the masses.[66] Officially, it was grouped under 'formalism', a bourgeois-type of artistic deviation incomprehensible to the Soviet workers and peasants, of which other artists, filmmakers or Dmitrii Shostakovich and fellow Soviet composers were found guilty as well.[67] A key objection from the Soviet ideological leaders towards abstract renditions was fiscal: given the outlay on posters, the message needed to be effective and straightforward. Their target audience should not be puzzled. Klutsis's work and that of his acolytes such as Viktor Koretskii (1909–88), Vera Gitsevich (1897–1976), and Boris Knoblok (1903–84) were difficult to decode.[68] Their artistic whim and photomontage's stylistic conventions confused spectators who mostly had attended no more than a few years of primary school or its equivalent.

Or so at least seems to have been the sentiment about art, literature, and music among the highest leaders, including the ultimate arbitrator, Stalin himself. Platon Kerzhentsev wrote a memo to Stalin and (then prime minister) Molotov in 1936 lamenting 'formalist' painting exhibitions in the Tretyakov Gallery and applauding a recent exhibition of the Wanderer Ilya Repin (1844–1930)'s work as being adored by 'worker visitors'.[69] He assured his chiefs that he would organize more 'realist' special exhibitions of artists such as Repin, Vasily Surikov (1848–1916) and, somewhat incongruously, Rembrandt.

Still, some photomontage posters passed muster even in 1939, as Figure 3.5 shows.[70] Made by Dmitrii Moor and Sergei Sen'kin, 70,000 copies of this poster were printed and sold for the fairly low price of 70 kopecks each. Its main text reads, 'Long Live the Great, Invincible Banner of Marx, Engels, Lenin, and Stalin! Long Live Leninism!' and announces on the five banners carried by the crowd to the right that 'The USSR Is the Shock Brigade of the Global Proletariat'. On the smaller red banners left of this, it says, 'Passionate Greetings to Our Leader and Teacher the Great Stalin!' It is an unusually popular late example of photomontage in the style of Klutsis, who had been executed in the previous year. Its theme, besides promoting Stalin to the pantheon of great Communist heroes, appears to be both underlining

FIGURE 3.5 *'Long Live the Great, Invincible Banner of Marx, Engels, Lenin and Stalin! Long Live Leninism!'*.

the success of the previous ten years of socialist construction, lifting up the Soviet masses and showing the world the awesome power of the proletarian masses within the context of the looming war.

Its theme of juxtaposing Stalin with Lenin, Marx, and Engels may have been a cause for authorizing its printing, despite its form. Perhaps as well in this case, its production was allowed because its creators were well-respected artists, namely Dmitrii Moor and Sergei Sen'kin (1894–1963), whose survival by 1939 meant that they had passed the loyalty test. Unlike many others, they had not been eliminated in the Great Terror on accusation of belonging to the many hostile groups that had been conjured up by the regime. At the Great Terror's height in 1937 and 1938, it seemed countless people were arrested as foreign spies, bourgeois nationalists, counterrevolutionaries, saboteurs, Mensheviks, SRs, Trotskyites, Zinovievites, Rightists, *kulak*s, or as belonging to the more generic rubric of anti-Soviet elements. A former Suprematist, Constructivist and member of the *LEF* collective, Sen'kin had collaborated with Klutsis in the early 1930s, but whereas the great photomontagist had been killed for being an alleged Latvian nationalist in early 1938, Senk'in survived into the 1960s and managed to see some of his recollections about the 1920s published.[71] As more often with the Great Terror, which saw millions arrested and at least 700,000 people executed within a year-and-a-half (June 1937–November 1938), the precise details about its reckoning with the Soviet community of poster artists are murky. Altogether, one gains the impression that the poster artists were relatively spared in comparison with, for example, writers of fiction and poets. Again, Stalin's perfunctory interest in this form of art may have played its part: despite Klutsis's lamentable fate, Stalin did not home in on any collective hostile mood among its creators that needed to be eradicated.[72]

Friendship of the Peoples

While Stalin rid himself of any potential enemy who at one point or another might have questioned his wisdom, an official façade was erected to reiterate that the Soviet Union was the beacon of human freedom and equality. A new constitution was introduced in December 1936, which nowhere mentioned the crucial role played by the Communist Party in determining the country's fate and was already for that reason alone a wholly mendacious screed. The fundamental laws it outlined burst with democratic principles and emphatically guaranteed human rights and freedoms in the Soviet Union.[73] Its Article 13 suggested that 'the Union of Soviet Socialist Republics is a federal state, formed on the basis of the voluntary association of Soviet Socialist Republics having equal rights ....'[74] It was a restatement of how the Soviet Union did not tolerate any racism. As Terry Martin has suggested, the Soviet Union even engaged in 'affirmative action' long before the term became fashionable in the late twentieth century.[75] There was equality between the 'nationalities' and a 'Friendship of the Peoples' within the USSR on the basis of such strict equality. This stood of course in stark contrast to the overt racism of the Nazis and even the Western colonial powers, or the United States with its segregation laws. It remained long after the Second World War a key reason why many outside political movements Europe looked to the Soviet Union as their guide for independent development, not least in the newly independent states in Africa and Asia.

Ethnic harmony was, of course, played up as well on Soviet posters. Whereas this was in part for foreign consumption, it also had a very clear domestic purpose. One could proclaim an end to ethnic strife, but, as with religion, that did not mean that people immediately discarded their beliefs. Stalin, a native of the multi-ethnic mosaic that is the Caucasus region and, as People's Commissar of Nationalities from 1917 to 1924, responsible for drawing the territorial borders of the various Soviet republics, autonomous republics and autonomous regions within the Soviet Union, knew all too well about the simmering ethnic tension. On posters throughout the entire existence of the Soviet Union, therefore, one finds assurances to non-Russians that they were 'full members of the team', and images and slogans for primarily Russian consumption to consider non-Russians their equals.

Colour Plate 7 shows a poster by an unknown artist, which reads, 'Long Live the Brotherly Union and Great Friendship of the USSR Peoples!'[76] All red banners, in the language spoken by the largest ethnic community in each of the then eleven Soviet republics, state: 'Greetings to the Great Stalin.' Lenin's Mausoleum on Moscow's Red Square appears in the background, making it seem as if this is an illustration of an actual parade. Perhaps unwittingly, the poster-maker did indicate that despite all the professions of ethnic equality, a pecking order remained in force among the Soviet peoples, for the three carriers at the front are (from left to right) Belarusyn, Ukrainian and Russian. This reflects perhaps more than just their population size (during the 1930s, Russians were most numerous in the Soviet Union, followed by Ukrainians and Belarusyn), for Russians did enjoy greater opportunities than non-Russians and Eastern Slavs had better career chances than non-Slavs in the USSR. And, indeed, only the Russian portrayed is dressed in modern style, all others wearing traditional dress (the Ukrainian man wears a sort of workers' cap, cleverly showing how a transitional developmental phase had been reached in his native land). In 1945, giddy with the victory over the Nazis, Stalin could not stop himself from calling the Russian nation the leading nation of the Soviet Union, which undermined the strict equality principle. It is interesting to note that the predominantly Muslim republics used at first a Latin (Roman) script after 1917 as reflected on the banners, but that exactly at this time the Latin letters were replaced by Cyrillic, another sign of the increasing Russian dominance in the Soviet Union.

Colour Plate 8 renders a 1950 or 1951 poster by Mariia Alekseevna Marize-Krasnokutskaia (1902–86), propagating the smooth modernization of the non-Russian ethnicities (in this case the Kazaks) within the Soviet Union.[77] Its text reads, 'The Endless Steppe Woke Up from Its Dream, and Happiness Is Brought to Us by the Spring of Communism!' The old man in traditional Kazak dress is Dzhambul (Zhambyl; 1846–1945), a famed Kazak traditional folksinger (*aqyn*; he plays a *dombra*), who was embraced by the Soviet communists. The Russian text, which rhymes, may be a reference to a song by Dzhambul. Dzhambul's authorship of his songs has been questioned, as has been their authenticity as actually traditional Kazak songs. The 1930s Soviet leadership in Kazakhstan sought someone who voiced Kazak songs in authentic fashion, albeit in pro-Soviet style and designated the most modestly known Dzhambul to serve as such. The message on this postwar poster is how much Kazakhstan had benefitted from its development in Soviet times, and how harmoniously traditional Kazak culture had merged with modern Soviet culture (as represented by the younger man in his distinguished suit who is standing next to Dzhambul). The dam depicted in the background may be one built in Soviet times in the Syr Darya, Irtysh, or Ural River. The picture is a sort of fantasy, hardly reflective of Kazakhstan at this time. The indigenous Kazak population had been reduced by one-fifth in the 1932–3 famine, while its territory harboured numerous Soviet labour camps. It was also used, without much thought for its consequences for human life, flora and fauna, as the testing ground for Soviet nuclear weapons. And the Syr Darya (which drains in the Aral Sea) was quickly drying out as its waters were siphoned off into large-scale irrigation projects in an attempt to turn the arid soil into fertile ground to grow crops such as cotton (and perhaps grapes …). The poster artist Marize-Krasknokutskaia was of noble stock but managed not to be stigmatized for this ancestry by the Soviet authorities. She predominantly made posters regarding motherhood, education, and child-care after the war, which makes this poster a bit of an anomaly in her *oeuvre*. It is unlikely she knew the Kazak language, which makes the reason for the poster's Russian text understandable. But it does raise the question of who its intended audience was (and the poster was printed in Moscow): Russians living in Kazakhstan? Russified Kazaks? Or Kazaks who knew Russian as a second language?

Based on his painstaking research and encyclopaedic knowledge about cultural expression in Stalin's Soviet Union, Leonid Maksimenkov plausibly suggests that Stalin did not always necessarily seek to be the supreme judge in artistic matters, but that his minions found ways to draw his attention to deviations that no longer were acceptable in the socialist-realist canon.[78] If sufficiently irritated by a work and if having some time to spare (during the Second World War, artistic expression enjoyed a greater degree of freedom because he did not have time to attend to it), Stalin might then interfere and impose his set of rules according to which artists would subsequently have to make their art. Some of those guidelines were purely a matter of personal whim, but Stalin did not claim to be an infallible expert: in literature, he allowed Maksim Gorky to impose the standard, for example. But Stalin does appear to have sought a Soviet art that appealed to his subjects: modernist experimentation had no place in it, as it alienated them. No doubt this was a consequence of his own traditionalist (even philistine) tastes. One of its best illustrations of this is the perhaps apocryphal anecdote that in 1948 Andrei Zhdanov, who after the war oversaw a lot of the renewed cultural straight-jacketing at Stalin's behest, suggested to composers such as Shostakovich, Prokof'ev, and Khachaturian that you could identify good music if you could hum it. Zhdanov was not a complete ignoramus in music, for he played piano himself, but like his boss seems to have missed (or disliked) the direction modernist classical composition had taken after 1900. At the same time, of course, Stalin's (or Zhdanov's) instinct that modernism could not readily find a mass audience was not wrong: in the liberal democracies of the Western world Marcel Proust's or James Joyce's novels, Alban Berg's compositions, or Kurt Schwitters's art did not acquire massive popularity in the interwar period either.

Themes from pre-Soviet Russian history were gradually woven into the imagery during the 1930s. Often, abstract imagery was replaced by concrete depictions, and symbols became more unambiguous. Even if *kulak*s, capitalists, Trotskyites, or Nazis were lampooned as grotesque caricatures, they were recognizable, or legible.[79] The far more narrowly defined aesthetic guidelines affected both the state's censors and the artists themselves, who could ill afford to fall foul of the authorities. Nonetheless,

> the unpalatable truth is that the artistic avant-garde was not incompatible with totalitarianism. The naïve view of the avant-garde's relationship to totalitarianism was rooted in the anti-modernist stance of the Nazi and Stalinist regimes (from 1934 onwards), [and within the USSR] radical artists actually play ... an important initial role in ... forming cultural models embodying the new ideology.[80]

We *grosso modo* agree meanwhile with Konstantin Akinsha's above appreciation about the motivation of a considerable amount of the artists to fall in line behind the Stalinist cause (even if we object to his somewhat simplistic use of the term 'totalitarianism'). Coercion, or the fear or threat of arrest, played a part perhaps, but might not have always been the main driving force behind their support for Stalin's communist utopia as expressed in their work. Some were unlucky, such as Klutsis, but most escaped his fate. Klutsis championed the photomontage style of poster-making, but that was not the key cause of his downfall, or so it appears, for he was scapegoated as a Latvian nationalist. Photomontage posters continued to be made after 1938. Poster-makers found their peace of mind in what to them amounted to only slightly circumscribed creative work on behalf of a worthy cause, with any moral qualms about it being offset by often very generous remuneration. For those unionized artists who calibrated their output to the desires of the regime, life was good, living in privileged enclaves with access to scarce commodities and perquisites otherwise unavailable to the Soviet population. And by the late 1930s they themselves indeed had often developed the templates according to which they designed their posters without much threat of being ideologically condemned.

4

Nazi Posters and the Construction of the *Volksgemeinschaft* ('National Community')

Once Hitler came to power in January 1933, the *NSDAP* began a concerted effort to homogenize German society and to bring the general population to an acceptance of National Socialist ideology. The Nazi movement had been driven by its convictions about the future of Germany and intended to convey the sense of the urgency of its mission to the nation. The National Socialists aimed to create consensus for their regime and conformity to its ideological goals. In the construction of the *Volksgemeinschaft* ('national community'), the regime not only utilized propaganda and popular enlightenment to create conformity, but also employed coercion and repression where consensus failed. Propaganda was an important tool, accompanied by the physical presence and menacing stance of the *SA* and the *SS*, as well as censorship and control of cultural output by Joseph Goebbels, Nazi Minister for Propaganda and Popular Enlightenment. Mass communication became a crucial way of bringing the German populace on side with the Nazi government. Nazi propaganda was extremely sophisticated, even when its output appeared relatively simple and uncomplicated. Hitler maintained: 'The art of propaganda lies in understanding the emotional ideas of the great masses and finding, through a psychologically correct form, the way to the attention and thence to the heart of the broad masses.'[1] Nazi propaganda was carefully designed to appeal to different sectors of society and to influence and sway millions of people. As Birgit Witamwas notes, from 1933 onwards, 'self-presentation and idealisation of National Socialism' became the focus of Nazi poster artists.[2] Nazi posters were largely ubiquitous and they did not have to compete with other sorts of iconography in the public sphere. Certainly, there were no other political messages for the obvious reason that all other political parties had been outlawed and banned.

This chapter explores the role of Nazi posters in the creation of the 'national community' and uses the posters as a point of entry into the policies of the regime. An analysis of the strong images and slogans employed by the *NSDAP* in its posters introduces the related Nazi policies, especially through the message of national unity as expressed, for example, in the poster '*Ein Volk, Ein Reich, Ein Führer*', which emphasized a key Nazi slogan. Here we examine an array of posters designed to appeal to different groups in German society across a range of ideological aims – these include posters aimed at helping to create a cult of the leader; posters to encourage a sense of duty to the nation, for example, to promote autarky and other Nazi alimentary policies, including the *Eintopf* ('one-pot dish'); posters directed at the German youth, encouraging membership of the Nazi youth groups, the Hitler Youth (*Hitler Jugend* or *HJ*) and the League of German Girls (*Bund Deutscher Mädel* or *BDM*); posters urging Germans to benefit from the holidays, trips and cultural opportunities offered by the *Kraft durch Freude* (Strength through Joy) organization; to save for the *Volkswagen* or 'people's car'; to listen to the 'people's radio'; and posters which reified the Nazi Party as the protector of the German family and which promoted large German 'valuable' families. Posters were also used to advertise exhibitions, sports events, and Party festivals.

As Wunderlich notes, 'in the public sphere, posters and announcements pasted on walls were the most popular formats for disseminating Nazi propaganda'.[3] As well as walls, propaganda posters were pasted onto kiosks and advertising columns, sometimes in multiple copies. For Hitler, the function of posters consisted of 'attracting the attention of the crowd'.[4] While the receptivity of the audience is harder to pinpoint, the barrage of propaganda methods employed by the regime, including posters – and underpinned by the use or threat of terror – certainly acted to influence the German population. The aesthetic language of the Nazi posters was difficult to ignore. The National Socialist party instrumentalized the power of this visual propaganda through its use of repeated slogans and striking colours. Cost-effective and easy to distribute widely, posters were 'an ideal advertising and propaganda instrument for influencing the masses'.[5] The effectiveness of posters as bearers of political propaganda relied on central party guidance, for example, a work on political posters for internal use produced by the Party's Central Propaganda Office. Erwin Schockel's *Das politische Plakat* (1938) disseminated advice on the production of political posters and noted their use in 'helping to suppress liberal Marxist ideology and enabling National Socialism to win over the *Reich*'.[6] In this way, daily life in the Third *Reich* became permeated with political and ideological content and slogans. Wunderlich argues that posters 'made a significant contribution to the acceptance of National Socialist policies'.[7]

The posters encouraged people to behave in a way that conformed to Nazi ideals across a range of policy initiatives. Of course, in the construction of the 'national community', it was important from the point of view of the Nazi regime to make it extremely clear to its citizens which groups were outside the 'national community' and did not fit in or belong. Posters that advertised the Degenerate Art Exhibition and Degenerate Music Exhibition, for instance, exemplify how this exclusion impacted cultural life in Germany. The Jews were the primary group of those excluded from the *Volksgemeinschaft* and because of this, anti-Semitic posters are considered in this chapter, including *Der Ewige Jude* ('The Eternal Jew'). Finally, this chapter investigates posters that were used to publicize and indeed to justify the regime's eugenic policies, including sterilization, indicating that certain groups, even those of German ethnicity, were 'inferior' and should not be allowed to reproduce, and paving the way for the Nazi 'euthanasia' campaign. Posters on these subjects clearly and graphically portrayed inclusion or exclusion from the 'national community'.

Hitler's view of the receptivity of the German masses was quite dismissive. He believed that 'their intelligence is small, but their power of forgetting is enormous'.[8] Hence, it was important to keep reminding them of the Nazi message – 'only after the simplest ideas are repeated thousands of times will the masses finally remember them'.[9] Hitler maintained that effective propaganda had to be restricted to a few points, but that this had to be repeated 'in slogans until the last member of the public understands what you want him to understand by your slogan'.[10] To be sure, posters offered an ideal form in which not only could slogans be employed, but also through which their visual and psychological effects could be enhanced through the use of powerful imagery. Posters played their role in the dissemination of Nazi propaganda because they were on public display and acted as advertising for the *NSDAP* and its policies.

Creating National Unity and the Cult of Hitler

David Welch has shown that Nazi propaganda was successful in the construction of the *Volksgemeinschaft*.[11] The building of this 'national community', the need for racial purity, the hatred of 'enemies' and the leadership cult were among the most consistent themes of the Nazi propaganda machinery, as well as its emphasis upon the regime's domestic and foreign policy successes. Posters and slogans called for allegiance to the nation and its leader. Nazi propaganda appealed to national unity, by requiring people to place the needs of the 'national community' ahead of their own selfish desires.

The *Volksgemeinschaft* was a central component of Nazi ideology. Its achievement meant the unification of the nation. The Nazis wanted to break down traditional class loyalties, or loyalties to region or church, and replace all of these with an unswerving allegiance to the regime. In this way, they intended that people should put the nation ahead of everything else, encompassed by the oft-used slogan '*Ein Volk, Ein Reich, Ein Führer*'

('One People, One Empire, One Leader') (see cover image). This poster was designed not only to encourage the cult of the *Führer* but also to emphasize the central importance of a unified people. Here we see a stern-faced Adolf Hitler, with his determination to accomplish his mission for the nation, looking off into the distance. His shirt and tie, with the tiepin detailed with a symbolic Nazi eagle, under a military-style jacket, complete with swastika armband, all very neat and tidy, depict a dependable leader. His pose is also very firm and balanced, as his left arm rests on the back of a chair and he holds his right arm – with his hand formed into a fist – into the right-hand side of his body. This is a no-nonsense posture, intended to convey certainty, reliability, and a commitment to the future, not only of the leader himself, but also of the nation that followed him.

Hitler himself, as *Führer* (leader), was the most important legitimizing and rallying force within the regime. Ian Kershaw has argued that 'the "Hitler myth" was consciously devised as an integrating force by a regime acutely aware of the need to manufacture consensus'.[12] Hitler was portrayed as the leader of Germany's destiny. Hitler's followers bestowed upon him his 'charismatic authority', based upon the popular perception of his 'exceptional powers' or 'exemplary character'.[13] Pierre Ayçoberry concurs that 'the construction of the Hitlerian myth resulted from a combination of autosuggestion, deliberate fabrication and a quasi-universal acceptance'.[14] And in this presentation of the *Führer*, posters continued to play their part, as they had done in the years leading up to the Nazi *Machtergreifung*.

Joseph Goebbels knew very well how to use words and images effectively to create an aura around Hitler as an infallible leader. An important photomontage poster from 1934, which was designed to promote the cult surrounding Hitler, featured large bold red lettering in blackletter font: '*Ja! Führer wir folgen Dir!*' ('Yes! *Führer*, we will follow you!'). A large image of Hitler looking to the future, dressed in military uniform with his Iron Cross – taken in 1933 at the Hoffmann studio in Munich – was superimposed upon thousands of people, very small-scale by comparison, behind him giving the Hitler salute. The Hitler salute and 'Heil Hitler' greeting became an important part of daily life, with the expectation of loyalty to Hitler and the regime expressed in this manner.[15] This poster underlined the key messages of uniformity, allegiance, and conformity.

The Nazi posters also aimed to show the German people that they had been right to vote for Hitler, contrasting '*Früher*' and '*Heute*', the situation 'Before' and 'Today'.[16] 'Before: Unemployment, Hopelessness, Neglect, Strikes, Lockouts. Today: Work, Joy, Order, National Camaraderie', concluding '*Darum Deine Stimme dem Führer!*' ('Thus, Your Vote for the Leader!'). A characteristic poster showed poverty, despair, and unemployment as a bleak background of the past, superimposed with a strong, large image of a Nazi German man, with a spade and a swastika armband, representing the present and a message that projected a good future thanks to Hitler.

Another key aspect of the promotion of the nation and national duty was exemplified by the Nazi policy of autarky or economic self-sufficiency. The poster urging Germans to 'Buy German goods', in line with Nazi autarky, is powerful in its imagery. It depicts a man constructing a wall of stone blocks with the words '*Hitler baut auf, helft mit. Kauft Deutsche Ware*' ('Hitler is building. Help out. Buy German goods'), designed by Gunther Nagel (see Colour Plate 15). A strong, muscular, and determined German man is shown playing his part in building the nation and the 'national community' in stone, with an agricultural background showing farming activity in the production of German foodstuffs. Complete with the symbolism of the red, white, and black swastika flag, this poster presented a clear message and demand for the German population. This appeal to Germans to buy German goods was part of a wider propaganda and policy programme that had two key aspects: the first was autarky which formed a core aspect of Nazi alimentary policy; the second, unsurprisingly, contained the racial aspect of Nazi ideology that Germans should not buy from Jews. That Germans should not purchase from Jews was clear from the earliest days of the National Socialist government. The National Boycott of Jewish Businesses on 1 April 1933 had set the stage for the economic harassment of Germany's Jews.[17] The boycott was instigated by Party radicals, especially the Nazi stormtroopers (*Sturmabteilung* or *SA*), who were euphoric after the *NSDAP*'s 'seizure of power'. Posters and placards were put up outside Jewish shops and businesses, saying 'Germans defend yourselves! Do not buy from Jews!' *SA* men placed themselves in front of Jewish shops to deter customers.

Once in power, from the outset, 'achieving nutritional autarky became a Nazi priority'.[18] This had an impact on the German diet. Personal purchasing decisions were closely linked to the needs of the national economy. Posters to promote Nazi alimentary policies formed part of a wider effort to educate and encourage a change in German eating habits in line with the priorities of the Nazi government. The annual harvest festival, held from 1933 onwards at Bückeberg in Lower Saxony, also had its part to play in influencing German society under National Socialism, and the theme of *Blut und Boden* ('Blood and Soil') was strongly presented in this context, as was the promotion of German agriculture and autarky. Goebbels carefully selected the location for the festival, with a simple design intended to 'emphasize the peasant character of the event'.[19] Posters reified the harvest festival and encouraged Germans to join in the glory of the German harvest and its celebration.

Another significant aspect of Nazi policy-making in relation to consumption was the *Vollkornbrot* ('whole-grain bread') campaign, instigated by *Reich* Physicians' leader, Gerhard Wagner. This policy was also promoted through posters. Wagner attacked 'the recent shift from natural whole-grain bread to highly refined white bread' and advocated a return to whole-grain bread.[20] In 1935, he ordered German bakeries to change over their production to whole-grain bread and launched a campaign to promote this as the *Volksbrot* ('people's bread'). It was a purposeful attempt to change consumption and production patterns. In 1937, Hans Reiter, president of the *Reich* Health Office, banned the bleaching of flour. Wholegrain bread was regarded as the food of the 'national community' and consumption of the patriotic loaf increased by 50 per cent by 1939.[21] The German whole-grain bread campaign was also partly about strengthening the health of the German *Volk*. Individual Germans, *Volksgenossen* ('national comrades'), as building blocks of the nation had a duty to be healthy in order for it to be great, healthy, and strong.

The introduction of the *Eintopf* ('one-pot dish') was designed to encourage national unity and foster a sense of 'national community'. On one Sunday each month, German families were urged to make savings against their usual Sunday lunch by having a 'one-pot dish' and to give a donation to help their needy 'national comrades'. This 'meal of sacrifice for the *Reich*' was an expression of the 'national community'. One-pot Sundays came to be observed, with magazines publishing recipes and regions developing their own particular variants. One common recipe was a split pea soup, made from dried peas, bacon cubes, and potatoes. The Nazi women's magazine *NS-Frauenwarte* included features on and recipes for the *Eintopf*, such as 'fish one-pot dish' and 'macaroni one-pot dish'.[22] The *Eintopf* was intended to symbolize the 'national community'. It was reified as 'the meal of sacrifice for the nation'. *Eintopf* Sundays changed the drive for autarky into a social ritual that aimed to unite the 'national community' through sacrifice. The Nazi Party leadership was photographed eating the *Eintopf* too. In addition, *Eintopf* meals held in communal settings, such as town squares, further appealed to the Germans to support the campaign. A propaganda poster for the *Eintopf* encourages Germans to observe the one-pot Sundays. It shows a steaming pot of stew, at the centre right of the poster, with five coins below, stating: 'We eat the one-pot meal ... no one shall starve.' Donations went to the *WHW* (*Winterhilfswerk* or Winter Relief Agency). The *WHW* more generally too encouraged wealthier Germans to give food, money, and clothes to distressed and impoverished 'national comrades'. The Party's involvement in these types of activities gave its members a role and purpose. The aim was for all charity work to be carried out by the official Party charity, not church or private charities. During the war, the *KWHW* (*Kriegswinterhilfswerk* or War Winter Relief Agency) continued charitable work and enlisted volunteers, especially women and Nazi youth group members, to help out in a variety of roles.

Youth

The Nazi movement and administration attached great importance to German youth.[23] At the end of 1932, just before the Nazis came to power, the Hitler Youth had a comparatively small membership of 107,956.[24]

Meanwhile, between 5 and 6 million young Germans belonged to an assortment of youth groups.[25] On 17 June 1933, Baldur von Schirach was made Youth Leader of the German *Reich*. His main objective in 1933 was to build a state youth organization and to try to consolidate all of Germany's youth into the Hitler Youth. At first, the Hitler Youth appeared attractive. It gave German youngsters the opportunity to participate in a new and exciting movement and escape from parental control and boredom at home. It offered them a sense of purpose, belonging, and unity. The Hitler Youth also created a new chance to take part in youth activities to some young people, who had not previously had access to youth movements. By the end of 1933, the Hitler Youth had more than 2 million members. While some of the explanation for this quick growth of the movement was its attraction to youth after the Nazi 'seizure of power', a large part of the reason was the process of *Gleichschaltung* ('co-ordination') of youth by the Nazi regime, which banned other youth groups. By the end of 1936, the Hitler Youth had 5.4 million members.

On 1 December 1936, the Law on the Hitler Youth stated, 'The future of the German nation depends upon its youth and German youth must therefore be prepared for its future duties.' On 25 March 1939, a further Youth Ordinance decreed: 'All young people are obliged from the age of 10 to their 19th birthday to serve in the Hitler Youth.' Boys aged ten to fourteen had to join the *Deutsches Jungvolk* (*DJ*), while boys from fourteen to eighteen had to join the Hitler Youth. German girls were to join the corresponding Nazi girls' organizations, the *Jungmädelschaft* (*JM*) for girls aged ten to fourteen and the *Bund deutscher Mädel* (*BDM*) for girls aged fourteen to eighteen. In the Nazi youth groups, boys and girls took part in a variety of activities and carried out duties too, which became more arduous and time-consuming as the years progressed.

The posters aimed at influencing the German youth quite simply advertised the Party and its youth formations. They were eye-catching and worded with strong messages, aiming to attract German youth to the Nazi Party youth organizations: the Hitler Youth and the League of German Girls. They were directed at boys and girls separately. For example, the 1937 poster, designed by Spindel, '*Auch Du gehörst dem Führer*' ('You too, belong to the *Führer*'), depicts a young blonde German girl, with plaited hair in her *BDM* uniform – an image of health and wholesomeness – against a blue background.[26] The lettering is mainly in red fraktur font, apart from the word 'you', which is set down in white lettering and in a larger size, for emphasis, directed at every single German girl who was not yet a member of the *BDM*. This was one of several key posters directed at Germany's youth.

Another such poster, designed by Hein Neuner, was '*Jugend dient dem Führer: Alle zehnjährigen in die HJ*' ('Youth serves the *Führer*: All ten-year-olds in the *HJ*'). A young and purposeful boy in *HJ* uniform is shown in the foreground, against a background of a photograph of the *Führer*. Hitler and the young boy in the poster both look in the same direction, to the

FIGURE 4.1 *'Youth Serves the Führer'*.

future. This poster encouraged the younger boys to join the movement – boys aged ten years old and upwards. An equivalent poster, also created by Hein Neuner, was directed at girls. It portrayed a bright, smiling blonde girl looking upwards, against a more faded background depicting dozens of *BDM* girls. 'Youth serves the *Führer*' was lettered in a broken font of mainly lower-case letters at the top of both posters; 'All ten-year-olds in the *HJ*' was placed at the bottom of the posters in antiqua capital letters (see Figure 4.1).

An important propaganda poster directed at youth once again emphasizes the significance of youth (and specifically in the Nazi youth movement) to Germany's future: 'Hitler Youth: Germany's Future'. A finely chiselled, well-proportioned face of a strong and young man looks off sideways into the future, accompanied by Nazi symbols in the form of swastika flags and an eagle (see Colour Plate 16). In a colourful poster, designed by Hermann Witte, a fresh-faced, smiling, blonde member of the *BDM* (*Bund Deutscher Mädel*) is wielding a collection tin adorned with a swastika. The caption reads, '*Baut Jugendherbergen und Heime*' ('Build youth hostels and homes').

The *BDM* girls had a wide variety of duties and collecting in this way was one of them. In the case of this poster, it was for the building of youth hostels; other examples included collecting for the *Winterhilfswerk*, the Nazi state-sponsored charity organization.

Another poster, designed by Ludwig Hohlwein, depicts a young boy in his *HJ* uniform, with his right arm raised, carrying a rucksack over his shoulder. Behind him is an idyllic German bucolic scene of a village and fields at the bottom of the picture, with blue sky and white clouds completing the background image. In red broken font at the top and bottom are two phrases: '*Schafft uns Jugendherbergen*' ('Build us Youth Hostels'); '*Wir sind die Garanten der Zukunft*' ('We are the guarantors of the future') – a powerful message that fit Hitler's view that German youth was crucial to the future of the nation.

The poster '*Bund Deutscher Mädel in der Hitler Jugend*' ('League of German Girls in the Hitler Youth'), also designed by Hohlwein, shows a blonde girl with her left arm outstretched and holding a flag pole in her right hand, with swastika banners behind her. The white antiqua lettering is placed in a block at the centre of the girl's body, contrasting with and standing out from her navy-blue uniform (see Colour Plate 17). In addition, posters directed at German youth emphasized sporting events and activities, such as the 'Sport Day of the *BDM*', because the Nazis aimed for the German youth to be as fit, athletic, and healthy as possible. These depicted *BDM* girls in uniform, in formation, bearing flags or engaging in sporting activities. For example, in a poster designed by Klotz, promoting a *BDM* sports day in Obergau in Westfalen, a colourful image of a *BDM* girl carrying a swastika flag is set against a monochrome photograph background, showing rows of *BDM* girls in uniform. Further posters directed at youth advertised sporting competitions, as exemplified by the poster by Ludwig Hohlwein, from 1934, depicting the '*Reichsberufs-Wettkampf der deutschen Jugend*' ('*Reich* Vocational Competition for German Youth'), held from 9 to 15 April 1934.[27] In the same year, Hohlwein also produced a poster for the *BDM Reichssporttag* (National Sports Day), 23 September 1934.[28] It foregrounds a young female athlete in *BDM* sporting uniform, poised in mid-air against a light blue sky. Nazi imagery is provided in the form of a swastika flag at the bottom-right-hand side of the poster, with the lettering in fraktur and gothic fonts.

Hohlwein also produced a powerful poster in 1936 aimed at German students and designed to garner their support for the Nazi regime. It bears a strong slogan: '*Der Deutsche Student kämpft für Führer und Volk in der Mannschaft des NSD-Studentenbundes*' ('The German Student fights for *Führer* and nation in the team of the National Socialist German Students' Association'). A strong, blond young man carries a swastika flag in his right arm. His left hand rests at his waist. His black tie sports a small black swastika on a white background. The lettering is all capitalized in black and red. The National Socialist students' association, which had been founded in 1926, aimed to promote the study of Nazi ideas and to disseminate Nazi ideology in the German universities, but its true ambition was nothing short of controlling the entire student population. This poster played a part in the Nazi campaign to appeal to German students.

Events Posters

The graphic artist Ludwig Hohlwein was commissioned to create the poster designs for the 1936 Olympic Games, hosted by Germany and regarded by the Nazi leader and propagandists as an excellent opportunity to showcase the achievements and greatness of the Third *Reich*. His colourful poster for the Olympic Winter Games held at Garmisch-Partenkirchen (6–16 February 1936) depicts a proud athlete in the foreground, wearing a shirt with the Olympic rings, raising his right arm and carrying his equipment aloft in his left hand. A purple sky in the background contrasts with mountains in bright yellow to create an evocative image. It is noteworthy that the lettering is in antiqua script – red capital letters for Germany 1936, followed by white capital lettering for the title, location, and dates – and thus intended for an international audience, not a purely German one (Fraktur broken font was the norm for internal German consumption). A competition was held for the poster design for the summer games in Berlin. First prize was awarded to Willy Petzold, a graphic artist, whose design did not nevertheless meet the overall requirement, but was used as an exhibition poster and catalogue cover for an Olympics Art Exhibition held in Berlin.[29] Franz Theodor Würbel's striking poster of the Berlin Olympic Games (1–16 August 1936) has the Olympic rings at the top, with a large golden figure of a chisel-featured, muscular athlete, wearing a laurel wreath around his head. Behind him, a yellow sky contrasts with the Brandenburg Gate in black, at the bottom right hand corner of the poster. Another impactful poster was designed to advertise Leni Riefenstahl's film *Olympia: Fest der Völker* ('Olympia: Festival of Nations'), which showcased the Berlin Olympic Games on the cinema screen. The poster portrayed the golden figure of a discus thrower against a blue and white background, atop an impressive column.[30]

The annual Nazi Party rallies at Nuremberg were a significant and focal point in the Nazi calendar and thus also for the German people. The Party Congresses began in 1929, before the Nazis had come to power, but after 1933 they became encompassing of the nation, as well as the Party. They were advertised and promoted through a variety of means, including posters. Richard Klein, a favoured graphic artist of the Nazi regime, designed the posters. Wunderlich notes that his party rally posters 'use medal-like motifs and reliefs, probably modelled in plaster, on red or black backgrounds, which, when photographed, give the images a strong, three-dimensional effect'.[31] These were strong images, portraying the power of the *NSDAP* and its leader, as well as the strength and vitality of the German *Volk*. A brief analysis of a selection of posters from the years 1934, 1935, 1937, and 1938 provides a decent measure of their design and purpose. The poster design for the 1934 rally showed the figure of a knight, carrying an upright sword in his right hand and bearing a shield with a swastika in his left hand. Five oak leaves on the shield symbolize connection to the German land. The motto of this rally was 'unity and strength'. The poster for the following year depicted three heads in relief: Hitler at the centre facing forward, a *SA* man on the left in profile and a soldier on the right, also in profile. The symbolism in the 1935 poster was provided by a large eagle with its arms stretched wide above the three figures, as though protecting them. It holds a wreathed swastika in its talons.

The poster for the 1937 Party Rally, 'The Rally of Labour', features a medallion depicting three strong men with arms raised, holding up the *Zeppelinfeld*, the location of the Nuremberg Party Rally, designed by Albert Speer. The *Zeppelinfeld* as a site was striking – built on a vast scale, it could hold 100,000 people and edged on three sides with flag platforms. In the poster, the top of the image shows an eagle with outspread wings, holding a garlanded swastika in its claws. Beneath its wings, on the left is a vine and on the right a cereal sheaf. Together here, Klein neatly symbolized labour on the land and the strength, fortitude and hard work of the German *Volksgenossen*, as well as including strong and recognizable Party symbolism. The 1938 Rally was named the 'Rally of Greater Germany', following the *Anschluß* of Austria to Germany. The poster for this rally depicts two strong, muscular, naked men, standing on a platform which bears the eagle and swastika symbols. The first man, representing Germany, holds aloft a very large swastika flag with his left arm, while his right arm rests on the shoulder of the second man, symbolizing Austria, bringing him onto the platform and into the fold of the Greater German *Reich*. They both face the same direction and the second man points in this direction too, indicating unity of purpose and destination.

An important day in the Nazi calendar was 9 November, which came to be a national holiday known as the Memorial Day of the Movement, commemorating the unsuccessful 'beer hall putsch' of 1923, in which Hitler had attempted to seize power by force. This commemoration day was promoted by a photomontage poster designed by Friedrich Franz Bauer and Karl Ferdinand Bauer, at the Bauer studio in Munich. It depicted an *SA* man in front of the *Feldherrnhalle*, with red antiqua lettering diagonally across the whole width of the poster in front of the building, stating simply '9 November'.[32] Sombre and dark, it recreated an atmosphere of loss and called for the memorialization of the fallen Nazis on that date in 1923.

Furthermore, an array of celebration days, including *Gau* (regional) Days and Festivals, were organized by the *NSDAP*, as well as the annual Day of the Police and Day of the Armed Forces. Such events on the Nazi calendar were promoted by posters. These events, whether local, regional, or national, formed an integral part of daily life and were orchestrated and managed carefully by the Party. In addition, Jupp Wiertz designed a special poster in 1937 to advertise the Bayreuth Festival, held from 23 July to 21 August 1937. He silhouetted the conductor, the members of the orchestra and their instruments in dark brown and dark orange at the bottom of the poster. Rays of light emerged from the middle of this image, flooding the rest of the poster with yellow and orange. A bust of Richard Wagner's head, also in orange, adorned the top centre of this very colourful and striking poster.[33] Wagner was Hitler's favourite composer and his works were considered the most suitable *völkisch* music during the Third *Reich*.

Strength through Joy, the People's Car, and the Radio

Very swiftly after the *Machtergreifung* in January 1933, the Nazi Party outlawed and decimated the parties of the political left, the *SPD*, and the *KPD*, as well as destroying the German trade-union movement. It tried to garner support among workers for the new regime. One of the ways in which it did this was through the activities of its *Kraft durch Freude* (*KdF* or 'Strength through Joy') organization. Posters showed the opportunities offered to German workers by the *KdF*, depicting its varied activities, including mass tourism and leisure (see Figure 4.2). The *KdF* arranged hikes and sporting activities. It organized holidays to the Black Forest and other regions of Germany, which were partly designed to reverse German regional particularism by encouraging people to visit other parts of their homeland. Together, these promoted the overall goal of the organization at 'community building'.[34] The *KdF* arranged steamship tours on the Rhine and the Danube. By 1938, the *KdF* arranged cruises to Madeira and the Norwegian fjords, as well as trips to other destinations in Europe.

One *KdF* poster states: 'Now you too can travel!' (see Colour Plate 18). *KdF* offered new travel opportunities to those who were unable to take such trips before, through subsidizing the cost. The chance to travel to the fjords of Norway or even to take holidays inside Germany was appealing. Mass tourism was part of the regime's attempt to create a classless society. It was a sign of the upward mobility of the working class, as such travel opportunities had previously been the privilege and preserve of the middle and upper classes. By 1939, 43 million Germans had travelled with Strength through Joy. Furthermore, there was greater accessibility to the theatre, cinema, and other cultural activities. Between 1934 and 1938, the number of participants in *KdF* cultural events 'grew from over nine million to over fifty-four million'. The opportunities provided by the *KdF* were all designed to enhance the esteem of the workers, to raise their productivity, and to give them a sense of their importance to the 'national community'. The *KdF's* organization of leisure time served to keep workers occupied, to divert their

FIGURE 4.2 'Kraft durch Freude' ('Strength through Joy') Travel Poster.

attention from the loss of their trade unions, to persuade them that the government was concerned with their well-being and, therefore, to decrease the possibility of disaffection or political opposition.

The Nazi regime was also determined to bring about the modernizing motorization of the nation. A 1936 poster by artist Werner von Axster-Heudtlass, with the words '*Der Führerversprach: Motorisierung*

FIGURE 4.3 *Propaganda Poster for the* KdF *Car.*

Deutschlands', depicts the motorization of Germany. It shows the development of the automotive industry from 1932 to 1935, leading up to the creation of the 'people's car'.[35] From August 1938, workers were encouraged to save for a *KdF* car or *Volkswagen* ('people's car') (see Figure 4.3). The scheme entailed a weekly payment of 5 RM over four and a half years for the acquisition of a 'people's car'. This made the ownership of an automobile potentially available to every German. This was symbolically significant, as previously car ownership had been reserved only for the upper echelons of society. By 1939, 270,000 people were participating in this scheme. The *Volkswagen* was intended as 'a car for free time and leisure' and as a means to shift the German car from the business sector to the private sector as a consumer item. One poster, designed by Christian Minzlaff, states: 'You have to save five Marks per week if you want to drive your own car!', showing a black people's car in the foreground, with a large coin behind it and a voucher card in the background, against a blue sky with white clouds, and green grass on both sides of the road. Another poster depicts two happy young Germans with wide, bright smiles exploring the German countryside in their *KdF* car. However, the outbreak of war in 1939 precluded the production of the *KdF* cars, as the economy geared to armaments and the factory output turned to military vehicles.

The *Schönheit der Arbeit* ('Beauty of Labour') department of the *KdF* played a significant part in influencing the everyday life of German workers.[36] Geraniums were placed at factory entrances to brighten them up, wholesome canteen food was provided and factory hygiene was improved. 'Beauty of Labour' was concerned with the hygiene and the functionality of industrial spaces. It became involved in factory architecture and design, as well as putting into place a variety of campaigns to ameliorate industrial workplaces, including 'Battle against Noise' (1935), 'Good Light – Good Work' (1935), and 'Hot Food in the Factory' (1938). These measures were designed both to create a sense of attachment of the workers to their workplace and to convince any doubters among them to accept Nazism. Timpe argues that 'beautification campaigns in both factories and villages were another important element of *KdF's* "joy production"'.[37] Posters such as 'Sun and Green for All Workers' (1934) – which depicted a worker opening the factory doors to a bright day with other factories in the background, in a pleasant and ordered landscape – advertised these campaigns. Another *Schönheit der Arbeit* poster showed the German factory before and after its activities to clean up and improve it, stating that 'Beautiful Workplaces' created great 'joy at work'. A well-organized factory replaced the gloominess and miserable conditions of the past. Posters played their part here in disseminating knowledge about the activities of these Party organizations and, in effect, advertising them.

Posters were also put out to encourage radio listening. For example, a striking black and white poster, with Nazi symbols, signed 'Uhlen', from the mid-1930s, states: '*Jeder Volksgenosse Rundfunkhörer*' ('Every National Comrade a Radio Listener'). Here, to be sure, was a clear emphasis on the duty of all 'national comrades', to listen to the radio. The radio was an important vehicle for Nazi propaganda. The *Volksempfänger* ('people's receiver') was a cheap radio set produced to greatly extend the number of households with a radio set. The Nazi regime commissioned manufacturers to produce two new types of cheap radios, costing 76 Reichsmarks for the larger set and just 35 Reichsmarks for the smaller set. In 1933, 1.5 million radio sets were produced. The cheaper version, the People's Receiver, cost approximately the weekly wage of a blue-collar worker and could be paid for in instalments. The People's Receiver sets had a very limited reception capacity so that they were unable to receive foreign radio broadcasts. A

FIGURE 4.4 *Poster for Radio Listening 'All of Germany Listens to the Leader with the People's Receiver'.*

poster advertising the new, cheap radio sets read: 'All Germany listens to the *Führer* with the People's Radio' (see Figure 4.4).

The emphasis on national unity was explicit. If 'all Germany' listened to the People's Radio, as this poster suggested, then there would be a sense of expectation or pressure on someone who saw the poster but did not. In 1933 alone, Hitler made at least fifty radio broadcasts. By 1939, 70 per cent of German households had a radio. This was three times as many as in 1932. Hence, the regime succeeded in creating a mass radio audience, with a rapid growth of radio ownership across all social classes. Radio was transformed from a small scale into a mass medium of communication. In addition, communal radio listening was encouraged to heighten the emotional impact of listening to speeches, with loudspeakers set up in town squares or other public areas for this purpose. The Nazi posters encouraging radio listening played their part in its promotion.

The Family

The National Socialists had capitalized on the conservative backlash against the changes in sexuality and family life during the Weimar years and claimed that they would restore traditional models of the family. Point 21 of the *NSDAP*'s Programme stated: 'The state has to care for the raising of the nation's health through the protection of mother and child.' The family was extolled in National Socialist ideology and propaganda as 'the germ cell of the nation'. The Minister of the Interior, Wilhelm Frick, stated in 1934: 'The family is the primordial cell of the *Volk*, that is why the National Socialist state places it at the centre of its policy.'[38] This declaration encapsulated a firm and solid commitment to family life. With very few exceptions, the Nazi leadership publicly exalted the ideological status of the family throughout the Nazi era. And indeed, Nazi propaganda underpinned this.

One key poster shows the Nazi eagle spreading its wings in protection of the 'valuable' German family (see Colour Plate 19). In parallel to the eagle, the father also has his arms around his wife and one of his children, while the mother holds a baby in her arms, with a third young child smiling and facing out at the viewer. This is an ideal young German family, already comprising three healthy looking children, reversing the trend of small families during the Weimar Republic. The type of family desired by the Nazi regime was termed *kinderreich* ('rich in children'), with four or more children. The family was regarded as the source of 'national renewal' through reproduction. There was a call for women to become valuable mothers of large families. In the Third *Reich*, parents of large families were to be proud and such families were promoted. However, the regime was careful to endorse only 'hereditarily healthy', 'racially valuable', politically reliable and socially responsible families as *kinderreich*. 'The *NSDAP* protects the National Community' is the headline slogan here. The subsequent wording here suggests that if 'national comrades' required help or advice, they could turn to their local *NSDAP* group and indeed the Party did provide assistance and counsel to families, with the proviso that they were 'pure' German families of good blood and character.

Paul Ginsborg notes the 'extraordinary combination of strategies' that the Hitler regime directed at German families.[39] Johann Chapoutot argues that procreation was central to the Nazis' overall aims and ambitions: 'The Aryan race had to be fertile and to produce as many children as possible, especially as a defense against the Slavic enemy; it also had to be attentive to the quality of the biological substance it produced, which was to be free of all foreign and degenerate elements.'[40] And so, although the Nazi administration claimed to protect and support families, it did this imperfectly for two main reasons. Firstly, Nazi policies intervened in German family life in an unprecedented way and one in which the family as a private unit was undermined, with the function of the family being reduced to simply reproduction. Secondly, they offered protection and support only to those German families deemed to be 'valuable'. For the rest, they implemented a policy of exclusion and at the most radical, a policy of *Ausmerze* ('eradication'). Hence, this poster which shows the Nazi protection of German families belied the truth to a very large extent.

Posters and Cultural Life

Posters were used to publicize the cultural policy of the Nazi regime, especially to advertise exhibitions and to distinguish between acceptable German art and 'degenerate art'. The desire of the Nazi regime to purify and cleanse society was reflected in its policy towards the arts, with its simultaneous process of encouraging pure and wholesome contemporary German art and purging *Entartete Kunst* ('degenerate art') that was regarded as decadent and unwholesome. Cultural officials aimed to eliminate all forms of art that they regarded as 'alien' or 'degenerate'. The Degenerate Art Exhibition opened in Munich on 19 July 1937. Ziegler and his commission confiscated some 16,000 works of art. In all, the campaign confiscated works by 1,400 artists, while works by 112 of these artists were selected for the exhibition. Among the most prominent of the artists whose works were seized were Max Beckmann, Ernst Barlach, Otto Dix, Georg Grosz, Paul Klee, Oskar Kokoschka, and Emil Nolde. Ziegler, in his opening speech, described the works that had been produced by modern artists as 'monstrosities', 'the crippled products of madness, insolence, lack of ability and degeneration'. The paintings were displayed in a deliberately poor manner, crammed into crowded galleries, many without frames, accompanied by pejorative captions. The exhibition was advertised by a red, black and white poster designed by Hans Vierthaler. He deliberately used geometric shapes to make the poster visually appealing and the text, all in lower case, explains the nature of the exhibition, to set right what the Nazis regarded as popular misconceptions about art, claiming that Judeo-Bolshevik influences had destroyed the essence of true German art and culture.

The Great German Art Exhibition opened simultaneously in the summer of 1937 at the House of German Art in Munich. The opening of the Great German Art Exhibition was marked by a large public ceremony and a parade. The eight exhibitions held in the House of German Art in Munich between 1937 and 1944 offered what the regime considered to be a cross-section of the best artistic work in Germany. There were relatively few paintings depicting specifically National Socialist themes or figures. Landscape paintings and depictions of 'womanhood' and 'manhood' dominated the exhibition. There were also portraits, still life paintings, and paintings of animals. The regime thus made it very clear which kind of art was acceptable and which was not, employing posters here too to publicize its cultural policy. Richard Klein designed the posters for the Great German Art Exhibitions. As Wunderlich notes, the posters for these shows all featured 'classic sans-serif antiqua lettering with a shadow, centred and on a light or brown background'.[41] The classical image and lettering on these posters for German Art contrasted very clearly with the extremely modern design on the 'Degenerate Art' poster.

The same applied to music and this was exemplified by the *Entartete Musik* ('Degenerate Music') exhibition, which opened in May 1938 in Düsseldorf.[42] While the *Entartete Musik* exhibition attracted considerably less attention than Munich's 1937 *Entartete Kunst* exhibition, it nevertheless remained one of the clearest examples of musical repression during the Third Reich.[43] The exhibition centred on a series of photographs and portraits of the contemporary composers deemed to have had the most destructive impact upon German music. Schoenberg, Stravinsky, and Hindemith were among the main figures included in the exhibition, as well as Jewish operetta composers Oscar Straus and Leo Fall, and some less well-known musicians. The organizer of the exhibition, Hans Severus Ziegler, opened it with the following declaration:

> The *Entartete Musik* exhibition presents a picture of a veritable witches' Sabbath portraying the most frivolous intellectual and artistic aspects of cultural Bolshevism ... and the triumph of arrogant Jewish impudence ... Degenerate music is thus basically de-Germanised music for which the nation will not mobilise its involvement'.[44]

Ziegler firmly believed German musicians were being tainted by 'degenerate' music and called for them to be able to 'breathe, live and work freely in a clean atmosphere' and the musical profession was purged of 'alien' and 'undesirable' influences. The poster advertising this exhibition shows a caricatured black jazz saxophonist with a prominent Star of David badge on his right lapel, indicating the negative and tainting influence of the Jews on music and their association with jazz music, regarded by the Nazis as 'inferior'.

Anti-Semitism and Eugenics

Nazi anti-Semitic propaganda in a variety of forms permeated the German population, creating an acceptance – tacit or active – that Jews were 'inferior', 'subhuman', 'alien' and essentially unwanted. For example, the poster 'Out with the Jewish Haggling Mind', created by Hans Schweitzer (signed 'Mjölnir') from *c*. 1936–7 encouraged the 'Aryanization' of the economy and businesses, as well as the kicking out or removal of the Jews from German society more generally. This poster coincided with policies designed to impel Jewish businesses and concerns to close down or to sell up at giveaway prices to German buyers, as well as preparing the ground for the Night of the Broken Glass and subsequent faster 'Aryanisation of the economy'.

The poster to advertise the exhibition '*Der ewige Jude*' ('The Eternal Jew'), by Horst Schlüter, was especially graphic and striking (see Colour Plate 20). Against a bright yellow background, a stereotypical bearded Jew, with hunched shoulders and a hooked nose, carries the symbols of both capitalism and communism – a handful of gold coins and the hammer and sickle, respectively. The poster advertised a political exhibition held at the library of the German Museum in Munich from 8 November 1937, open daily from 10 am until 9 pm. The evocative phrase '*Der ewige Jude*' in bright red, in a design intended to resemble Hebrew script, stood out against both the yellow background and the large, long black coat of the figure in the poster. The poster advertising the Nazi anti-Semitic film *Jud Süss* (1940), designed by Bruno Rehak has those title words in bright red lettering over a black background, with a single figure of the Jewish character depicted with a green face and yellow eyes, looking evil and shady. It is a powerful poster, aiming to evoke anti-Semitic sentiments.

The displays of the tabloid *Der Stürmer* in the streets of German cities had a similar aim to posters, by publicizing as widely as possible Nazi anti-Semitic ideology: 'The Jews are our misfortune.' These types of displays acted to permeate and spread anti-Semitism among the German populace, reinforcing anti-Semitic beliefs where they existed and creating them where they did not. This constant barrage of propaganda served to heighten anti-Semitic sentiment at the same time as Nazi policies towards Germany's Jews placed more and more restrictions upon them. As the years passed, and Nazi anti-Semitic policies became increasingly radical, the regime intensified its propaganda efforts to depict the Jews as 'inferior', as 'alien' and as 'enemies'. We shall consider further Nazi anti-Semitic posters – from the wartime period – in Chapter 5.

Sterilization was the principal method used by the Nazi regime to prevent people it considered 'undesirable' from having children. In one poster from *c*. 1936, promoting sterilization, the Nazis proudly headlined: 'We are not alone.' A strong German man, with his arms protectively around his wife and baby, holds a shield with the words 'Law for the Prevention of Hereditarily Diseased Offspring 14.7.33'. This law came into effect the following year, on 1 January 1934. The poster aimed to show that there was nothing outlandish or wrong with this policy, demonstrating that sterilization was widely accepted in other European countries and elsewhere in the rest of the world. It claimed that similar policies existed in a number of other countries: the United States, Denmark, Norway, Sweden, and Finland; and that several more, Hungary, Switzerland, England, Poland, Lithuania, Latvia, and Japan, planned to introduce similar legislation. The intention was to show that this was not a policy that was unique to Germany. Another poster shows three children with disabilities, with the caption 'Who would be responsible for this?', again with the suggestion that sterilization could prevent such births (and with the unwritten text that this would be better for the nation). The sterilization law is shown on the left-hand side of the image, with the words 'Not punishment but liberation'.

The Nazi law called for the compulsory sterilization of anyone that suffered from 'congenital feeble-mindedness, schizophrenia, manic depression, hereditary epilepsy, Huntington's chorea, hereditary blindness, hereditary deafness, serious physical deformities' and 'chronic alcoholism'. Between January 1934 and September 1939, approximately 320,000 people (0.5 per cent of the population) were forcibly sterilized under the terms of this law. The majority of them were of German ethnicity; however, they were considered to be 'hereditarily ill' or simply 'feeble-minded' by the regime and its eugenic experts. The 'feeble-minded' made up two-thirds of all those sterilized, of which about two-thirds of these were women.

Sterilization was not unique to Germany. On the contrary, as Marius Turda notes, the desire for a healthy national body was 'central to eugenic discourses across Europe' and beyond.[45] Sterilization came to attract considerable attention from both the medical profession and social reformers who wanted to protect the nation from biological and social decline. Eugenics came to be considered as a way in which a particular society or nation could improve itself and was motivated by economic factors as well. In the United States, Canada (in the province of Alberta, eugenics were only debunked in 1971 by the government), as well as in Europe, eugenics, or the science of better breeding, informed sterilization programmes. Indeed, by 1935, thirty American states had enacted laws to allow for compulsory sterilization of those in state institutions such as prisons and asylums. Madison Grant, president of the New York Zoological Society, wrote in 1916 that 'the laws of nature require the obliteration of the unfit and human life is valuable only when it is of use to the community or race'.[46] In Europe, Romanian eugenicist Eugen Relgis claimed that 'with the help of science, degenerates could be exterminated through euthanasia [but i]t is … preferable, from all points of view, that degenerates should not be born, or even better, not conceived'.[47]

The common aims of the eugenics movement were to promote and increase the nation's 'fit' elements and to eliminate the 'unfit', the 'antisocial' and the 'asocial'. This reflected the middle-class prejudices of the eugenicists and like other movements in North America and elsewhere in Europe, and racial hygiene in Germany before 1933 had been more concerned with class than race. Advocates of eugenics believed that the rational management of the German population, by controlling the reproductive capacities of various groups within it, would lead to the attainment of a healthier and more productive nation. The social, political, and economic problems that had beset Germany during the Weimar Republic required radical solutions and it was during this time that eugenics or racial hygiene had flourished – as a means of boosting the level of productivity and fitness within the German population. The course and scope of racial hygiene changed dramatically, however, once the Nazis had come to power. No longer just the concern of a fairly narrow elite of intellectuals and medically trained professionals, racial hygiene played a central part in Nazi state policy in line with Nazi ideology and Hitler's obsession with the preservation of the 'Aryan' race.

Beyond its sterilization policies, the Nazi regime also endeavoured to eliminate the 'hereditarily ill'. In particular, they created resentment towards mental patients, stigmatizing them as a 'burden'. A number of propaganda films were produced to stigmatize the 'hereditarily ill' and the mentally ill, including *Sins of the Father* (1935) and *All Life Is a Struggle* (1937). Such propaganda starkly contrasted the healthy and valuable 'national comrade' with the 'sick' and 'unproductive' asylum patients. Even arithmetic questions in school textbooks were used to emphasize to pupils the cost involved in maintaining 'ballast existences'. Posters were also employed to show the cost of bearing the 'hereditarily ill'. In one such poster, a tall and strong German 'national comrade' bears the weight of two 'hereditarily ill' people. The headline reads, 'Here you carry this along.' It states that a 'hereditarily ill' person who reaches the age of sixty years old costs on average 50,000 RM. The suggestion here is that this represents a huge burden on Germany and that the money 'wasted' on this could be better spent in other ways.

The Nazi press too advocated the killing of mentally ill patients. Conditions in the asylums deteriorated rapidly after January 1933, as the regime closed down specialist facilities, removed patients from private and religious sector care and packed patients into cheaper state-run institutions in order to centralize control and to save resources. The Nazi government did not want to continue spending money on those individuals it considered to be 'incurable' and the question of eliminating the 'burden' continued to be raised. For example, in a discussion on the subject with Dr Gerhard Wagner, the *Reich* Physicians' Leader, Hitler, said that the question of 'euthanasia' would be taken up 'in the event of war', as 'such a problem would be more easily solved in war-time'.[48] Indeed, Stephan Kühl has argued that once war broke out, influential eugenicists such as Otmar von Verschuer, Eugen Fischer, Fritz Lenz and Ernst Rüdin

> saw the necessity not only for an economic and military mobilisation, but especially for a biological one …. The killing programme was the symbiosis of an economic, military and race hygienic mobilisation at the 'home front'.[49]

The 'euthanasia' campaign (code-named T4) was implemented at six killing centres – Bernberg, Brandenburg, Grafeneck, Hadamar, Hartheim, and Sonnenstein.

The mentally ill and physically disabled were stigmatized as 'hereditarily ill', 'unproductive' and ultimately 'unworthy of life'.[50] The 'children's euthanasia' programme claimed the lives of at least 5,200 children, including adolescents, but the total number of victims may have been as many as 6,000. Operation T4, the adult 'euthanasia' campaign claimed 70,273 lives. Burleigh has argued that the 'euthanasia' programme was 'a carefully planned and covertly executed operation with precisely defined objectives'.[51] Its practitioners believed that they were carrying out a necessary task for the benefit of the *Volk*.[52] They also justified their work in terms of benefitting the patients' families. While some parents may have wanted to remove the burden of handicapped children – either so that they could give more attention to their other healthy children or because they wanted to eliminate any blemish such offspring had on their family's value – the 'euthanasia' murders had a tragic impact upon countless families.

The Nazis employed an array of sophisticated propaganda techniques to influence the German population. The poster was one of these. While it is difficult to determine the exact level of the impact of poster propaganda on the populace, nevertheless, posters played a crucial role in the Third *Reich* and in the acceptance of Nazi policies – whether passive or active. This is because they effectively advertised the Nazi regime and its policies in the way that a company might have advertised its products at that time. They were everywhere in the public domain, on buildings and hoardings, and they influenced and seduced people both consciously and subconsciously.

The Nazis used poster propaganda to disseminate information, sway popular opinion, and, importantly, influence the relationship between the regime and the German population. Posters harmonized the subject matter into an easily understandable combination of words and images. Softer, pastel colours were used for consensus; for example, in cases in which it was easy to sway loyal and hardworking 'national comrades' with images and slogans about holidays or improved conditions in German factories. Bold, strong colours and more complex font styles were employed for the depiction of 'enemies'. As Aristotle Kallis has noted, propaganda is 'not a matter of one-directional communication between the person who transmits the message and passive receivers but a complex process of negotiation, shared knowledge and trust, reassessment and reformulation'.[53] The next chapter investigates Nazi posters in relation to foreign policy and war. The National Socialist government utilized posters as part of its overall propaganda strategy in order to promote its foreign policy, to underline the necessity for war and to maintain popular support for the war once it began. In time and in particular, posters were employed to depict the ultimate enemy of the regime and the nation, the Union of Socialist Soviet Republics.

5

Nazi Posters, Foreign Policy, Militarism, and the Second World War

This chapter examines posters relating to Nazi foreign policy (such as the poster for the commemoration of the annexation of Austria, 13 March 1938), the *SA*, the *SS*, and the *Wehrmacht*, as well as posters produced during the war. Important Nazi wartime posters included 'Into the Dust with all Enemies of Greater Germany!' depicting a strong fist smashing the French, the British, and the Jews; and the 1943 poster '*Adolf Hitler ist der Sieg!*' ('Adolf Hitler is Victory!'). Posters were utilized to emphasize the important struggle of the Nazi war effort, to excoriate and vilify 'enemies' and to encourage mobilization on the home front. The most salient subjects of Nazi wartime posters, unsurprisingly, were their 'enemies' – first of all, Britain and France; then from June 1941, the USSR (and 'bolshevism'); then, from December 1941, the United States; and consistently throughout, the Jews. Nazi wartime posters directed at the home front captured a variety of themes including the evacuation of the cities, the enrolment for the 'people's army' towards the end of the war, the discouragement of women from hoarding and 'hamstering', making trips to the countryside to barter non-perishable items for food from the farmers, and the curbing of 'black' radio listening. Poster displays were a key conduit through which the regime appealed to the German population. We can see in the wartime period an evolution of techniques and styles. Once again in this chapter, key Nazi posters are analysed and utilized to investigate related Nazi policies and aims particularly within the context of the Second World War as it progressed.

To be sure, the Nazi regime won people to the national cause by means of its foreign-policy successes. German nationalists who were dismayed by the punitive Treaty of Versailles in 1919 could only rejoice in Hitler's wholesale revocation of its terms. The treaty had been deeply resented by German nationalists in the years that followed, partly fuelling radical groups on

Germany's far right and especially the *NSDAP*. Particularly galling was Article 231, the 'war-guilt clause', which stressed Germany's position in starting the First World War:

> The Allied and Associated Governments affirm, and Germany accepts the responsibility of Germany and her allies for causing all the loss and damage to which the Allied and Associated Governments and their nationals have been subjected as a consequence of the war imposed upon them by the aggression of Germany and her allies.

The treaty also contained provisions for heavy reparations to be paid by Germany for the damage done. In addition, Germany lost a considerable amount of territory in Europe, including Alsace-Lorraine to France. Furthermore, the union between Germany and Austria was forbidden under the terms of the Treaty of Versailles. In addition to territorial losses and restrictions in Europe, Germany was stripped of her overseas colonies in Africa. Strict limits were imposed upon the German military: Germany was to have a maximum of 100,000 troops, conscription was prohibited, and its armed forces were to do without tanks, armoured vehicles, military aircraft and submarines. Germany had had little choice but to accept the treaty, although there were strong objections, and it was regarded as a *Diktat*. Once Hitler came to power, from the mid-1930s onwards, he essentially tore up the treaty, going against one provision after another. The 'bringing home' of the Saarland in 1935 and the march into the Rhineland on 7 March 1936 met with rapturous popular approval.

The *Wehrmacht*, the *SA*, and the *SS*

In March 1935, a new law changed the name of Germany's armed forces from the *Reichswehr* to the *Wehrmacht*. These events signified success and recovery for the German military under their 'great leader'. The Hitler government introduced conscription and proceeded to reverse each of the treaty's clauses regarding Germany's armed forces. The *Wehrmacht* grew rapidly. The first *Tag der Wehrmacht* (Day of the Armed Forces) was held in 1936. Posters advertising this event were put up right across the land. The *Wehrmacht* played a significant public role from the start – parading, taking part in the Nuremberg Party rallies and engaging in military drills and manoeuvres. The posters associated with the Day of the Armed Forces each year were striking. The 1940 poster designed by Blasius Spring depicts a uniformed German soldier holding up his bayonet in his right hand. Against a black background, a protective eagle in red and cream colours spreads its wings, as the soldier in turn protects the German farmer with his horse and plough.

The *Wehrmacht* grew rapidly to thirty-six divisions with 555,000 soldiers. Military planning in 1935 and 1936 'envisaged a quantitative and qualitative transformation in the German armed forces', in order to prepare the nation for war.[1] The *Wehrmacht* quickly developed into a powerful and well-equipped army. In September 1939, Germany mobilized an army of 2,750,000 men in 103 divisions, including six armoured divisions and four motorized infantry divisions. The *Wehrmacht* had changed from an elite military cadre into a veritable 'people's army'. It was the institution in which 20 million German men experienced and fought the Second World War. Thirteen million of these soldiers fought or served 'in the east' at some point in their careers. Omer Bartov has shown that 'the *Wehrmacht* was the army of the people, and the willing tool of the regime, more than any of its predecessors'.[2] The *Wehrmacht* succeeded in creating highly disciplined and motivated soldiers out of its recruits, whatever their social class. Its recruits, as Hitler's soldiers, became part of a *Kampfgemeinschaft* ('fighting community'), a construct through which the Nazi regime mobilized the whole nation for its war of expansion, conquest, and destruction. The *Wehrmacht* convinced the majority of its men, just as the regime convinced the majority of the civilian population, that they were fighting a justified and necessary war against racial and political enemies and an essential and existential war for the German nation. Nazi posters that depicted the *Wehrmacht* often showed soldiers alongside civilians, indicating not only that the army was protecting the nation, but also that the 'fighting front' and the 'home front' shared one common goal: to win the war, as we shall see later on in this chapter.

The regime also utilized posters to promote the Party's own paramilitary formations, the *SA* and the *SS* (*Schutzstaffel*). The *SA* (or stormtroopers) had been founded on 3 August 1921, organized and led by Ernst Roehm. Dubbed the 'brownshirts', due to the colour of their uniforms, the *SA* started out in Munich, the early stronghold and base of the *NSDAP*, where it meted out violence to opponents of the Nazi Party and was closely associated with the local army units, which trained the storm troopers in military skills. Once the Nazis came to power, the first six months of their rule was characterized by a period of unrestrained street violence by the *SA*. The regime's opponents were beaten up, arrested and imprisoned. During this period of 'national revolution' after the 'seizure of power', the activities of the *SA* increasingly met with the disapproval of leading conservatives and army officers. Hitler officially called an end to the revolution in July 1933, but the *SA* continued to act in the same violent manner as before. It became clear to Hitler that he had to bring the unruly Party rank and file in the *SA* under control. The *SA* was purged on the Night of the Long Knives (30 June 1934). Many prominent Nazis lost their lives that night, including Ernst Roehm, the leader of the *SA*. The strength of the *SA* was reined in and Himmler's *SS* became increasingly forceful as the Nazi paramilitary arm in its stead. As a reward for its loyalty in the Roehm purge, the *SS* became completely independent from the *SA* on 20 July 1934 and thereafter grew from strength to strength. Nevertheless, the *SA* continued to exist and to recruit new members. An *SA* poster from this period, designed by Sepp Semar, shows a brown-uniformed *SA* man looking to the future.[3] Against an orange background, his strong facial features make him appear both determined and menacing. The words '*SA-Voran*' ('*SA* – Take the lead') appear in large jaunty yellow letters at the bottom of the poster. The colours are striking and harmonious in Semar's poster, aiming to attract new members to the *SA*. Other graphic artists including Ludwig Hohlwein also designed *SA* posters.

Created by Julius Schreck shortly after Hitler's release from Landsberg Prison in 1925, the *SS* originated as the internal party protection squadrons that formed Hitler's personal bodyguard. Heinrich Himmler joined the *SS* in that same year and was appointed head of the *SS* on 6 January 1929. At that time, the organization had approximately 250 members. Himmler had exceptional organizational skills and was determined to increase the power of the *SS* within the Nazi movement. The original *SS* had been made up of 'early fighters' of the *NSDAP* and ex-servicemen, but Himmler intended to create an elite organization. In order to emphasize the social and ideological status of the *SS*, Himmler distributed honorary commissions to a number of prominent figures. He also incorporated some elite riding clubs into the *SS*. While actively recruiting high-status new members, Himmler simultaneously eliminated undesirable elements from his organization. Under Himmler's leadership *SS* membership expanded quickly to 10,000 in 1931; 52,000 in 1933; and 200,000 in 1935. Although it was intended to remain an elite organization, the *SS* still needed to recruit new members and utilized posters for this purpose, especially when during the wartime period it became ever more active in a combat role and began to drastically expand its numbers.

A poster from 1941 showed a uniformed *SS* man against a cream-coloured background. His strong features and the insignia on his uniform stood out clearly, with the *Waffen-SS* rune also on his helmet and on a black flag behind him. The symbolism was impossible to miss. Ottomar Anton produced a series of posters in 1942 that aimed to encourage *SS* membership.[4] One such poster showed two uniformed *SS* men, armed and determined, with the words: '*Auch Du zur Leibstandarte-SS Adolf Hitler*' ('You too can be one of Adolf Hitler's Personal Bodyguards'). Another poster appealed to members of the *Reich* Labour Service to volunteer to join the *Waffen-SS*. It showed a civilian worker and an *SS* man in profile, standing side by side, both looking purposefully in the same direction. In his left hand, the *SS* man hoisted his weapon up over his shoulder; the German worker was shown in the same pose, with his tool raised in an identical manner. It was designed not only to recruit new members to the *SS*, but also to show that all Germans, whether on the home front or on the battlefields, were working towards the same goal. Anton produced a similar poster in 1943 to encourage members of the Hitler Youth to volunteer for the *SS*, with a depiction of a Hitler Youth boy standing in front of an *SS* man, both in their uniforms, both looking towards the future, with two simple words printed below: '*Auch Du*' ('You too'). The message to the Hitler Youth was clear – they too could become *SS* members.

PLATE 13 *Nazi Election Poster 1932 'Our Last Hope: Hitler'.*

PLATE 14 *Nazi Election Poster 1932 'National Socialists 1'.*

PLATE 15 *'Hitler Is Building Up. Help Out. Buy German Goods'*.

PLATE 16 *'Hitler Youth: Germany's Future'*.

PLATE 17 'Bund Deutscher Mädel in der Hitler Jugend' (*'League of German Girls in the Hitler Youth'*).

PLATE 18 'Kraft durch Freude' *Travel Poster.*

PLATE 19 *Nazi Family Poster.*

PLATE 20 'Der ewige Jude' *('The Eternal Jew')*.

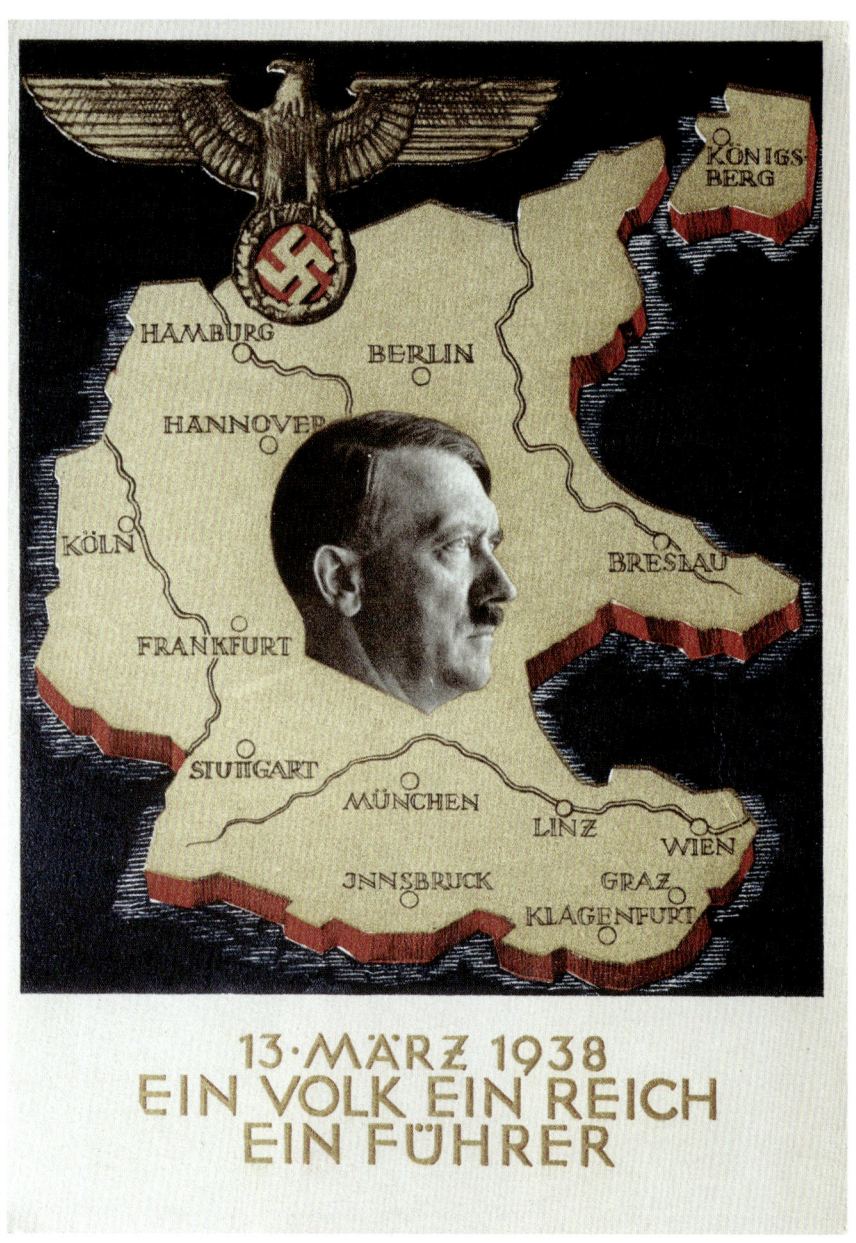

PLATE 21 *Annexation of Austria Poster 1938.*

PLATE 22 'Ein Kampf, Ein Sieg!' *('One Fight, One Victory!')*.

PLATE 23 'Sieg oder Bolschewismus' *('Victory or Bolshevism')*.

PLATE 24 'Adolf Hitler ist der Sieg!' *('Adolf Hitler Is Victory!')*.

The Expansionism of the Third *Reich* and the Second World War

In addition to these types of posters that aimed to recruit members to the *SA* and the *SS*, posters were put up that glorified the Nazis' staged destruction of the unpopular Treaty of Versailles. The *Anschluß* (union) with Austria in 1938 was a huge triumph for the 'national community' and its *Führer*. The poster designed to commemorate it shows a profile of Hitler looking eastwards, in the centre of a map of the unified Greater German *Reich* (including Austria) (see Colour Plate 21). The symbolic protective Nazi eagle appears in gold at the top of the poster, carrying a wreathed swastika in its claws overhanging the map. At the bottom of the poster is the date of the *Anschluß*, 13 March 1938, with the slogan '*Ein Volk Ein Reich Ein Führer*'. Hitler claimed that providence had singled him out to be the one to return his homeland, Austria, to the German *Reich*. The question of what the German nation should look like had been debated by German nationalists during the nineteenth century – whether Germany ought to take the form of a 'small Germany', without Austria, or a 'large Germany', that incorporated Austria. While a 'small Germany' was the one that had emerged in 1871, upon the unification of the nation under Kaiser Wilhelm I, Hitler had very different ideas and the map of 1938 reflected this. That Hitler looks to the east in this poster is suggestive of his further territorial ambitions.

After the *Anschluß*, Hitler continued his quest for '*Lebensraum*' ('living space'), annexing the Sudetenland and the rest of Czechoslovakia before setting his sights upon Poland. A Nazi poster titled '*Sieg über Versailles*' ('Victory over Versailles') showed a swastika cutting through chains in the Rhineland, Austria, the Sudetenland, Bohemia and Moravia, and Memel (Klaipeda, part of Lithuania until annexed by the *Reich* in March 1939). A poster on the same subject stated: '*Zug um Zug zerriß Adolf Hitler das Diktat von Versailles!*' ('Step by Step Adolf Hitler Tore Up the Treaty of Versailles!'). While Nazi foreign policy continued to succeed, the sense of national pride and 'national community' was enhanced and Hitler appeared to be infallible. Hence, even a nation hesitant to go to war again in September 1939 accepted Hitler's decision and reaped the benefits during the initial *Blitzkrieg* successes of the Second World War. In addition, Nazi propaganda conveyed the message that the German nation was 'being forced into a war' by Britain, France, Poland, and the Bolsheviks (even when a Non-Aggression Pact with the Soviet Union had been signed in August 1939), while Hitler himself was portrayed as 'desiring peace and having struggled to avoid war'.[5] To be sure, nothing could be further from the truth, but the Nazi propaganda machine mendaciously twisted the reality into a story that the population would find easier to accept. Through encirclement, Nazi propaganda maintained, Germany was being coerced into a war that was not of her choosing. By December 1939, Goebbels called for enemy statesmen, and in particular Neville Chamberlain, to be depicted as 'vengeful tyrants'.[6] Furthermore, Britain was portrayed as a cunning, devious foe. Nazi propaganda constructed Britain as a perfidious empire-builder. It resurrected images and themes from the nineteenth century to indicate Britain's sinister motives. Furthermore, hatred towards the Poles was whipped up with nationalistic and irredentist claims that land given to Poland at the end of the First World War (Danzig and the 'Polish corridor') had to be returned to Germany. An astute propagandist, Goebbels continually developed messages, slogans, and images to powerfully persuade the population into believing the Nazis' ideological tenets.

The poster '*In der Staub mit allen Feinden Grossdeutschlands*' ('Into the Dust with all Enemies of Greater Germany!') created by Hans Schweitzer in 1940 portrayed a strong fist smashing the French, the British, and the Jews. He chose a cream background against which the bright red letters stood out very clearly. The message was evident too – Germany, represented by the powerful fist, would defeat and pulverize her enemies, who were depicted as being small, insignificant, and easily beaten. But in reality, of course, Britain especially was to prove a difficult and indefatigable enemy, and much larger and more powerful enemies were to come, in the form of the USSR and the United States. By 1943 and 1944, as we shall see a little further in the chapter, Schweitzer's posters were spelling out a different message: the enemies still need to be defeated, but it was not going to be easy.

In the first half of 1941, Hitler tore up the non-aggression treaty that had been signed between the USSR and the Third *Reich* in August 1939 (the Molotov-Ribbentrop Pact). The Nazi invasion of the USSR (Operation Barbarossa) began on 22 June 1941. Unlike the Nazis' campaigns elsewhere in Europe, the invasion of the USSR was planned as a war of extermination from the start. It was conducted without reference to internationally accepted legal norms. Because the Soviet Union had neither acknowledged the Hague Convention on Land Warfare of 1907, nor ratified the Geneva Convention of 1929 on the treatment of POWs, the Nazis felt no restraints in their brutal treatment of the Soviet enemy, which resulted in millions of deaths. The Nazis conceived of the war against the USSR as an essential struggle for the existence of the German people, which was conducted with unprecedented brutality. It was mercilessly aimed at the complete extermination of the enemy, which the Nazis considered to be 'inferior'. But the German forces did not achieve the swift victory they had hoped for in the USSR. They experienced serious resistance from the start and although the USSR lost a great deal of territory, the Soviet armed forces did not collapse in the same way that the Polish, Dutch, Belgian, or French armies had done before them. Despite suffering huge numbers of casualties, Soviet troops were able to resist the Nazi forces and to inflict serious losses upon the *Wehrmacht*. Nevertheless, Nazi propaganda besmirched the Soviet enemy as brutal and barbaric, and posters played their part in depicting the Soviet or Bolshevik 'menace' in strongly negative terms. Significantly too,

Nazi anti-Soviet propaganda was, as O'Shaughnessy notes, 'more polemical and combustible than that directed against the West'.[7]

In the campaign on the Eastern Front, the Soviet counterattack at Stalingrad marked a significant turning point in Germany's war, as the strategic initiative passed from the *Wehrmacht* to the Red Army. By the time of its conclusion in early 1943, hundreds of thousands of Germans, Romanians, and Hungarians had become POWs. From that point onwards, the German army – on the defensive and without a realistic prospect of winning – had to keep on fighting. The Battle of Stalingrad had raged for more than five months, from the first German assaults in late August 1942 to the eventual surrender of the German Sixth Army under Field Marshal Friedrich Paulus on 31 January 1943. It was a brutal and bloody battle involving street-by-street fighting in bitterly cold weather conditions. Of the once 300,000-strong German Sixth Army trapped in Stalingrad, between 30,000 and 45,000 had been flown out wounded, half were killed or died of cold, and over 100,000 surrendered to the Russians (of whom only some 6,000 survived their captivity to return to Germany). Subsequently, during July and August 1943, a major tank battle between German and Soviet forces ensued on the Eastern Front near Kursk. At the Battle of Kursk, the German forces were outgunned and outmanoeuvred. Here, the Red Army may have won the most important single victory of the war. The *Wehrmacht* no longer enjoyed the advantages of better training, surprise, and tactical superiority, which had brought it successes in 1941 and 1942. The launch of the massive tank battle at Kursk effectively accelerated the defeat of the Germans because, although the Red Army suffered greater losses than the German army, the *Wehrmacht* had much greater difficulty in replacing men and weaponry.

During the course of the Second World War, and especially during the Nazi campaign against the USSR, the role of posters took on a new significance reflecting what was seen as a life-and-death struggle until the end. Nazi propagandists redoubled their efforts with vigour. In 1941, Goebbels noted the need to make the enemy appear brutal. The propaganda division of Goebbels's Ministry had always commissioned the German Propaganda Studio (DPA) to produce Nazi posters to ensure the maintenance of a high standard. The Ministry did not want local offices to produce the posters because they did not have enough resources to do this to a high quality. During the war, the budget allocation to the DPA increased from less than 1 million RM to over 1,400,000 RM.

Once the United States had entered the Second World War in December 1941, the Nazis created a new myth about this new enemy. The United States was presented as a ruthless and money-worshipping capitalist nation, motivated by consumerism and greed. Nazi posters emphasized this clearly. Moreover, the Nazis went back to the atrocity propaganda that the British had used against Germany during the First World War. They strongly believed in its power in bringing about victory for the Entente powers and defeat for

Germany. During the Second World War, Goebbels maintained that his anti-British propaganda was a reversal of this. While British propaganda again attacked Germany in the Second World War, Goebbels was ruthless and hard-hitting in his counterattack.

From 1942 onwards in particular, enemy bombing inflicted tremendous damage and terror on the German civilian population. The RAF had bombed German cities from as early as 1940, but the use of large phosphorous incendiary bombs in 1942 brought with it a significant change in the scale and impact of air raids. Starting with the raid on Lübeck in March 1942, the frequency and severity of Allied bombings increased. In the summer of 1943, the German city of Hamburg endured a relentless ten-day air raid in which 34,000 people were killed and more than a quarter of a million homes were completely destroyed. From 1943 onwards, the southern cities in Germany also became targets for Allied bombs. Instead of continuing their attacks on the industrial Ruhr region, the Allies turned their attention to Berlin in the summer to autumn of 1943. On the night of 18–19 November 1943, the Battle of Berlin took on greater vigour. Between that night and 2 March 1944, sixteen major raids were mounted on the city. No more than 200 acres of its built-up area had been damaged in all the previous raids since August 1940: Berlin had continued to function normally as the capital of Germany and of Hitler's Third *Reich*. Goebbels, as *Gauleiter* of Berlin, persuaded 1 million of its 4.5 million inhabitants to leave before the Allied bomber command main attacks began. Those who remained began to undergo the most sustained experience of air attack undergone by any urban population throughout the Second World War. Berlin did not suffer a firestorm, but relentless high explosive bombings, six times in January 1944 alone, resulted in devastation. As many as 9,000 Berliners were killed in this battle (a greater death toll prevented by the solid construction of shelters), but 1.5 million Berliners were made homeless, and 2,000 acres of the city lay in ruins by the end of March 1944.

The successful bombing operations carried out by the Allies represented a serious indictment of *Reichsmarshall* Hermann Goering's air defences. Once Hitler's favourite, Goering's standing within the party leadership and also his reputation in the population at large began to decline sharply. Soon all kinds of jokes were circulating about him. Under day-time and night-time attacks by the USAAF and the RAF, each deploying over 1,000 aircraft during the autumn, winter and spring of 1944–5, German economic life was paralysed by strategic bombing. The *Luftwaffe* was overwhelmed, and anti-aircraft systems dwindled into ineffectiveness. The cost of strategic bombing on Germany's civilian population was very high in terms of both casualties and the physical destruction of urban areas. Few aspects of the Second World War made so deep and lasting an impression on Germans as the bombing of their cities. In the first months of 1945, the bombing reached its peak in terms of tonnage dropped with the destruction of Magdeburg in January

1945 and Dresden in February 1945. The devastation was enormous. In the last four months of the war alone, when the bombing campaign was at its most ferocious, at least 130,000 people died.

The Ministry of Propaganda stoked the fires of hatred with a vicious propaganda campaign against the Allied bombing crews and their political leaders. Goebbels described the Americans as 'gangsters' and the air crews as uncultivated mobsters and criminals. The British men were castigated as members of the effete ranks of the aristocracy. But both, Nazi propaganda claimed, were in the service of Jewish conspirators who were manipulating Roosevelt and Churchill in order to bring about the total destruction of Germany. The propaganda had some effect. For example, there were widespread reports from 1943 onwards of people demanding reprisal attacks on London.

July and August 1944 proved the bloodiest months yet for the *Wehrmacht*. Over 215,000 German soldiers were killed in July and nearly 350,000 were killed in August. With defeat unavoidable, the Nazi regime continued to send its soldiers to their deaths in hundreds of thousands. The Battle of Berlin was one of the last major land offensives in the Second World War in Europe, in April–May 1945. German military strategy consisted of trying to ward off the inevitable collapse, while shedding as much blood as possible. In the end, Nazi Germany achieved total defeat surrendering only once enemy troops had captured the seat of government in street-by-street fighting which cost both the invaders and the defenders hundreds of thousands of casualties.

Posters were utilized to appeal to the populations of Nazi-occupied lands. For example, in a reassuring and unthreatening poster by Theo Matejko from 1940, aimed at civilians in occupied France, a German soldier is shown holding a smiling French child eating bread, with two further French children close by his side, looking up at him. The caption, in red and black lettering, reads, '*Populations abandonnées, faites confiance au soldat allemand*' ('Abandoned populations, place your trust in German soldiers') (see Figure 5.1). This was shrewd propaganda, offering a possibility of assurance about the occupying forces, which belied the truth of their aims. This gentle image of the German soldier was very different from propaganda posters in Germany, which showed the *Wehrmacht* to be ruthlessly determined in the face of its enemies. Slogans intended for a German audience were powerful and memorable: 'Life or Death'; 'For Freedom and Life'; 'Perish Judah'; 'Victory at any Price'.

Moreover, there were posters aimed at young men in Nazi-occupied territories across Europe to join the *Waffen-SS*. These were captioned in different languages so that local populations would be able to read them. For example, a poster campaign in the Netherlands encouraged Dutch volunteers to join the *Waffen-SS*. The poster shows a uniformed SS man against a background of a blue sky, with aircraft above, and

FIGURE 5.1 'Populations abandonnées, faites confiance au soldat allemand!' *('Abandoned Populations, Have Confidence in German Soldiers!').*

tanks and infantrymen below, with the wording: '*Nederlanders Voor uw eer en geweten op tegen het Bolsjewisme! De Waffen SS roept u!*' ('Netherlanders – For your honour and conscience, up against Bolshevism! The *Waffen-SS* is calling you!') (see Figure 5.2).[8] Anti-Semitic posters were also put up in territories in the USSR – regarded as being set free from Bolshevism by the invaders – for example, in the Baltic states and in Ukraine, in order to encourage local populations to join the Nazi campaign against the Jews.

FIGURE 5.2 SS *Recruitment Poster in the Netherlands:* 'Nederlanders'.

'Total War'

The '*Ein Kampf, Ein Sieg!*' ('One Struggle, One Victory!') poster from 1943 by Hans Schweitzer has the dates 30 January 1933–43 at the top, suggesting that the war was simply an extension of Hitler's continued aim from the date he took power, to make Germany great and to defeat her enemies (see Colour Plate 22). Here a brown-shirted *SA* man stretches his right arm out beside a swastika flag, as a *Wehrmacht* soldier at the height of the war does the same, evoking this continued battle from the early days of the Nazi success in seizing power in 1933, to project victory on the battlefield. In this way, the 'interpenetration of conflict with communication', which permeated Nazi ideology from its origins, extended with a certain degree of ease into the wartime period, as the war itself became 'a formulaic meld of punch and publicity'.[9] This striking martial and belligerent poster was intended to keep up popular endurance, by showing the prowess, fortitude, and ideological determination of German soldiers, as they held their right arms up in the Hitler salute.

Through a variety of propaganda media, including posters, the regime alarmed its population into action, in particular, by showing frightful Soviet hordes. This was the creation of an enemy that differed from reality. True, the Soviet armed forces were numerous and powerful, but the Nazis' satirized version of the enemy portrayed a demonic adversary that was unreal. Nazi propaganda claimed that the 'Judeo-Bolsheviks' intended the destruction of Germany and that the nation had to fight a 'total war', as Goebbels maintained in his speech in Berlin on 18 February 1943, to the bitter end in order to defend the fatherland from this threat. Indeed, at the height of the war, Nazi propaganda posters harked back to the anti-Communist theme of those in the period before 1933. The 1943 poster *'Sieg oder Bolschewismus'* ('Victory or Bolshevism') by Hans Schweitzer ('Mjölnir') exemplifies this well (see Colour Plate 23). It was part of a vast poster campaign launched by Goebbels in 1943, designed to urgently impart the need for success on the battlefield as well as diligence on the home front. 'Victory', in big red letters, was depicted as a smiling, blonde mother holding up her happy and healthy golden-haired child, while 'Bolshevism', in black letters, showed misery, desperation, and capitulation at the hands of a dark and menacing Bolshevik figure. The idea of Communist victory was unimaginable. Schweitzer's poster was designed to keep up popular morale and a determination to resist the enemy at all costs, to keep the nation fighting in a life-or-death struggle against Bolshevism and to win the war. Millions of these posters were put up across the land (sized 3 feet by 5 feet). In addition, posters were displayed on buses and trains, kiosks, walls and shop windows.[10] These poster campaigns were implemented in the aftermath of the defeat of the German 6th Army at Stalingrad. The tide of the war had turned against Germany and the Nazi propaganda response was to double down upon its excoriation of the twin enemies of 'Bolshevik barbarism and US consumerism'.[11]

Posters proclaiming 'Adolf Hitler is Victory' also appeared during 1943. Hitler was portrayed as a great military leader, destined to lead the nation to victory. A huge amount of money and effort was put into these poster campaigns. The poster, designed by R. Gerhard Zill, shows a serious and determined looking *Führer* standing behind a chair with his hands resting on the top of the chair. The simple and clear caption reads, *'Adolf Hitler ist der Sieg!'* ('Adolf Hitler is Victory!') (see Colour Plate 24). This slogan was also particularly utilized again in the aftermath of the assassination attempt on Hitler on 20 July 1944, after which, as O'Shaughnessy notes, 'Hitler is victory' became 'the revived slogan'.[12] This was an illusory or an imagined leader, self-sacrificing and dutiful; honourable and idealized. Hitler was presented as a great military strategist. This type of poster propaganda was designed to maintain support for Hitler and for the war effort.

A wartime poster by Werner and Maria von Axster-Heudtlass shows a German soldier shielding the nation from its brutal enemies. Standing firm against four fierce dragon-like creatures with sharp teeth and fangs, depicted in black and grey at the bottom right-hand corner of the poster, with a large shield bearing a Nazi symbol in one hand and wielding a large weapon in his other hand, he protects the German *Volk* depicted behind him at the top left-hand side of the poster. The *Volk* is represented in colour, by marching Hitler Youth bands, those at the front carrying large swastika flags. The caption at the top in black lettering reads, '*Hass und Vernichtung unserer Feinden*' ('Hate and Destruction of our Enemies'), while the caption at the bottom in red lettering states '*Freiheit, Recht und Brot unserer Volk*' ('Freedom, Justice and Bread for our *Volk*'). The enemies are labelled as 'Judaism', 'Bolshevism', 'Plutocracy', and 'Capitalism', clearly indicative of both a hatred of the Jews and their alleged affinity and connection to the external foes of National Socialism, the USSR, Britain, and the United States. Britain and the British were continually portrayed as duplicitous and cunning, with their perfidious plutocracy. Together, these three enemies represented an existential menace to the Third *Reich*.

The *Wehrmacht*, as we have seen, was a major institution within German society that had a bearing on the 'national community' and was deeply affected by National Socialism. Furthermore, the position and role of the *Wehrmacht* in Nazi Germany were especially significant because the attributes of the *Wehrmacht* as a 'fighting community' were very closely linked to those of the wider 'national community'. Hans Schweitzer's 1944 poster, '*Alle Kraft gespannt! Totaler Krieg – Kürzester Krieg*!' ('All Power Ahead! Total War – Shortest War!'), aimed to mobilize the whole nation together into the war effort. This was 'total war'. The poster showed the German soldier and the German worker together, looking resolute and determined, bent on achieving final victory. The Nazis told the nation that all power and every resource had to be used, that 'total war' would make the conflict a shorter one. There was a great sense of solidarity between the home front and the *Wehrmacht*, both consciously contributing to the Nazi war effort, albeit in different ways.

The German nation's heroic and courageous soldiers had to be supported on the Home Front. Many wartime posters were produced with the aim of keeping up popular morale and encouraging particular, desired forms of behaviour among the German population, as well as discouraging unwanted ways of acting. From 1940 onwards, the RPL distributed a series of posters bearing the 'Motto of the *NSDAP*', with words from Robert Ley, the head of the *DAF* (German Labour Front), aimed at keeping up the morale of industrial workers. As well as Ley's speeches to German workers, posters played their part in mobilizing German workers. For example, one *DAF* poster depicted a German soldier, with the slogan: 'He is fighting harder!

We are increasing our performance.'[13] In May 1943, with the cooperation of Albert Speer, a renewed propaganda effort was directed at factory workers with the slogan 'Hard Times, Hard Work, Hard Hearts', aiming to appeal to blue-collar workers in bombed German cities. This was another clear message, in very difficult times.

In the wartime years, rationing and the decreasing availability of foodstuffs also had an impact on people's daily lives. This situation led many women to buy food on the 'black market'. In addition, urban women bought and hoarded up non-perishable items for use in bartering, for example, exchanging soap products for food from farmers. They exchanged children's toys and table linen for potatoes, milk, vegetables, or fruit. The growth of a black market of barter in Germany indicated the seriousness of food shortages within the industrial cities. Urban women made 'hamstering trips' by train from the cities to the countryside to look for food or to exchange goods for food, in order to supplement their rations, which grew increasingly meagre as the war years went on. The Nazi propaganda poster, stating 'Hoarder, you should be ashamed of yourself!' discouraged hoarding or 'hamstering'. These women were guilty of selfishness at a time, the regime maintained, when it was more crucial than ever to put the needs of the nation before those of the individual. Hoarding was frowned upon by the regime. A 1939 poster by Max Eschle depicts a German woman with a white scarf and brown dress with a hamster's face. She is laden with two baskets brimming with non-perishable goods, as well as a box containing a pair of shoes under her right arm. The vivid, orange wording stands out clearly against the black backdrop.

Another 1939 poster encouraged women to enrol in air raid protection. Ludwig Hohlwein's poster shows a smiling, uniformed young German woman playing her part for the nation. With the swastika symbol and acronym of the National Air Raid Protection League displayed behind her against a sky-blue background, the Gothic font wording simply says: '*Frau im Luftschutz!*' ('Women in air-raid protection!'). It exhorted German women, who were not obliged to undertake war work yet at this point, to volunteer in a useful service to the *Volk*. An impactful poster designed by the same graphic artist was intended to encourage people to observe 'blackouts'. It depicted a German city at night time, with purple and black buildings against a sepia-toned night sky with three stars. At the foreground of the image, three bombs rain down on the city from the sky. Showing two of the buildings with lights on, the poster asks: '*Kannst Du das verantworten?*' ('Do you want to be responsible for this?'). A further message below clearly stated that by leaving lights on at night, when there ought to be a 'black out' to prevent air raids on German cities, '*Du hilfst dem Feind!*' ('You help the enemy!').

A poster titled '*Hilf auch Du mit!*' ('You help out too!'), depicted three German women in the foreground, with linked arms, ready to help out with the harvest in the countryside, against the background of a much larger figure of a soldier, depicting the fighting front. Women's Labour Service became compulsory from January 1943 and posters with this type of theme served to encourage German women to do their duty and contribute to the war effort as required. It was important for the regime to garner all possible support on the home front. Another noteworthy wartime poster campaign centred upon the theme of the enemy listening. One such poster depicted two men on a train talking, with the simple caption (and instruction) 'Be Quiet', in this campaign against rumours and spying. People were urged to be cautious while travelling and while at work, even amongst family, friends, and acquaintances. 'Pst! Keep Quiet' and 'The Enemy Is Listening!' were some of the key slogans on posters of this type, designed by Richard Blank and other graphic artists throughout the war years.[14] Depictions of a shadowy figure in the background warned the public to be careful of being overheard. This kind of government warning against enemy listening was not unique to Nazi Germany, of course.[15] Similar campaigns were afoot in the Soviet Union, Britain, and other belligerent nations.

Throughout the war, the Nazis were determined to win over public opinion, and it therefore became illegal for Germans to listen to foreign radio stations. This was known as 'black listening'. Despite the risk of severe punishment, people did listen to foreign broadcasts, for example, from the BBC or Radio Moscow. These people were regarded as 'traitors', as portrayed on posters to discourage this practice. A poster from 1944 showing an ordinary German citizen tuning in furtively to foreign radio broadcasts depicted this as a shady occupation.[16] At the bottom of the dark image, in large capital letters, the word '*Verräter*' ('Traitor') was printed in bright red. Again, this was designed to show up non-conformist behaviour and to make people feel ashamed of their actions. But some German people risked punishment in their desire to find out what was really going on in the war. It was perhaps one of the least dangerous forms of dissenting behaviour because it was very difficult to detect illegal listening; most of those found and punished had been denounced to the authorities by neighbours, acquaintances or even by family members.

During the last months of the war, remaining civilian men were drafted into a national militia, the *Volkssturm* ('people's army'), in a last-ditch attempt to defend the fatherland. A poster by 'Mjölnir' called to arms young teenagers and older men with the slogan '*Um Freiheit und Leben*' ('For Freedom and Life') (see Figure 5.3). Both the older man and the youth in the first image wear the *Volkssturm* uniform, looking in the same direction, ready to defend their nation to the end. The powerful wording is presented in broad, bright red lettering. In the second image, the 'people's army' men join in the 'shoot back' of the German *Volk* (1944), reflecting the strong *Wehrmacht* soldier with his gun, shown in the background, all working together towards the same aim.

FIGURE 5.3 'Volkssturm'.

Anti-Semitic Posters during the Wartime Period

Nazi propaganda encompassed a wide range of allegations against the Jews. Building on the traditional religious anti-Semitic belief that Jews were Christ-slayers, they added a much more uncompromising racial component to anti-Semitism. The Jews were depicted as an 'inferior' and alien race that insidiously threatened the 'master race'. Incongruently, they were considered the evil geniuses behind both capitalism and communism, depicted as dirty and as carriers of disease, and caricatured in hideous and pernicious ways. Nazi anti-Semitic posters offer a clear view of this aspect of Nazi propaganda and policy. The Nazis manufactured a myth that the Jew was everywhere, a sinister and pervasive threat, not only to the German nation, but likewise to the world. The Jew was the scapegoat for all that had gone wrong in Germany and Hitler repeatedly blamed the Jews for both the First World War and the Second World War. With lurid colours to represent the Jewish 'enemy', anti-Semitic posters on the streets of both Germany and Nazi-occupied territories affected the public mind daily as people went about their activities and errands. It was impossible to escape from the images, which made it impossible also to escape from the Nazi anti-Semitic myth.

Three Nazi anti-Semitic films *Die Rothschilds (The Rothschilds)*, *Jud Süss (Jew Süss)* and *Der ewige Jude (The Eternal Jew)* screened in 1940 were part of a wider propaganda campaign to justify the increasingly harsh and discriminatory treatment of the Jews by the regime, and to prepare the German population for more radical anti-Semitic policies. Posters advertising the anti-Semitic films portrayed the Jews in a sinister fashion.[17] *Die Rothschilds* showed the rise to power and wealth of the Rothschild family and the emergence of the 'Jewish-British plutocracy'. It revealed the 'historical fact' that Jewish financiers had profited from the death of German soldiers. The Jews were portrayed as both a racial and an economic threat. Veit Harlan's *Jud Süss* (1940) showed the inherent rootlessness of 'the Jew' and his ability to assimilate himself into any society. Süss, the elegant and fashionable lawyer, personified 'the Jew in disguise'. The rest of the Jews in the film were portrayed as dirty, hook-nosed, and physically repellent. They represented 'authentic Jewry'. The poster for *Jud Süss*, designed by Bruno Rehak, makes the title character look untrustworthy and devious, with shifty, hooded eyes and caricatured with sidelocks and a long beard. Large bright red lettering at the top was used for the film title. *Der ewige Jude* was one of the most virulent propaganda films ever made. It claimed to be a documentary film about world Jewry. The main tenet of the film was that 'the Jew' had cunningly assimilated himself into European society. The film showed pictures of Jews with beards and traditional garb. Each shot faded into one of the same men 'disguised' in European clothing. Hence, the Jews were represented as an insidious threat to the nation. Moreover, they were associated with vermin to emphasize to the audience that they were 'disease-bearers' and 'subhuman'. The film covered the entire gamut of Nazi allegations against the Jews. The poster for *Der ewige Jude* shows the faces of five stereotyped and sinister-looking Jewish men overprinted with a large, red Star of David, on a black and red background, with the title words below, *Der ewige Jude*, printed in a font resembling Hebrew script, in which *Jude* is double sized. The poster states this is 'a documentary film about world Jewry', directed by Fritz Hippler.

This type of visual propaganda started to prepare the way for more radical policies against the Jews. This radicalization enormously accelerated after the invasion of the Soviet Union on 22 June 1941. In Germany, once Jews were obliged to wear a Yellow Star on their clothing, from 1 September 1941, propaganda posters simply carried an image of the Yellow Star with

'*Jude*' printed in the centre of it, with the words 'Whoever wears this symbol is an Enemy of our *Volk*'. This was an unambiguous message, helping to prepare the way for the Nazi policy of 'resettlement', which was in reality the deportation of the Jews to the East and ultimately, for most, to their death. In Nazi-occupied Poland, ghettos, into which Jewish communities were forced to live, had been established earlier than June 1941. Nazi posters underlined the threat of the Jews to the local Polish communities by pointing out the health risk posed by the Jews in the ghettos as carriers of disease. For example, one such poster read: 'Beware of Typhus – Avoid Jews'. These words, printed in Polish in bright red lettering, accompanied an alarming, dark image of a Nazi stereotype Jewish man, against a sinister black background, with a Star of David symbol, shown with eight huge, over-sized lice crawling over him in different directions, for emphasis. Thousands of these types of posters were distributed and put up in Warsaw, where there was a large Jewish ghetto. They were designed to instil fear and hatred of the Jews among the local Polish population.

As the war of extermination in the East raged on, special mobile killing squads, the *SS Einsatzgruppen*, operated in the rear of the *Wehrmacht*, engaging in the wholesale slaughter of Jewish populations within their reach by mass shootings on former Soviet-held territory. From late 1941 and especially after the Wannsee Conference of January 1942, the 'Final Solution' was systematically carried out through the establishment of six death camps located in Poland – Auschwitz, Majdanek, Chelmno, Belzec, Sobibor, and Treblinka – where the Nazis used poison gas, Zyklon B, to gas to death the Jews in sealed chambers. After they had died, their bodies were taken to specially constructed crematoria where they were burnt.

During this time, anti-Semitic propaganda continued to foment hatred in German-occupied Europe. The 1943 Nazi anti-Semitic poster epitomized the manner in which the Jews were held responsible for the war and for that reason (among others) subject to the Nazis' genocidal policy. Here, Hans Schweitzer creates a caricature of the 'capitalist' Jew, presented as hook-nosed, fat, and repellent, in his black hat and suit, marked with the Yellow Star with the word '*Jude*' ('Jew') in the centre. This Nazi poster clearly points the finger at the Jewish scapegoat, with the words '*Der ist Schuld am Kriege!*' ('He is Responsible for the War!'). In white font, the word 'he' is presented in a much larger size for emphasis (see Figure 5.4).

Another anti-Semitic wartime poster from 1944, created by Bruno Hanich, is particularly striking. It depicts a typical image of a Nazi caricature of a Jew, with a gold Star of David hanging from a golden chain at his waist, and wearing a bowler hat. He is shown skulking as a dark shadow behind the flags of Great Britain, the United States and the USSR. The reprehensible character partly emerges from behind the flags of the three enemy nations, with the caption '*Hinter den Feindmächten: der Jude*' ('Behind the Enemy Powers: the Jew'). The first words are printed in white text against the background of the Union Jack and the Stars and Stripes

FIGURE 5.4 'Der ist Schuld am Kriege!' *('He is Responsible for the War!')*.

flags, while the words 'The Jew' are in a bigger cursive script, as if daubed on in paint in yellow gold, to match both the golden chain and star, and the yellow hammer and sickle on the Soviet flag. Here, the Jew was the ultimate enemy, working behind the scenes of the Allied powers to destroy Germany. According to Nazi myth, the Jews were manipulating the Western plutocratic nations, as well as the communist USSR, in order to attain their own world domination. Such views were not new, and indeed *The Protocols of the Elders of Zion* (a forgery concocted by the tsar's secret police in pre-First World War Russia), which had circulated in the years before the First World War, had made similar claims about the aims of international Jewry to obtain global dominance. But this graphic poster made the point very clearly.

Fighting to the Bitter End

In addition to national propaganda campaign efforts, posters were put up in individual towns and cities urging the German population to fight on, with slogans such as *'Frontstadt Frankfurt wird gehalten!'* ('Front City Frankfurt will be held!'), with an image of an older man and two youths representing the *Volkssturm*, looking grim and determined, holding up a swastika flag. The *Volkssturm* represented a further Nazi myth, a 'motley army of old men and youths were incorporated into yet another campaign, the symbol of popular will, the quintessence of demotic rage, the German masses empowered, vengeful'.[18] But while there was no collapse of the home front and the nation was defended street by street, it was delusional to think that the *Volkssturm* could stop the Allied forces in the last months and days of the war. As Aristotle Kallis has noted, 'during the period of "defeat" National Socialist propaganda was gradually deprived of its monopoly of truth if not on a purely organisational level, then certainly in mass psychological terms'.[19] Finally, the 'Hitler myth' started to crumble.

The Nazi leadership, despite the fact that the German armed forces were on the defensive by now, became ever more desperate in their response to the Allied advances. Hitler was determined to fight to the bitter end. His apocalyptic rhetoric of victory or annihilation continued, even though, or perhaps indeed because, Germany was in a position of desperation. Hitler had committed the German armed forces and its population to so much, not only in terms of the warfare, but also in terms of genocide and crimes against humanity committed at the same time. There was a sense that they had to keep on going, because the retribution, particularly meted out by the Red Army, would be too great. They had to fight on to the end. The home front, as we have seen, also had to endure rationing, Allied bombing, the destruction of German cities, loss of life and the separation of families. And so Hitler called on both the home front and the German armed forces to continue their struggle and maintain their fortitude. Fighting ended at different times in different places at the end of the war, due to Hitler's insistence that the Germans defend every last town and village of the land. Most obeyed, not only or necessarily out of loyalty to Hitler and his regime, but mainly due to the fear and dread of the Red Army's revenge. Sheer terror of the Soviet hordes inspired the German people to hold out and fight to the bitter end. By this time, as we have noted, remaining civilian men had been drafted into the *Volkssturm* in a last-ditch attempt to defend the fatherland, while the Hitler Youth also played its part in anti-aircraft activities and in the final defence of Berlin. To be sure, this conclusion was not what the smiling young Germans had anticipated when they joined the Nazi youth movement in the early years of the regime. Nazi propaganda had duped the population as a whole, but its indoctrination of the youth, in particular, was devastating.

At the end of the war, after Germany's capitulation, the Allied powers were determined to bring to justice leading Nazis, which they did at the International Military Tribunal at Nuremberg and other postwar trials. Of course, the Nazi Minister of Popular Enlightenment and Propaganda, Joseph Goebbels, had already taken his own life, but Hans Fritzsche was tried at Nuremberg as a representative of this ministry. Julius Streicher was also brought to trial at Nuremberg for his incitement of hatred towards the Jews, particularly in his malevolent and pernicious publication *Der Stürmer*. In later trials, other Nazi propagandists, including press magnates, filmmakers, photographers and journalists, stood before German courts. What happened to the Nazi poster artists after the fall of the Third *Reich*? Philipp Rupprecht, creator of anti-Semitic caricatures in *Der Stürmer*, was already a POW who was in US custody at the time of Germany's surrender. In 1947, he was tried and convicted in Germany, receiving a sentence of ten years in a work camp.[20] However, following an appeal, his sentence was reduced, and he was released in 1950. Hans Schweitzer ('Mjölnir'), one of the most prolific Nazi poster artists, was fined 500 marks by a German court after the war. But this was reduced on appeal and his record was cleared in 1955.[21]

Posters were one segment of a massive propaganda campaign both to publicize Hitler's polices and to legitimize Hitler's war. While they appeared in front of the eyes of German citizens on a daily basis as they went about their lives, on shop fronts, walls, kiosks, buses, trams, and trains, they have received comparatively little attention from historians of the era, even those writing on propaganda. Yet they created in Germany, both in peacetime and at war, 'an energised, politicised and vividly pictorialised public space'.[22] In this way, the power of the Nazis' carefully constructed images, symbols and slogans pervaded the popular mind. The Nazis understood the power of this relatively simple medium of propaganda. Posters were effective because they were not burdensome for the viewer – and because of their ubiquity, people saw them all the time. They were easily understood and did not challenge the viewer. People knew straightaway who fitted into the 'national community' and who did not. They were often attracted by the feeling of belonging to it and by the sense of being guided and steered (although in reality, deftly controlled) by their visionary leader, Adolf Hitler. This diminished the effect on both individual Germans and the nation as a whole of the more unpleasant aspects of the regime and its policies. The Hitler regime aimed to reach the whole population through every means possible. It was important to keep up the morale of the German populace, especially during a time of 'total war'. The intention was also to keep up productivity, to underline the necessity for the triumph of the Third *Reich*, and to emphasize the evil nature of the nation's enemies. Losing the war was portrayed as inconceivable in Nazi propaganda. It was essential to maintain the struggle to the bitter end. The power of Nazi propaganda, in all its forms, somehow achieved this goal of Hitler, to keep fighting, and the Third *Reich* capitulated in May 1945, only after it was invaded and occupied by the troops of its adversaries. The ubiquitous nature of Nazi posters in public spaces throughout the Third *Reich* played an important part in Nazi propaganda, both in the creation of the nation and in the construction of enemies, generating a considerable impact upon the German population.

6

Soviet Posters in the Second World War and Beyond

By the time of the outbreak of the Second World War, the Soviet poster, in a sense, was ready for it. Poster-makers knew their audience and, after a quarter century of developing their art, knew how to produce the images and message required by the regime. And even when they inadvertently crossed the ideological line or delivered a poster that was weak, pre-publication censorship officials and *agitprop* workers would correct them before much damage was done.

Posters against the Nazis

While in the official discourse of the regime Soviet participation in the Second World War began on 22 June 1941 with the Nazi invasion of the Soviet Union, the Soviet involvement in this war actually began not long after the German attack on Poland on 1 September 1939.[1] On 17 September 1939, guided by the secret clause of the Non-Aggression Pact (Molotov-Ribbentrop Pact) of the previous August, Soviet forces crossed the international border between Poland and the Soviet Union, marching into what they called 'western Belarus' and 'western Ukraine'. The Soviet claim was that the inhabitants of these territories were predominantly Belarussian (Belarusyns) and Ukrainian, who, because of the terms of the March 1921 Treaty of Riga between Poland and a then feeble Soviet Russia, had unjustifiably fallen under Polish rule. At that time, it was implied, the Soviet regime had been forced to allow this, as it no longer wanted to continue the bloodshed of the war with Poland in which it had been engaged since 1919. Now, citing ethnic and historical grounds, and with the rest of Poland falling under Nazi occupation, the Soviets took back what allegedly should have always belonged to them. In addition, the Soviet invaders argued, the population was now liberated from both the rule of the

Polish landlords and non-Ukrainian or non-Belarusyn bourgeoisie in these territories' cities, and would be treated to the blessings of a classless society.[2] The somewhat strenuous contortions of Soviet propaganda justifying these moves are illustrated by Figure 6.1.[3]

It shows a poster from September 1939 in the Ukrainian language, albeit made by the Russian Viktor S. Ivanov. The poster was produced within a week after the Soviet invasion of eastern Poland. The text reads, 'It is Our Sacred Obligation to Extend a Helping Hand to the Fraternal Peoples of

FIGURE 6.1 *'It Is Our Sacred Obligation to Extend a Helping Hand to the Fraternal Peoples of Western Ukraine and Western Belarus'*.

Western Ukraine and Western Belarus.' No fewer than 200,000 copies were produced, the number indicative of the clear intention to blanket the newly annexed territories' Ukrainian population with professions of the goodwill of the Soviet soldiers and their government (its price of 70 kopecks a piece must have been paid by Soviet military and *agitprop* officials rather than by any Ukrainians, who did not use Soviet currency before mid-September 1939). Ivanov became a two-time recipient of the Stalin Prize for his wartime posters, the highest honour for artists in the Soviet Union. It should be noted that the Soviet soldier depicted is immaculately dressed and equipped, which rather belied the situation on the ground. Similarly, the traditionally dressed Ukrainian peasant family's feet are bare, not a likely scenario in the cold and muddy autumn of 1939. Additionally, the parents' faces look rather emaciated, contrasting with the well-fed Soviet soldier. It can further be said that the poster idealizes the 'Friendship of the Peoples' (*Druzhba Narodov*) that supposedly prevailed among the many ethnic communities living with the Soviet borders.

The occupation of these territories was then followed by the intimidation of the Baltic countries into subjugation in the autumn of 1939, the Soviet-Finnish War (November 1939–March 1940), the annexation of the three Baltic countries (June 1940), followed by that of northern Bukovina and Bessarabia (both taken from Romania, in the early summer of 1940). Soviet troops, in other words, were everywhere on the march in eastern Europe, long before the Nazis launched their Operation Barbarossa.[4] On 22 June 1941, then, a Nazi-led alliance of armed forces invaded the Soviet Union. Despite plentiful warnings, the Soviet leadership and its military were caught by surprise. The Soviet air force was destroyed on its airfields and Soviet land forces were rapidly defeated in battle after battle during the first weeks of the war. Instead of allowing timely withdrawals, Stalin's stubbornness to deny reality left hundreds of thousands of Soviet soldiers caught in pincer moves by the rapidly advancing Nazi armies. Leningrad was almost entirely cut off from the rest of the Soviet Union by 8 September 1941, while Kyiv fell not long after in the same month.

Somehow, though, the Soviet defenders managed to stop the Germans from reaching Moscow, and by late 1941, the Soviet counteroffensive in the Battle of Moscow pushed the front line further back from the capital. Overoptimistic because of this success, Stalin decided on a premature military offensive campaign in the late winter of 1942 which failed at great cost once again in casualties and materiel. During the spring of 1942 in a desperate lurch, Hitler decided that a new offensive aiming for the Caucasian oilfields and the city of Stalingrad might decide the war in his favour. Neither the oilfields nor Stalingrad ever effectively fell into Nazi hands, however. Instead, as we saw in the previous chapter, the military tide on 'the eastern front' (as the Germans called it) turned in Soviet favour. Stalingrad's victory was followed by the Battle of Kursk and the liberation of Kyiv in 1943. Leningrad was definitively relieved from its siege in January 1944. Operation Bagration of the summer of 1944 saw the Soviet armed forces comprehensively recover all territory lost after 22 June 1941 and brought Soviet forces to the gates of Warsaw. Sweeping southward through Romania and Hungary towards Vienna as well, by the spring of 1945, the Soviet armies neared Berlin, which fell into their hands in May. Nazi Germany had ceased to exist and Hitler was dead.

The war in eastern Europe saw bloodshed that was unprecedented in history. Soviet civilian and military losses are estimated at 27 million people, about one-sixth of the country's population in June 1941. The Nazi regime behaved with lethal brutality in implementing the Holocaust on Soviet territory, from the more than 30,000 Kyivan Jews executed in a mere few days in September 1941 at Babyn Yar, to the mass killings of Jews in lorries, and their slaughter by an almost infinite number of other methods (Soviet-Jewish victims of the Nazis were less frequently killed in the deathcamps than their central and western European counterparts, but more in such less systematic ways). But besides the Jews, millions of other Soviet civilians were killed by the Nazis, as real or alleged communists, as hostages in retribution for partisan activities, or because of sheer whim. For Slavs, too, were 'subhumans' (*Untermenschen*) in the Nazi worldview, hardly worthy of existence as human beings.

As a result, Soviet wartime propaganda found a ready audience. While at the outset of the war some may have been willing to give the new German rulers the benefit of the doubt, Nazi atrocities and their ruthless exploitation of almost all of the Soviet civilian population over whom they lorded it antagonized everyone. This hatred of the Nazis was almost universal, despite Stalin's cruel deportation of entire Soviet ethnic groups accused of collaboration with the Nazis (Crimean Tatars, Chechens, etc.), which already began when the war with the *Reich* was still raging. Soviet thirst for revenge then found an outlet in the mass rape and murder committed by the Soviet armed forces in Germany in 1945 (which was tacitly rather than openly encouraged).

In the light of events then unfolding, the January 1945 poster rendered on Colour Plate 9 may strike us with the benefit of today's hindsight as particularly disturbing.[5] Made by Stalin Prize recipient Aleksei A. Kokorekin (1906–59), it was released almost precisely at the moment Soviet troops moved into pre-1939 German territory and began to exact terrible revenge on the German population through mass rape and mass murder. A poster such as this one fanned the flames of hatred, even when it says, 'Kill him! He Killed Your Loved Ones, Burned Your House Down, Destroyed Your Workplace!', which is aimed primarily against Nazis or Germans in uniform, rather than women and children shown here as victims of German atrocities. Of course, the kind of bloodbath as depicted *had* been perpetrated by the Nazis on the Soviet population. But the Soviet Army might have been reined in more once it reached German territory in an attempt not to besmirch its heroics by lowering itself to the same level of moral depravity as its adversaries; instead, it showed no restraint whatsoever, and those few who did protest the Red Army's atrocities, such as the political commissar Lev Kopelev (1912–97), were prosecuted for defaming the military.

Rallying behind the Flag

The deep trauma that the war left within the Soviet population may to a degree explain why postwar posters acquired such a bland quality. It certainly explains why few voiced any protest when it appeared soon after May 1945 that Stalin had no plans to liberalize his regime and allow a greater measure of individual or religious freedom to his subjects (which had been fleetingly enjoyed during the war). People were stunned by what had occurred from 22 June 1941 to 10 May 1945 and barely had the strength to nurse their physical and psychological wounds; there was little to no desire to challenge the regime. Without many qualms, Soviet citizens participated in the postwar Soviet campaigns to rebuild their country and prepare for a new war, this time with the United States and the United Kingdom. By 1949, a Soviet atomic bomb was successfully detonated, although in 1947 the country had still experienced a lethal famine. The standard of living remained spartan all the way until Stalin's death in March 1953.

The Great Patriotic War, as the Soviets soon called it (adopting a name already used for the Russian war of 1812 with Napoléon) after the Nazi forces and their allies invaded in June 1941, triggered some of the best work ever made by Soviet poster artists. Emblematic of this is Victor Deni's output. His glory days had appeared long past, but once more he found his muse, as the figures rendered here show, with the second one distributed mere months before his death in 1946 (see Colour Plate 10 and Figure 6.2).[6] Colour Plate 10 is a poster by Deni dating from the first winter of the war (February 1942), when a Soviet victory seemed far away. It reads, 'What Does a Pig Need Culture and Science For? Its Mind Is After All Tiny: "Mein Kampf" Is the Limit for a Pig Snout, and its Ideal [Is] the Corporal's Boot!' The swastika-spurred boot tramples signs that say 'university', 'schools' and 'courses'. Obviously, a porcine Hitler's head pops out from inside the boot. Orwell's picture of the future from *Nineteen Eighty-Four* and pig dictatorship from *Animal Farm* seems to be conjured up here, but equating Germans with pigs (pork being standard fare in Germany, although hardly less so in Russia) was a bit of a cliché in the Soviet Union and elsewhere, while swine are considered especially unclean animals in most Eurasian cultures (think of the German swearword '*Schweinhund*'). The bestial metaphor required no great artistic invention, while Hitler as a corporal was another worn-out trope. Deni's greatest strength lay in his caricatures, as a consequence of which his 1930s posters, bereft of almost any satirical approach, were rather weak. Even if this poster signalled a return to his best work of the civil war and early 1920s, it is a rather crude effort that somewhat misses the mark. Surely, destroying educational facilities and assaulting learning, while bad things, were not the worst misdeeds of the Nazi regime.

Figure 6.2 displays one of Victor Deni's last works, released in March 1945. Deni's ability at demonizing assorted foes is at great display here. The text reads, 'Nowhere Can the Monster Hide! It Will Receive its Just Desserts! Everything Alive Hates Him! He Will not Receive Mercy!' From Hitler's pocket a swastika-marked paper emerges that reads, 'Under the Ground', indicating the dictator's hiding out in a bunker. Deni's rendition of Hitler as evil personified is powerful. Oddly, the ailing Hitler portrayed here might partially reflect the ailing artist himself, who was a hypochondriac whose paranoia was magnified by alcoholism and who went to an early grave in 1946.

FIGURE 6.2 *'Nowhere Can the Monster Hide! It Will Receive Its Just Desserts!'*.

Like Victor Deni, many poster artists answered the call and outdid themselves in this ultimate crisis, helping to stave off their country's and their own doom. Perhaps this was to be expected of Soviet poster makers: given the almost unimaginable bestiality of some of their acts, depicting the Nazis as demons did not require great imagination. And making caricatures out of their foes had been an old specialty of the Soviet poster-makers.

Figure 6.3 is a photomontage-style poster of the early days of the 'Great Patriotic War', as the Soviets called the Second World War (the date of its release was 8 July 1941, that is a mere sixteen days after the Nazi invasion).[7]

FIGURE 6.3 *'Our Forces Are Countless!'*.

The text announces that 'Our Forces Are Countless!' Its author was V. B. Koretskii, one of many leading prewar poster artists who threw himself at shoring up Soviet resolve in the jittery first year of the war. The turn to rehabilitate *Russian* history after war's outbreak became much more marked as can be seen in this image, for, in the right background behind the bearded worker, Moscow's monument to Kuz'ma Minin and Dmitrii Pozharskii can be seen. Minin and Pozharskii led the Muscovite-Russian liberation army that chased the Polish-Lithuanian army out of Moscow in 1613, upon which Mikhail Romanov was elected as tsar. Russian historical figures (up to and including the heroes from the 1812 French invasion of Russia such as Mikhail Kutuzov and Denis Davydov) were frequently used to boost Soviet morale during the war. The bearded figure as such is interesting; there was a marked preference for clean-shaven men on most Soviet posters of the 1930s and 1940s, even when especially in the countryside men tended to have moustaches and beards (noteworthy as well are a number of the armed workers drawn up behind him having facial hair). It appears that Koretskii, perhaps prompted by his *agitprop* chiefs, deliberately broke the mould to appeal to the collective farming population, whose loyalty to the Soviet regime was fickle, and who might recognize themselves more in a bearded than clean-shaven man. In addition, the poster seems intended as a call to arms to those who did not serve in the regular army, but in the home guard (*narodnoe opol'chenie*) that was set up upon the Nazi attack. Indeed, the name *narodnoe opol'chenie* was used by Soviet-Russian historians for Minin and Pozharskii's army of 1613.

Figure 6.4 renders another poster of the harrowing early days of the Great Patriotic War.[8] It was made in 1942 by M. A. Gordon and Boris Efimov for the occasion of the twenty-fifth anniversary of the 1917 October Revolution, which had unfolded in Petrograd (renamed Leningrad in 1924). It depicts a man and a woman serving in Leningrad's Home Guard, with behind them the contours of the city's admiralty, situated on the Neva River (as well as a factory – perhaps the famed Putilov arms factory, a revolutionary hotbed – and a bridge over the river). The words below are by Andrei Zhdanov, the Leningrad Communist Party boss from 1934 to 1946, who peers at the banner at his own quotation which announces, 'In Leningrad there is no difference between front and rear. All live by one thought, by one spirit, to do everything toward the enemy's destruction.' Leningrad's siege was already storied by 1942, as the city had been holding out against Germans and Finnish attackers for more than a year after it was almost wholly encircled on 8 September 1941; the siege was only to end formally in January 1944, after lasting 900 days (although the worst of the military threat had already diminished in its ultimate year). The horrendous death toll of its trapped inhabitants from the fall of 1941 until the middle of spring 1942 was not publicized in the Soviet Union; up to 1 million people may have died of hunger. After 8 September 1941, the city could

FIGURE 6.4 *Andrei Zhdanov and Besieged Leningrad.*

solely be supplied through (and people could only be evacuated by way of) a small north-eastern route that went across Lake Ladoga, which could no longer be navigated by vessels after mid-October. Only when it was solidly frozen in December the famous Ice Road was opened, when lorries (trucks) could drive across the frozen lake, resuming its supply, albeit in piecemeal fashion. Leningrad's citizens had not been evacuated in time because Soviet leaders (not least Zhdanov) had underestimated the speed of the German advance in the summer of 1941 and only realized the danger of Leningrad's encirclement when people no longer could leave in any great number. It is relatively rare to encounter Zhdanov's image (or any of Stalin's cronies) on posters, despite his prominent role alongside Stalin.

After the Nazi attack, Soviet posters revolved around the singular uniform theme of the war, regardless of the style in which their images represented the subject matter of Nazi perfidy and Soviet tenacity in the face of adversity. Uniformity was additionally ensured through the Soviet press agency *TASS*, which had a monopoly on distributing the news, launching a regular display of wall-window posters to boost morale that echoed *Rosta*'s wall windows of the civil war period.[9] One of *TASS*'s main artists was, indeed, Mikhail Cheremnykh, who thus returned to the limelight of poster-making.[10] Most of the posters were in the satirical style, not only drawing from the *Rosta* traditions such as in the sequence of scenes, but also from the satirical magazines such as *Krokodil*. Perhaps having in mind Mayakovsky's verbal antics, the texts of the *TASS* posters were composed by well-established poets such as Samuil Marshak and Demyan Bednyi, and usually consisted of one or more stanzas.

Despite the popularity and quality of the *TASS* posters influencing other poster production, control was slightly eased by the highest authorities, allowing artists a measure of freedom to choose what they wanted to design.[11] *TASS* posters were far from the only posters produced during the war. We have already discussed Irakli Toidze's legendary poster calling Soviet men to arms (see Colour Plate 1). Thematically, appeals to patriotism regularly drew on archetypical Russian heroes, who were identified with a Russian struggle for survival in times past, such as Aleksandr Nevskii (already immortalized by Eisenstein on film in 1938), Kuz'ma Minin and Dmitrii Pozharskii, Generalissimo Aleksandr Suvorov, and Marshal Kutuzov. In terms of the social values they reflected, the posters were quite traditional, as for example in rendering women as 'manning the homefront' and men serving in the armed forces or home guard.[12] Together with children, women often appeared on Soviet posters as feminine objects, the helpless victims of Nazi atrocities. Once again, gender equality seemed to remain an ideal of legal principle rather than a practical reality. This was somewhat odd, as a not insignificant number of women served in the active army (as air-force pilots, infantry snipers, and tank personnel) or in the partisan movement, in addition to their incalculably important roles as nurses and doctors, or as army administrative staff.

While drawn designs remained popular, posters using photomontage were equally common during the Great Patriotic War, as is evident from some of the figures herewith included. Photomontage posters had shed most of their experimental guise, leading Konstantin Akisha to suggest that they reminded in their composition more of early modern masters' canvases than of their Dadaist or Constructivist early days.[13] Ultimately, once the pupils of Heartfield and Klutsis aged in the postwar era, photomontage posters did become rarer in Soviet poster-making.[14] Meanwhile, the socialist-realist guidelines for poster-making remained dominant until even after Stalin's death in 1953.[15] As Masha Kowell writes, '[t]he posters patently resemble one another on a formal level, defined by realist form, mixed colors, muted palette, and iconographic level, dominated by the presence of idealized and frontally ... oriented Soviet bodies'.[16] She does note the rise of more independently minded posters in the 1950s 'Thaw', moving away from the relentless political messaging of the pre-1953 poster.[17] It was in that period especially the well-connected survivor Boris Efimov who oversaw a return to an artistic freedom and a level of original creativity in poster-making that had disappeared in the 1930s.[18] The *Agit-Plakat* group that Efimov supported was allowed to move away from the conservatism imposed by the revived *Izogiz*, the state publishing house for art (from 1938 to 1953 the publication of poster art had been done by the state publisher *Isskustvo*).

And, indeed, to today's viewer it seems that the immediate postwar poster lost almost every creative spark. The poster-makers drew on safe, bland stereotypes, truly clichés, which had in the past been given the stamp of approval when they were first invented. Many show Stalin, who was now cast as the infallible *generalissimo* (a title he was awarded in 1945 as the architect of the Soviet victory), the coryphaeus of all sciences, and the political genius on a par with Marx, Engels, and Lenin in every which way in Soviet public discourse (Lenin himself became decidedly less a topic).[19] He usually wears a greatcoat and, half of the time, his army (or worker's) cap (see Colour Plate 11). A slight grey tinge runs through his moustache and hair, adding to the cachet of great wisdom that he is supposed to radiate (and representing a younger version of himself, as he had gone quite grey by 1945).

Colour Plate 11 renders a somewhat unusual wartime poster in which Stalin is the towering figure.[20] Issued in July 1942, its creators were V. S. Baiuskin and A. F. Shpir, who hark back to the composition of the *Rosta* windows by Mayakovsky and his friends in the civil war, as well as to the 1930s experimentation with photo novellas. It was number eleven of a poster newspaper (*gazeta*) called 'The Great Patriotic War', of which 10,000 copies were printed. Its subtitle (to which Stalin points) quotes part of an Order of the Day previously released by the commander-in-chief himself, which says, 'Under Lenin's Banner Go Forward toward the Destruction of the German-Fascist Aggressors!' The Red military's progress after October 1917 is narrated, with various battle scenes sequentially depicted and juxtaposed to the growing industrial might of the USSR, churning out ever more advanced arms in ever greater numbers. The first panel starts with the brief fight against the advancing Central Powers by the nascent Red Army in February 1918, followed by a depiction of the civil war against the White forces and the 'foreign interventionists' on the third panel, after which the story moves on to the tanks built in the Five Year Plans, and ends with the fighting of the Second World War. Stalin strikes a sort of mirror of the classic Lenin pose.

The Character of the Postwar Poster

After 1945, only by exception did Stalin's political comrades, the wartime Red Army commanders or friendly foreign political leaders (such as the Bulgarian communist leader Georgi Dimitrov, the Yugoslav boss Tito, or the Chinese chief Mao Zedong) appear on Soviet posters. During Stalin's final years, the equally frequently depicted generic workers and collective farmers are well-proportioned and handsome square-jawed men or soft-jawed women, while they are given a few ethnic markers (such as moustache, hat, headdress, darker skin pigmentation, high cheekbones) when the poster's target audience was not Slavic or Baltic. Stalin and these generic proletarians usually stare in the distance, often looking up to what is the radiant future, one presumes, in their, and the viewer's, imagination. In the early postwar years, the facial expression of the workers was somewhat grim and determined, accompanied by slogans that the country would be quickly rebuilt, and the Fourth Five Year Plan (1946–50) would be completed early and over-fulfilled. They seem to have softened a bit subsequently, once the worst of the debris was cleared by 1950.

After 1945, far fewer posters were produced that portrayed various enemies luridly. In the early days of the Cold War, the fate of the wartime alliance was not yet decided and the Soviet leaders appeared to have held the door open to renewed cooperation until 1948.[21] Even after the spring of 1948 (and despite the outbreak of the Korean War in 1950), the foreign threat was felt to be far less acute than it had been before May 1945. The Soviet Union was no longer isolated after V-E Day and acquired powerful allies, most prominent among which was the Chinese People's Republic in 1949. It also gained formidable military might with its own atomic bomb in the same year.

Soviet posters, then, acquired a peaceful appearance because of a changed context, but one is struck as well by the lack of inspiration that seems to have befallen their makers (see as well Figure 1.1 again). Colour Plate 12 may serve as typical, representing 'High Stalinism' at its finest.[22] It is from 1952, and made by Boris Naumovich Belopol'skii (1909–78). Its text reads, 'Study the Great Path of the Party of Lenin-Stalin!' Its print-run was a whopping 300,000, the highest of any Soviet posters shown in these pages. The image depicts what Nikita Khrushchev in 1956 would call 'the cult of personality' at its most graphic. The reader's pose is typical for the postwar poster, with the protagonist staring into the distance, supposedly pondering the marvel of Lenin with Stalin at his side leading his country to the promised land and the two leaders depicted behind him as a relief in almost Greco-Roman style. (Are there echoes of Mussolini's aesthetic preferences here?) The well-dressed young man (almost the twin of the man portrayed on the radiofication poster, it seems) again represents the postwar ideal, with workers (or their children) becoming part of what was called the 'Soviet intelligentsia', the learned vanguard of the proletariat, eagerly studying the key works by Lenin and Stalin, one of each of which lies on the table. The book that the man holds in his hands is the 'Bible' of Stalinist Communism, the *Short Course of the History of the All-Union Communist Party (Bolsheviks)*, published in 1938 first in *Pravda* and then in bookform, and written by a not further identified 'commission of the Communist Party's Central Committee'. Tens of millions of copies were subsequently sold in numerous languages before it was withdrawn from circulation after Stalin's death in 1953. Stalin certainly oversaw its drafting, although he modestly left others to sing his praises on its pages, perhaps only suggesting the deletion of a few overly sycophantic sentences.

It is a matter of speculation in how far the poster-makers felt constrained by the postwar 'cultural crackdown', engineered by Zhdanov and others on Stalin's urging, and played it safe in response.[23] From the middle of 1946 until early 1949, writers, composers, theatre critics, philosophers and scientists were all disciplined for overly generously interpreting the greater freedom of expression the wartime crisis had allowed them. Religious houses of worship were no longer (re-)opened after a brief wartime (from approximately 1943 to 1947) relaxation of the regime's anti-religious policies. Too zealous affirmations of ethnic identities were condemned and curbed, not merely in the newly acquired territories in the west, but also in Bashkortostan, Georgia, or Tatarstan, and, by extension, desires for genuine self-determination in the satellite states in East-Central Europe (which led to Yugoslavia's early defection from the Soviet camp). A spontaneous eruption of Jewish enthusiasm for Israel's foundation in 1948 was quickly suppressed as a betrayal of loyalty to the Soviet Union, a campaign that soon became a barely camouflaged anti-Semitic outburst drummed up by the authorities. And even Stalin's closest comrades were put in their place, with Vyacheslav Molotov and Anastas Mikoyan gradually leaving the limelight, Zhdanov succumbing to the shock about the public dressing down of his son by Stalin himself (which led to the return of Georgii Malenkov to a high post, after he had been briefly demoted), and, most notoriously, the Leningrad Affair, which cost the lives of a number of prominent bosses, such as Nikolai Voznesensky and Aleksei Kuznetsov.[24] Finally, the hero of Stalingrad and the fall of Berlin, Georgy Zhukov (1896–1974), was demoted (on accusations of unauthorized plundering) as was naval chief Nikolai Kuznetsov (1904–1974), while Marshal Grigorii Kulik (1890–1950) was executed, and air force commander Aleksandr Novikov (1900–76) was arrested: the armed forces' brass was therefore likewise shown that it was disposable.

Although poster artists avoided most of the cultural crackdown after 1945, not all escaped. 'Formalism' in poster-making was condemned in a Central-Committee decree of late 1948, with the leaders' criticism more concretely singling out the anaemic production of posters depicting the hard work conducted in the city and countryside in resurrecting the country after the war.[25] Posters' poor artistic and printing quality was furthermore attacked. Almost exactly three years later, in October 1951 a meeting in Moscow was held to discuss the state of the political poster. Photomontage was now fully rejected by a leading Soviet art official, Vladimir Kemenov (1908–88), who even dismissed most use of photography in posters.[26] The Stalin Prize winner Viktor Koretskii, who had made his name as a photomontage artist, was singled out in this harsh criticism. Still later, in the spring of 1952, Koretskii once again was publicly criticized as the ringleader of photomontage posters in *Pravda*.[27] It certainly did not help Koretskii's case that he was Jewish, as the final years of Stalin's life were hallmarked by a virulent anti-Semitism.

Perhaps as a result of the withering criticism of his work, Koretskii became after Stalin's death one of the patrons of the *Agit-Plakat* movement that tried to produce posters without excessive ideological interference.

In this fearful environment, it seems that poster-makers exercised the greatest caution, as is underlined by the post-1953 rise of the *Agit-Plakat* group, who revolted against the milquetoast posters of the final Stalin years. Altogether, this strategy may have paid off: most makers of plastic arts, including Koretskii, remained at liberty. The Soviet authorities' renewed imposition of ideological and aesthetic uniformity or conformity did not need a massive arrest wave to make its point.[28] The memory of the Great Terror was still fresh. Besides an official like Kemenov, the printers and publishing houses, or the censor agency *Glavlit*, other gatekeepers remained as well in power, such as the painter A. M. Gerasimov (1881–1963), who was the chairman of the Soviet Union's artists' union; M. B. Khrapchenko (1904–86), Kerzhentsev's successor as the chairman of the USSR's government's committee of art(istic) affairs; and the latter's own successors Polikarp I. Lebedev (1904–81) and Nikolai N. Bespalov (1906–80).

After 1945, posters became part of a standard package of propagandistic tools that were meant to enthuse the Soviet masses for the pre-ordained moments when the expression of a true Soviet spirit was expected. Thus, we see many posters which call for electoral support for the only voting options in the elections of the rubber-stamp parliaments at various levels. Others call for the expeditious fulfilment of the Fourth or Fifth Five Year Plans (respectively 1946–50 and 1951–5). And many exhort people to celebrate the anniversary of the October Revolution, or to express their love for motherland and the great Stalin.

Both Edward Cohn and Serhy Yekelchyk have investigated the degree of genuine enthusiasm among the Soviet population and concluded that in this period not all of it had yet devolved into pure cynicism, but it is to be severely doubted that posters still added very much enthusiasm to such support.[29] Rebuilding the country was an inevitable task, the necessity of which was never in doubt as the logical corollary of the military victory of 1945. No convincing was necessary on this score. Additionally, many still felt that the Soviet project deserved another chance, after having been so brutally assaulted and almost dismantled by the Nazi regime (and perhaps after having learned from some of the blunders of the 1930s): indeed, Stalin's successor, Nikita Khrushchev, seems to have been of such mind and appears to have believed even in the mid-1950s that his subjects would agree with his sustained enthusiasm for the cause.

Despite the efforts by *Agit-Plakat* from 1956 onwards, posters may have passed the apex of their popularity by 1945. The 'radiofication' of the Soviet Union rapidly grew after 1945. With ever greater ease, films could be seen and radio programmes could be heard. The literacy rate of the country neared 100 per cent, but what was even more important was that children attended school for a much longer time than previously. Soviet citizens became avid readers (as they still were even after their country collapsed), and all-Union and local newspapers and magazines were made ever more readily available, often with colour photography (and coloured films, too, became the standard). Of course, the power of images did not diminish, but even in this regard the poster encountered growing competition.

Some of the optimistic mood at the end of the war is reflected in the poster displayed in Figure 6.5. It is forecasting the idyllic turn most posters were to take after 1945 (and in its soft colours, not visible here).[30] But its key aim was to aid the Soviet regime's effort to have their country recover

FIGURE 6.5 *'Glory to the Mother Heroine'*.

from the wartime devastation.[31] It dates from September 1944 and was created by Nina Nikolaevicha Vatolina (1915–2002; she was Deni's one-time daughter-in-law) in immediate response to the introduction of a new government award for mothers giving birth to a great number of children (it reads, 'Glory to the Mother Heroine'). Vatolina earlier acquired fame for the wartime poster *'Ne Boltai!'* ('Do not Blab!'), depicting a woman holding a finger to her lips warning that the enemy might be listening. It bears mentioning here that in 2022 Russian President Vladimir Putin reintroduced this pro-natalist Soviet policy, which decorated mothers of ten children or more as heroes (heroines) of the Motherland (or, then, the Soviet Union). This measure of 1944, of course, was provoked by the tremendous loss of life in the Second World War (and, perhaps, the decade prior to it). Even the population increase from the renewed 1945 territorial annexations of the Baltic countries, Bessarabia, Bukovina, and the former eastern Poland could not compensate for this demographic catastrophe. Violence, famine, and disease may have cost 35 million Soviet inhabitants their lives from 1929 to 1945, amounting to one-fifth of the country's population. The policy of awarding benefits and perquisites to such exceedingly fecund women was not very successful. Soviet urban housing was utterly cramped, hardly allowing for the accommodation of two children, let alone ten, and food scarcities persisted for long after 1945 (a famine hit several regions of the country in 1946 and 1947). In addition, very few men had survived to partner the mother-heroines, without whom, despite some daycares and other facilities in the towns, a large family was hard to manage. Likewise, on the collective farms women performed most of the manual labour after the men had vanished in the war: grandparents if present might fill in, but to raise more than five children seemed impossible given this burden.

The Poster after Stalin

Agit-Plakat was not as innovative – neither politically nor aesthetically – as it claimed to be, as is also evident from the close supervision exerted over it by Boris Efimov, who always remained a loyal Soviet subject, keeping his doubts about his country to himself. Indeed, another influential figure within *Agit-Plakat* was Mikhail Mikhailovich Solovyov (1905–90), who had headed the *NKVD* art studio [sic!] during the height of the Great Terror from 1936 to 1941. Originally a painter, Solovyov's art is never anything more than conventional. Politically, he seems to have been the ultimate sycophant. Figure 6.6 is one of his products.[32] This 1956 poster celebrates International Women's Day (March 8). It depicts a female collective farmworker (*kolkhoznitsa*) chalking up the productive triumphs of her farm. Its slogan reads, 'We Will Meet 8 March by the Highest Standards in Our Work!' On the chalkboard the names and jobs of six *kolkhoznitsy* of the collective farm 'The New Life' are listed, who carry typical Russian

FIGURE 6.6 *'The New Life'*.

names (Morozova, Stepanova, Nikolayeva, Mironova, Eliseyeva, and Orlova) and of the jobs done by the farm workers that have been completed by 100 per cent or more of the planning target (spring grain preparation; equipment repairs; increase in heads of cattle; milking; and ensuring the survival of dairy cattle). A realistic touch is the artist listing the six women's typical *kolkhoz* jobs (two are brigadier – a sort of team leader of teams that ploughed, sowed, harvested, and weeded; one is a cattle expert; one a milkmaid; one an animal-keeper; and one a head of a smaller team – or link). Many a *kolkhoz* like this was called 'The New Life', so it may be pure coincidence that not long after, in the early 1960s, the writer Fyodor Abramov (1920–83) wrote a novella about a collective farm with that very name.[33] Abramov is sometimes scathingly critical in his portrayal of how poorly collective farms operated under Stalin (readers suspected that Abramov was actually taking a swipe at collective farms in the 1960s). The book surprisingly passed the censor.

Solovyov was a supreme Soviet loyalist. His poster accurately reflects the overwhelming numerical preponderance of women in Soviet agriculture after the Second World War, especially in Russia, Ukraine, and Belarus. Both the design and its execution may reflect how poster art continued to ossify after Stalin's death, despite the *Agit-Plakat* movement with which Solovyov was associated. It is also noteable that the image conveys how the style of dress of rural women began to resemble that of their urban sisters. It is not clear that this was indeed the case in reality. In other words, much of what the viewer sees here reflects an ideal, which rarely materialized in Soviet reality.

Ultimately, the *Agit-Plakat* movement walked in lockstep with Nikita Khrushchev's efforts to revivify the revolutionary enthusiasm of the early years of Soviet communism, to which a considerable number of Soviet poster artists involved in *Agit-Plakat* may have looked with a certain tinge of nostalgia (Efimov and Solovyov had been in their twenties in the 1920s). It succeeded to some degree in reinvigorating the Soviet political poster, but it found itself now in a much more crowded field of means by which the Soviet regime could spread its propaganda.

Soviet poster-makers, despite the sometimes stunning effect of their posters or their great creative powers, were ultimately no different from artists or architects who in other times created work to the greater glory of their employers, from the builders of the pyramids or the gardens of Versailles, to the poems of Simeon Polotsky (1629–80) at the court of Tsar Aleksei, or of Vasily Zhukovsky (1787–1852) at Tsar Nicholas I's court. Enjoying a certain artistic talent, they proved after 1917 to be willing to resolutely support the revolutionary cause, even when this cause (or its minders) demanded the sacrifice of innocent people who stood in its way. Indeed, Soviet poster artists made little distinction between demonizing alleged foes or displaying their skills in denouncing actual enemies, like the Nazis and their leader. Whether or not poster artists themselves even saw any difference between supposed capitalist cronies such as *kulaks*, priests, mullahs, and the Nazis is a moot point. In hindsight, after Stalin's death, many, like Efimov, lamented the victims of collectivization or the Great Terror, but they showed little hesitation in supporting such policies when those events unfolded. Perhaps it is easier for us today to enjoy the inner city of St Petersburg (built at the expense of thousands of dead forced labourers) than Soviet poster art because Peter the Great's age is so far in the past. Certainly, the aesthetic pleasure in looking at Soviet posters is much diminished when their link to one of the most criminal regimes that ever ruled is considered.

Conclusion

This book has examined the utilization of posters as a medium of political propaganda in the USSR and the Third *Reich*. The poster offers a strong visual point of entry into the two regimes. Posters' images and texts signalled shifts of the historical context in which they were produced, charting, besides evolving aesthetic taste and technological ability, the often violent circumstances in which they were conceived. In the Soviet case, we see how they reflected the civil war's brutality and the NEP's lull, followed by the epochal changes of the Great Turn and the Great Terror's fear of imagined foes, who eventually materialized in a real war in 1941. The Soviet mindset can be read in posters made during the Second World War and postwar reconstruction, while they illustrate the absurd dimensions of the Stalin cult. In the Nazi case, posters in the Weimar era in the period leading up to Hitler taking power, especially 1930–3 revealed a deliberate strategy to respond to the anxiety of a country reeling from a deep economic crisis. From 1933 to 1939, Nazi posters were key in the creation of the cult of Hitler and the *Volksgemeinschaft* of a unified Germany, which rid itself from its foes. After 1 September 1939, Nazi posters reflected the triumphalism of the early war years and the growing desperation towards its end.

Posters were a significant part of life during the mid-twentieth century, employed as a modern medium to convey messages and political ideology to the populations in the Soviet Union and in Germany. Posters pasted onto walls proved to be a very popular and persuasive format for the broad distribution and dissemination of both Soviet and Nazi propaganda and slogans. Both regimes employed slogans that could be easily remembered, although the Soviet ones were often lengthier and more explanatory. Their propaganda harmonized the subject matter into an easily understandable combination of words and images on posters. They spent a considerable amount of effort, energy, and expense to get these to an extremely high standard – designs and slogans that looked simple had been very carefully chosen and created. The regimes employed the most skilled graphic artists, as long as they conformed politically. And so, posters were part of the spirit of the age.

This book has analysed the origins, development, and role of posters in the USSR: Soviet political poster art was born out of an existential crisis in 1918 and 1919, when posters found a keen audience both within the Communist Party and the Soviet populace. It has explored the experimentation in Soviet poster art during the 1920s and 1930s. It has shown how posters were utilized to advocate for Party programmes and policies. The combination of abstract and representative imagery in Soviet poster art demonstrates how it tried not only to appeal to popular taste, but also to conform to what the Party bosses, and especially Stalin, wanted. The presentation of Soviet posters changed over the course of time from an abstract or satirical style to a more popularly attractive and naturalistic one, in order to capture and entice their audience. In the USSR, despite differences in styles, poster-makers were all united in seeking to promote the communist message. Appeals to duty were conveyed on Soviet posters, not just of the Great Patriotic War, but of the civil war as well: join the army, work as hard as possible for the common cause, and watch out for foes. And Soviet posters remained a key medium to spread the Marxist-Leninist message long beyond the end of the Great Patriotic War.

This book has examined the use of posters by Hitler and the *NSDAP*, moving through three phases: first, the origins and development of early Nazi posters in the period before the 'seizure of power' in January 1933; second, in the years between 1933 and 1939 in the construction of the 'national community'; third, in the wartime period between 1939 and 1945. The style was distinctive in each phase, as the development of poster art and the requirements of the *NSDAP*, in terms of its key messages, changed over time as well. In the early years of the movement, the *NSDAP* utilized posters simply to advertise political fixtures and events. These posters were very simple, giving out information about the time and location of a meeting or rally. As the years progressed, Goebbels, already chief of Party propaganda, employed posters more effectively and creatively, as a way not only of bringing attention to the Party, but also of generating popular appeal. Posters were used to attract voters to the Nazi Party. The slogans and images put across clear messages that chimed with the emotions of the German population, particularly during the years 1930–2, when Germany was beset by economic misery, political incapacity, and social distress.

Once in power, the Nazis used posters as an important part of their propaganda machine in the creation of the *Volksgemeinschaft*, not only to create consensus and conformity among *Volksgenossen* ('national comrades') but also to vilify their 'enemies', particularly the Jews. An analysis of the strong images and slogans used by the *NSDAP* in its posters has introduced the related Nazi policies. The key message of national unity, as expressed, for example, in the poster '*Ein Volk, Ein Reich, Ein Führer*', emphasized a central Nazi slogan. We have examined a range of posters designed to appeal to different sectors of the German populace across a range of ideological imperatives, including posters designed to create the cult of the *Führer*; posters to instil a sense of obligation to the nation, for example, to promote autarky and other Nazi alimentary policies, including the *Eintopf* ('one-pot dish'); posters directed at the German youth, encouraging active membership of the Nazi youth groups, the Hitler Youth and the League of German Girls; posters urging Germans to benefit from the holidays and excursions offered by the *Kraft durch Freude* (Strength through Joy) organization; to save for the *Volkswagen* or 'people's car'; to listen to the 'people's radio'; and posters which extolled the Nazi Party as the protector of the German family and which promoted large German 'valuable' families. Posters were also used to advertise exhibitions, sports events, and Party festivals. In addition, we have seen how they were employed to promote particular policies or ideas in relation to groups who did not fit into the Nazis' 'national community', such as the physically and mentally ill, and, in particular, the largest group of victims of the regime, the Jews.

During the wartime years, Nazi poster propaganda both venerated the armed forces and called upon the home front to do its part for the war effort. The two were regarded as strongly interconnected, as the posters from these years clearly illustrate. We have noted an evolution of techniques and styles in the wartime period. We have examined important wartime posters, including 'Into the Dust with all Enemies of Greater Germany!' depicting a strong fist smashing the French, the British, and the Jews; and the 1943 poster '*Adolf Hitler ist der Sieg!*' ('Adolf Hitler is Victory!'). Such posters were employed to emphasize the critical struggle of the Nazi war effort, to vilify the 'enemies' of the regime, and to encourage popular mobilization on the home front. The most significant subjects of Nazi wartime posters were their 'enemies' – first, Britain and France; then from June 1941, the USSR (and 'bolshevism'); then, from December 1941, the United States; and consistently throughout, the Jews. In addition, Nazi home front posters depicted a variety of themes including the evacuation of the cities, the enrolment for the 'people's army' towards the end of the war, the discouragement of women from hoarding and 'hamstering', and the curbing of 'black' radio listening. Posters were a crucial conduit through which the regime appealed to the German populace.

The Nazi posters used pastel colours for consensus, for example, in cases in which it was easy to sway loyal and hardworking 'national comrades' with images and slogans about holidays or improved conditions in German factories. Bold strong colours and more complex font styles were reserved for the depiction of 'enemies', particularly the Jews, but also Germany's wartime enemies, Britain, the USSR, and the United States. Indeed, oftentimes, the Jews were portrayed as manipulating those nations too. In both Soviet and Nazi posters, aesthetically pleasing artwork could be wielded towards the aim of subjugation, suppression, and humiliation of 'enemies'. Soviet posters used softer colours as well once the existential challenges of the Great Turn and the Second World War were overcome. After 1945, the posters emphasized an emerging socialist world, in which neither class nor gender nor race was to stop people from developing all their talents for the sake of the common good.

Soviet posters were born in the cauldron of the civil war. From the beginning, they demonized those opposed to the communist cause, making their foes into caricatures. Their form at first varied. While Constructivists left a significant imprint on their outlook, they might also display traces of the *lubki* tradition, or sport a more realistic representation. Eventually a sort of hybrid poster developed, in which both abstract concepts and concrete images were reflected, or even merged, as in the photomontage images. How well these posters worked in rallying the Soviet population to the cause and of Marxist-inspired modernization is moot. Likewise, we cannot truly assess the contribution posters made to the Stalin cult. Certainly, Stalin had become a mythical, almost divine creature in the eyes of the Soviet inhabitants after the Soviet victory in the Great Patriotic War, but in how far he had acquired this status before 22 June 1941 is less clear. Calls for a unified resistance against the foreign invaders initially were bereft of images of Stalin, who only began to reappear when victory came more clearly in sight by early 1943. Zhdanov's portrayal as a determined chief is a bit of an anomaly in showing one of Stalin's lieutenants as a wartime leader on his own, but it was produced when the worst of the Leningrad siege was over and the city appeared to have survived the Nazi onslaught. And perhaps it should be seen as the exception proving the rule; few posters were made foregrounding leaders other than Stalin (besides sometimes the deceased Lenin) after 1929. Rodchenko was reprimanded for his glorification of Voroshilov and Budyennyi, and, if portrayed at all, one sees the boss's cronies mainly in the background, dwarfed by their boss.

The war certainly allowed Soviet poster-makers to show off their strengths, perhaps because their art had been born in another war (and some of the same poster artists had already been active in the civil war). After May 1945, Soviet posters acquired a certain blandness in an attempt to have harmony replace strife. They referred to people's daily existence, emphasizing how much life had improved under the wise leadership of Stalin and how hard work and study might lead to the promised land of plenty. But their artistic quality and mass appeal may have declined in displaying such subject matter, lessening their effect, that is, 'the deliberate, systematic attempt to shape [their audience's] perceptions, manipulate cognitions, and direct behaviour', as Jowett and O'Donnell define it.[1]

Soviet authorities did not practise what they preached in terms of equality. Men enjoyed greater chances to get ahead in life, received better wages, occupied the highest ranking positions in the Party and government apparatus, and were not expected to contribute much of anything in terms of child rearing or household chores. Similarly, Russians (or those fluent in the Russian language) had much greater opportunities for social mobility, while even ascribed class markers might handicap one's chances for a good education or career, better housing and so on (even after the 1936 constitution officially did away with such discrimination). *Kulaks* or (former) priests and their offspring, or those who had pre-1917 noble or middle-class ancestors, had to make way for blue-collar workers or poor peasants. These realities of Soviet society were reflected on posters. And as with the portrayal of enemies, both demonizing their foes into ugly caricatures, Nazi and Soviet posters also showed remarkable similarity in the way in which they portrayed women as child carers, for example. Nonetheless, far more than women depicted in the *Reich*'s propaganda, Soviet women were routinely shown as workers, too. For few women were not wage earners in the Soviet Union, which was hailed as a sign of gender equality, even when it was driven by economic necessity, in a country that was always short of workhands in industry and agriculture. Even before the Second World War, women were more frequently shown farming than as factory workers, a trend reinforced after 1945 when they indeed formed the great majority of collective-farm workers. By contrast, in Nazi Germany women were called up relatively late in the war (in 1943) and even then, not uniformly.

Similarly, in showing the harmonious 'friendship of the peoples', ethnic equality was rendered, or, if there was a subtle hint at the 'leadership' of the Russian ethno-cultural community, it was shown as that of a gentle hand, indeed that of an older sibling, as it was phrased by postwar official proclamations, the highest in the land. Meanwhile, posters aimed at a non-Russian Soviet audience showed the firm conviction that Soviet-induced technological modernization was a leap forward in improving people's lives, who, except for a few rather quaint ephemeral traditions, embraced its blessings. A touch of desperation may be gleaned from Soviet wartime posters that tried to appeal to everyone to defend the motherland. Indeed, Toidze's poster shows a woman dressed in a sort of quasi-traditional garb, appealing to all Soviet citizens, not just those in blue coveralls. And bearded rural types inspired by the Russian-historical figures of Minin and Pozharsky were urged to join the counterpart of the Nazi *Volkssturm*, the *narodnoe opolchenie*.

The question cannot be conclusively answered as to which side was more effective in using this propaganda weapon, but the Soviet side may have counted more talented artists lending their hand at poster-making. Even if that is true, though, artistic merit does not necessarily mean that good art (even if it can be defined what that is, which is impossible) appeals to a mass audience. What we can say, given the enormous outlay both regimes spent on poster production, is that the images had at least to a degree the desired effect of rallying people behind their cause. After all both Nazis and Soviets did cut out wasteful or ineffective projects, from producing dirigibles (Zeppelins) to constructing useless railroads or canals, even when they never admitted to making any mistakes. More concretely, perhaps, funding for the Soviet photo-novella, initially heavily subsidized, was discontinued once its appeal appeared rather limited and its production prohibitively expensive.

Posters continued to be produced and relied upon by both regimes to put across their messages.

To what extent, then, did posters reflect real life in the Soviet Union or Nazi Germany? Of course, some posters had no intention of showing reality, as in the depiction of ugly class or race enemies, foreign, or domestic. Many posters did have the intention of illustrating the regime's and its ideology's desired society. On Soviet posters, farmers (unless 'liberated' Ukrainians, etc.) look healthy, are well dressed, organize their work effectively, or master their machinery and tools in a way that hardly reveals the operation of the collective farms of the era. Workers and soldiers are well proportioned, pictures of health, dressed in sober but immaculate fashion. The suits of the radio announcer or the student of Leninism-Stalinism are extremely well-cut, of a quality that was nowhere manufactured in the Soviet Union, where men tended to have ill-fitting suits made of polyester, if they had them at all. Such posters displayed the hoped-for prosperous and contented society, imagined rather than real. Nazi posters too portrayed an idealized image of for example, families and workers, which belied reality. Nazi family posters showed the protection of the state for German families, but firstly, this was not the case for all families (certainly Jewish, Sinti, and Roma families received the very opposite of state protection, but even families of German ethnicity who fell short of the 'hereditary health' requirements of the regime faced drastic eugenic policies); and secondly, the regime intervened in family life and the private sphere in a way that demeaned the family as an institution or unit. Nazi posters depicted an idealized life for the workers, owning their own cars and working in beautiful factories that resembled workshops before the Industrial Revolution, rather than the reality of the factories in the 1930s and 1940s, especially once armaments production was prioritized and accelerated. Once the war had broken out, those savings for the 'people's car' amounted to nothing as *Volkswagen* turned to production for the military. Yet the various exhortations on posters for people to play their part in the war effort were real. The 'total war' called for sacrifices and hardships; in addition, they had to act responsibly in terms of adhering to 'blackouts' and other necessary wartime behaviour, as posters reminded them constantly.

An essentially twentieth-century phenomenon, the poster captures its *Zeitgeist* and, more than anything, that of the century's two most infamous dictatorships of the extremist left and right. Their production reflects its technological possibilities (the lithograph press, the photograph, the use of railroad, lorry, and automobile for its distribution) and its artistic context and fashions in terms of its stylization, fonts, and colours. And, of course, posters highlight the tremendous importance placed upon propaganda. This was a time when posters often provided the central frame of reference for propaganda. Posters were harnessed as a crucial means to sell the respective regimes' messages. Their images fit the new age of 'mass politics' and its attempts to galvanize and mobilize their populations in supporting the ruling parties' political aims. Both regimes shared a deep appreciation for visual means, which could be utilized in a manner impossible before 1900. Posters were more easily displayed than film and provided images in a manner that radio signals could not (while radio receivers were in the Soviet Union rather rare before 1950). They were cheap to produce, visually appealing and their messages easily imbibed and absorbed. In Goebbels's twelve-year propaganda campaign to sway and seduce the German population once the Nazis took over power, the poster was an important tool. Posters were relatively cheap to produce and easy to distribute. Their effective messages and slogans made them an ideal means of disseminating Nazi ideology. The aims of the graphic artists and their Party handlers were clear. Of course, the popular responses and reactions to posters in both regimes are much more difficult to gauge. But certainly the ubiquity of the posters and the repetition of themes, words, and images had an impact because it was impossible for people not to see them and notice them on a daily basis, once they left their homes and entered public spaces.

The poster was not invented by these regimes, nor was propaganda more broadly, but these two regimes employed them in novel and distinctive ways. While the Soviet poster was somewhat more part of a modernist genre that was hugely influential in the 1920s and 1930s beyond its borders, as well as within them, the Nazi poster reflected the antinomy of Nazism as 'reactionary modernism', blending a tendency to the ultra-modern with one of traditionalism and parochialism.[2] While agricultural labour was a common theme in both regimes, the Nazi posters emphasized *Blut und Boden* (Blood and Soil) and old-style farm production, rather than the gleaming machines portrayed in the Soviet posters. The Nazi regime had an inherent contradiction – to restore traditional or even archaic values and mores on the one hand, yet to modernize and industrialize on the other. However, the Nazis did not experiment with the avant-garde and similar styles of abstract artistic representation because these were anathema to them and regarded as culturally degenerate and inferior. Both regimes used persuasive techniques of visual propaganda. Both idealized workers, peasants, and soldiers. Both had personality cults of their respective leaders.

Lastly, we should ponder the place of the artists who made the posters. Many of them were committed Nazis in Germany or true-believing Communists in the USSR. But not all, of course, were unflinchingly loyal. Apsis left the Soviet Union soon after the civil war, and Mayakovsky killed himself in 1930. Others, to be sure, were persecuted, such as Koretskii, or even more tragically, Klutsis. Still, others became consummate sycophants, like Boris Efimov, a Stalinist under Stalin and an adherent of the Thaw under Khrushchev. The temptation to profess one's loyalty as a poster-maker was great, indeed. Not only might it allow one to evade incarceration or the execution squad, but also the remuneration of artists in the Soviet Union was comparatively generous. If one did the regime's bidding, it was possible to lead a fairly quiet life in which one could enjoy a decent level of material prosperity, unlike the great majority of the Soviet population under Stalin. Such rewards might help soothe one's conscience when confronted by some of his regime's odious deeds. In Nazi Germany too, the graphic artists who designed posters for the regime not only benefitted from its patronage and were successful in their work, but also for the most part continued relatively unimpeded with their lives in the postwar period.

In the end, in both regimes we have established that posters depicted a reality of the leaders' choice, which was in fact an illusion. The depiction of workers, soldiers, and women, as we have noted, did not reflect reality. Even more, 'enemies' were grotesquely caricatured into monsters. The posters were utilized further to enhance the cult of the leader and to persuade the populaces to think and behave in particular ways set out by the regimes. People were directly confronted by Nazi and Soviet posters: it was impossible then to evade their messages, images and slogans. Public spaces were highly politicized visually by the posters utilized by both regimes to disseminate their propaganda. In both of these political systems, in which there was no prospect or opportunity for competing or oppositional ideas or images, propaganda posters were all-pervasive.

NOTES

Introduction

1. Toby Clark, *Art and Propaganda in the Twentieth Century: The Political Image in the Age of Mass Culture*, London: George Weidenfeld and Nicolson, 1997, 13.
2. The term at first had a religious meaning, when, soon after the Council of Trent (1545–63), the Catholic Church began to undertake a concerted effort to propagate its faith countering Protestantism (see for example Erwin W. Fellows, '"Propaganda": History of a Word', *American Speech* 3, 1959, 182–9).
3. Garth Jowett and Victoria O' Donnell, *Propaganda and Persuasion*, London: Sage, 2019, 1. See also below in Chapter 1 for Lenin's distinction between agitation and propaganda.
4. Ibid., 6.
5. Ibid., 31.
6. Ibid., 136.
7. Clark, *Art and Propaganda in the Twentieth Century*, 105.
8. Jowett and O'Donnell, *Propaganda and Persuasion*, 199.
9. Clark, *Art and Propaganda in the Twentieth Century*, 106.
10. Ibid., 103.
11. Ibid., 105.
12. Ibid., 105.
13. Ibid., 105.
14. Ibid., 111.
15. As in the UK's Ministry of Information, which employed George Orwell (Eric Blair) among its staff.
16. See Victoria Grieve, *The Federal Art Project and the Creation of Middlebrow Culture*, Chicago, IL: University of Illinois Press, 2009.
17. See the discussion furnished by the Hagley Museum in Wilmington, Delaware, 'The National Association of Manufacturers and Visual Propaganda', available at: https://www.hagley.org/librarynews/research-national-association-manufacturers-and-visual-propaganda, accessed 15 March 2024.
18. Clark, *Art and Propaganda in the Twentieth Century*, 74. See also, S. Heller, *Iron Fists: Branding the 20th-Century Totalitarian State*, London: Phaidon, 2008.

19 S. White, *The Bolshevik Poster*, New Haven, CT: Yale University Press, 1988, 34.

20 It seems pertinent to note that the architect of the diffusion of the cheap poster in the Western world was a former communist, the Dutchman Engel Verkerke (1924–2022), who left the Dutch Communist Party not long after Stalin's death when he was confronted with the stark reality of the Soviet regime. Verkerke had clearly understood the power of the poster by then; from 1957 his poster-making venture sold millions of copies worldwide.

21 See 'Vystavka "Plakat na sluzhbe piatiletki" (Pervaia vsesoiuznaia vustavka plakata)', available at: https://tramvaiiskusstv.ru/plakat/articles-plakat/item/868-06-12-2016-vystavka-plakat-na-sluzhbe-pyatiletki-pervaya-vsesoyuznaya-vystavka-plakata.html, accessed 5 September 2022.

22 Alan Bullock, *Hitler and Stalin: Parallel Lives*, New York: HarperCollins, 1991; Robert Gellately, *Lenin, Stalin, and Hitler: The Age of Social Catastrophe*, New York: Vintage, 2007; Richard Overy, *The Dictators: Hitler's Germany, Stalin's Russia*, New York: Norton, 2006; Laurence Rees, *Hitler and Stalin: The Tyrants and the Second World War*, London: Penguin, 2021.

23 H. Rousso, ed., *Stalinism and Nazism: History and Memory Compared*, Lincoln, NE: University of Nebraska Press, 2004; I. Kershaw and M. Lewin, eds, *Stalinism and Nazism: Dictatorships in Comparison*, Cambridge: Cambridge University Press, 1997.

24 Timothy Snyder, *Bloodlands: Europe between Hitler and Stalin*, New York: Basic Books, 2010.

25 Jan T. Gross, *Revolution from Abroad: The Soviet Conquest of Poland's Western Ukraine and Western Belorussia*, Princeton, NJ: Princeton University Press, 2002.

26 Abbott Gleason, *Totalitarianism: The Inner History of the Cold War*, Oxford: Oxford University Press, 1995; Hannah Arendt, *The Origins of Totalitarianism*, New York: Shocken, 1951; Zbigniew Brzezinski and Carl J. Friedrich, *Totalitarian Dictatorship and Autocracy*, Cambridge, MA: Harvard University Press, 1956.

27 Although a broad comparison (including Mao's China and Mussolini's Italy) of the art of twentieth-century dictatorships may be found in Igor Golomstock, *Totalitarian Art*, New York: HarperCollins, 1990. For a critique, see Roger Griffin, 'In the Shadow of the Megamachine: Reflections on Golomstock's "Iron Law of Totalitarian Art"', *Third Text* 51, Summer, 2000, 29–38.

28 K. Waschik and N. I. Baburina, *Werben für die Utopie: russische Plakatkunst des 20. Jahrhunderts*, Bietigheim-Bissingen: Tertium, 2003; and K. Vashik, N. Baburina, *Real'nost utopii: Iskusstvo russkogo plakata xx veka*, Moscow: Progress-Traditsiia, 2004.

29 Victoria Bonnell, *Iconography of Power: Soviet Political Posters under Lenin and Stalin*, Berkeley and Los Angeles, CA: University of California Press, 1999.

30 White, *Bolshevik Poster*. See also the recent brief overview by Judith Devlin (Judith Devlin, 'Visual Channels (1): Posters and Fine Art', in *Media and Communication in the Soviet Union [1917–1953]: General Perspectives*, eds. Kirill Postoutenko, Alexey Tikhomirov and Dmitri Zakharine, Cham: Palgrave Macmillan, 2021, 21–35.

31 For a long-term view of images' use in Russian culture (not least in political terms), see Valerie Kivelson, Sergei Kozlov and Joan Neuberger, eds, *Picturing Russian Empire*, Oxford: Oxford University Press, 2024.

32 Such roots are explored by, for example, Richard Pipes, *Russia under the Bolshevik Regime*, New York: Knopf, 1993, 299, 310; Sjeng Scheijen, *Diaghilev: A Life*, Oxford: Oxford University Press, 2010; and Laura Engelstein, *The Keys to Happiness*, Ithaca, NY: Cornell University Press, 1994.

33 A. Rosenfeld, *Defining Russian Graphic Arts: From Diaghilev to Stalin, 1898–1934*, New Brunswick, NJ: Rutgers University Press, 1999; Stephen M. Norris, *A War of Images: Russian Popular Prints, Wartime Culture, and National Identity, 1812–1945*, DeKalb, IL: Northern Illinois University Press, 2006.

34 Peter Kenez, *The Birth of the Propaganda State: Soviet Methods of Mass Mobilization, 1917–1929*, Cambridge: Cambridge University Press, 1985; Boris Groys, *The Total Art of Stalinism: Avant-Garde, Aesthetic Dictatorship, and Beyond*, New York: Verso, 2011; David Brandenberger, *Propaganda State in Crisis*, New Haven, CT: Yale University Press, 2012; Evgeny Dobrenko, *Late Stalinism: The Aesthetics of Politics*, New Haven, CT: Yale University Press, 2020.

35 Peter Kort Zegers and Douglas Druick, eds, *Windows on the War: Soviet Tass Posters at Home and Abroad*, New Haven, CT: Yale University Press, 2011; K. Toland, *Constructing Revolution: Soviet Propaganda Posters, 1917–1947*, Brunswick, ME: Bowdoin College Museum of Art, 2021.

36 See *Tramvai iskusstv*, available at: https://tramvaiiskusstv.ru/, accessed 9 August 2022. Its poster section is available at: https://tramvaiiskusstv.ru/plakat.html, accessed 9 August 2022.

37 See David Welch, ed., *Nazi Propaganda: The Power and the Limitations*, Croom Helm, 1983; Routledge Library Editions, 2015; David Welch, *The Third Reich: Politics and Propaganda*, London and New York, 1993, as well as his articles 'Nazi Propaganda and the *Volksgemeinschaft*: Constructing a People's Community', *Journal of Contemporary History* 2, 2004, 213–38; 'Propaganda and Indoctrination in the Third Reich: Success or Failure?', *European History Quarterly* 17, 1987, 403–22; and Clemens Zimmermann, 'From Propaganda to Modernization: Media Policy and Media Audiences under National Socialism', *German History*, 2006, 431–54.

38 Randall L. Bytwerk, *Bending Spines: The Propagandas of Nazi Germany and the German Democratic Republic*, East Lansing: Michigan State University Press, 2004.

39 Corey Ross, *Media and the Making of Modern Germany: Mass Communications, Society, and Politics from the Empire to the Third Reich*, Oxford: Oxford University Press, 2010; P. Swett, S. Jonathan Wiesen and R. Zatlin, eds, *Selling Modernity: Advertising in Twentieth-Century Germany*, Duke University Press, 2007; Pamela Swett, *Selling under the Swastika: Advertising and Commercial Culture in Nazi Germany*, Stanford University Press, 2013; S. Jonathan Wiesen, *Creating the Nazi Marketplace: Commerce and Consumption in the Third Reich*, Cambridge: Cambridge University Press, 2010; and Nicholas O'Shaughnessy, *Selling Hitler: Propaganda and the Nazi Brand*, London: Hurst, 2016.

40 Steven Luckert and Susan Bachrach, *State of Deception: The Power of Nazi Propaganda*, Washington, DC: USHMM, 2009.

41 Sylke Wunderlich, *Propaganda des Terrors: Plakate des NS-Staates zwischen 1933 und 1945 – Propaganda Posters of the Nazi Terror Regime*, Berlin: Berlin Story Verlag, 2020.

42 Werner Trostel, *Schlagwort Brot: Politische Plakate des 20. Jahrhunderts*, Ulm: Vater und Sohn Eiselen Stiftung, 1997; Hans Bohrmann, ed., *Politische Plakate*, Dortmund: Harenberg, 1984; *Politische Plakate der Weimarer Republik 1918–1933*, Darmstadt: Hessisches Landesmuseum; Friedrich Arnold, ed., *Anschläge: Politische Plakate in Deutschland 1900–1970*, Langewiesche-Brandt, 1977; Birgit Witamwas, *Geklebte NS-Propaganda: Verführung und Manipulation durch das Plakat*, Munich: De Gruyter, 2016.

43 See, for example, *Für Frieden und Sozialismus: Plakate der Parteien und Massenorganisationen der DDR*, Berlin: The Yorck Project, 2006; *Anschläge von 'Drüben': DDR-Plakate 1949–1990*, Essen: Steidl Verlag, 2015.

44 A. Hitler, *Mein Kampf*, London: Pimlico, 1992, 164.

Chapter 1

1 As said, the best overview is by Vashik and Baburina (see Waschik and Baburina, *Werben für die Utopie*; Vashik and Baburina, *Real'nost utopii*).

2 'Communism', 'Communist' and 'Communist Party' will be capitalized if we are discussing the Soviet Communist Party rather than when we focus on communism as an ideology, or as a movement in general.

3 In its chapter three, V. I. [N.] Lenin, *What Is to Be Done?: Burning Questions of Our Movement* [1902], available at: https://www.marxists.org/archive/lenin/works/1901/witbd/iii.htm, accessed 6 June 2022. For more on the historical origins, see Norman Davies, *Europe: A History*, Oxford: Oxford University Press, 1996, 500–1.

4 Lenin, *What Is to Be Done?*, chapter two.

5 Pipes, *Russia under the Bolshevik Regime*, 5.

6 This begs the question in how far Lenin *c.s.* were hypocrites, championing a cause whose ideals they did not believe in themselves but propagated to gain dictatorial political power. I [KB] suggest that they were wholly convinced that right was on their side, at least until the early 1960s. The Communist Party was a cult, an echo chamber, in which dissenting voices and opinions were not tolerated. Criticism of the Soviet project rarely was entertained by its zealots before Khrushchev's rule.

7 One of the best memoirs of such a zealot who ultimately abandoned the cause is that by Lev Kopelev (1912–97, see Lev Kopelev, *The Education of a True Believer*, New York: Harper & Row, 1980). He wrote further two books about his life in the *Gulag* and as a dissident (see Lev Kopelev, *To Be Preserved Forever*, Philadelphia, PA: Lippincott, 1977; and Lev Kopelev, *No Jail for Thought*, London: Secker & Warburg, 1977).

8   Manfred Hildermeier, *Geschichte der Sowjetunion, 1917–1991. Entstehung und Niedergang des ersten sozialistischen Staates*, Munich: Beck, 1998, 551–9; Masha Kowell, 'Agit-Plakat: The Destalinization of Soviet Posters (1956–1966)', unpublished PhD dissertation, University of Pennsylvania, 2013, 63.

9   A good example is the depiction of General Anton Denikin's allegedly brutal treatment of 'workers' in the Russian Civil War, available at: https://www.posterplakat.com/the-collection/posters/pp-262?src=categories/civil-war, accessed 24 June 2022. People are literally hanging from lampposts in this image.

10 The famine, too, is reflected in Soviet poster-culture; it was routinely the case linked to a political cause, as in the Soviet campaign against Russian Orthodoxy; see, for example, the graphic 1922 poster, available at: https://www.posterplakat.com/the-collection/posters/pp-410?src=categories/civil-war, accessed 25 June 2022.

11 The secret police running the camps, meanwhile, went through a quick sequence of renaming, from (United) State Political Administration *([O]GPU*, around 1930) to People's Commissariat of Internal Affairs (*NKVD*, 1934–46) to Ministry of Internal Affairs (*MVD*, 1946–53).

12 See for example Boris Efimov's drawing of 1938 (figure 5), available at: https://www.tate.org.uk/research/features/two-soviet-cartoonists, accessed 28 June 2022. Or see his linking of a swastika to Trotsky c.s. in Alice Nakhimovsky, 'Efimov, Boris Efimovich', in *The Yivo Encyclopedia of Jews in Eastern Europe*, available at: https://yivoencyclopedia.org/article.aspx/Efimov_Boris_Efimovich, accessed 20 July 2022. Efimov was Jewish himself, through which anti-Semitism is incidental rather than a recurring theme in his work. He lived a very long life, and somehow avoided falling victim to Stalin's bloodlust (unlike his brother Mikhail Kol'tsov).

13 See Boris Efimov's suggestions about the need for Stalin's 'personal approval', as recounted to Laurence Rees (Rees, *Hitler and Stalin*, xv).

14 *Soviet* means council, as in council of workers' deputies, or council of workers' and soldiers' deputies.

15 See Kenez, *Birth of the Propaganda State*.

16 See for a recent appreciation Maria Belodubrovskaya, *Not According to Plan: Filmmaking under Stalin*, Ithaca, NY: Cornell University Press, 2017, which is based on the same author's 2011 doctoral dissertation 'Politically Incorrect: Filmmaking under Stalin and the Failure of Power', defended at the University of Wisconsin in Madison.

17 See Kees Boterbloem, *Life and Death under Stalin: Kalinin Province, 1945–1953*, Montréal-Kingston: McGill-Queen's UP, 1999, 130–1; Vance Kepley, Jr, '"Cinefication": Soviet Film Exhibition in the 1920s', *Film History* 2, 1994, 262–77; and Peter Kenez, *Cinema and Soviet Society: From the Revolution to the Death of Stalin, 1917–1953*, London: I.B. Tauris, 2000.

18 For a scholarly comparison, see Richard Taylor, *Film Propaganda: Soviet Russia and Nazi Germany*, second rev. ed., London: I.B. Tauris, 1998.

19 There were some non-Russian filmmakers, but, apart from Oleksandr Dovzhenko, none reached anything near Soviet-wide recognition.

20 For more, see Konstantin Akinsha, 'The Second Life of Soviet Photomontage, 1935–1980s', PhD dissertation, University of Edinburgh, 2012, 78–9 and 130–7. Photography was often considered more an artistic than propagandistic medium, Akinsha suggests.

21 For a thoughtful discussion of Stalinism as a possible 'political religion', see Erik van Ree, 'Stalinist Ritual and Belief System: Reflections on "Political Religion"', *Politics, Religion and Ideology* 2–3, 2016, 143–61. For an (over) abundant collection of photographs of Lenin published in the very last days of the Soviet Union, see Iu. A. Akhapkin et al., eds, *Lenin: Sobranie fotografii i kinokadrov*, 2 vols, third rev. ed., Moscow: Panorama, 1990.

22 Akinsha, 'Second Life', 137–40.

23 The best book on this is David King, *The Commissar Vanishes: The Falsification of Photographs and Art in Stalin's Russia*, new ed., London: Tate, 2014.

24 Akinsha, 'Second Life', 79–122.

25 A particularly nauseating photo-story was made by Rodchenko about the White Sea-Baltic Canal project built by mainly political convicts (Akinsha, 'Second Life', 116). Even less successful was the photo-film, a sort of slide projection; slides, as in the contemporary West, did enjoy popularity as a form of domestic entertainment (ibid., 122, 124).

26 See Erika Wolf, 'When Photographs Speak, to Whom Do They Talk? The Origins and Audience of *SSSR na stroike (USSR in Construction)*', *Left History* 6.2, 1999, 53–82.

27 See Akinsha, 'Second Life', 11–12.

28 For these parades and their significance, see Malte Rolf, *Soviet Mass Festivals, 1917–1991*, Pittsburgh, PA: University of Pittsburgh Press, 2013; and Karin Petrone, *Life Has Become More Joyous, Comrades: Celebrations in the Time of Stalin*, Bloomington, IN: Indiana University Press, 2000.

29 For Rodchenko's activity in this regard, see Elena Barkhatova, '"Modern Icon", or "Tool for Mass Propaganda"?: Russian Debate on the Poster', in *Defining Russian Graphic Arts: From Diaghilev to Stalin, 1898–1934*, ed. Alla Rosenfeld, New Brunswick, NJ: Rutgers University Press, 1999, 132–65: 142, 144; and Akinsha, 'Second Life', 15, 74–5; and for Klutsis's influence, see Akinsha, 'Second Life', 141. See some of Klutsis's work on the wonderful *Posterplakat* website, available at: https://www.posterplakat.com/the-collection/artists/klutsis-gustav-gustavovich-klucis-gustavs, accessed 25 June 2022. An assessment of his significance can be found in Maria Gough, 'Back in the USSR: John Heartfield, Gustavs Klucis, and the Medium of Soviet Propaganda', *New German Critique*, Summer, 2009, 133–83. Gough writes how '[he] produced under Stalin some of the most haunting examples of visual propaganda ever executed in the service of modern, one-party state power' (ibid., 134). See as well Victoria E. Bonnell, 'The Leader's Two Bodies: A Study in the Iconography of the "Vozhd"', *Russian History* 1–4, 1996, 113–40.

30 See Akinsha, 'Second Life'.

31 See Stephen Lovell, *Russia in the Microphone Age: A History of Soviet Radio, 1919–1970*, Oxford: Oxford University Press, 2015; see, especially, ibid., 9–10; see also Boterbloem, *Life and Death*, 129.

32 Poster image provided by Poster Plakat.com. It was issued in 1950 in a print-run of 100,000.
33 Gough, 'Back in the USSR', 135.
34 It is therefore understandable that Stites makes no mention of posters, albeit less evident why posters are not discussed in Orlando Figes, *Natasha's Dance: A Cultural History of Russia*, New York: Picador, 2002 (see R. Stites, *Serfdom, Society, and the Arts in Imperial Russia: The Pleasure and the Power*, New Haven, CT: Yale University Press, 2005; and Figes, *Natasha's Dance*).
35 See Alla Rosenfeld, 'The Search for National Identity in Turn-of-the-Century Russian Graphic Design', in *Defining Russian Graphic Arts*, ed. Alla Rosenfeld, 16–38.
36 See Christina Lodder, *Russian Constructivism*, New Haven, CT: Yale University Press, 1983.
37 See Tarabukin's words as quoted in *In the Service of the State: Nikolai Dolgorukov and the Art of Persuasion*, ed. Alla Rosenfeld, New York: Merrill C. Berman Collection, 2020, 12.
38 See the juxtaposition of a 1944 satirical cartoon by Boris Efimov of Hitler and Goebbels and a 1792 English lampooning of the French *sans-culottes* in Zegers and Druick, eds, *Windows on the War*, 334.
39 See for example the first thirty-three colour plates in *Defining Russian Graphic Arts*, ed. Alla Rosenfeld.
40 Barkhatova, '"Modern Icon"', 158–9.
41 See for this benign explanation 'Khudozhniki reklamy. Sergei Sakharov', available at: https://tramvaiiskusstv.ru/plakat/articles-plakat/item/5936-3-12-2019-khudozhniki-reklamy-sergej-sakharov.html, accessed 9 August 2022.
42 Norris, *War of Images*, 4–5, 10–35.
43 Ibid., 54–163.
44 The Golden Age, mainly defined as literary epoch, being the age from Pushkin, Gogol and Lermontov in the late 1830s and 1840s.
45 See colour plate 35 of *Defining Russian Graphic Arts*, ed. Alla Rosenfeld as well as White, *Bolshevik Poster*, 4, figure 1.3.
46 See White, *Bolshevik Poster*, 75, figure 4.10.
47 For their Soviet iteration, see Norris, *War of Images*, 164–85.
48 Kowell, 'Agit-Plakat', 6. *Rosta* stands for *Rossiiskoe telegraficheskoe agenstvo*, or Russian telegraph agency.
49 This despite its middle-brow or even low-brow flourishing, see Stites, *Serfdom*. Still, several Wanderers such as Repin and Levitan did study printing (see Ekaterina Grishina, 'The Graphic Arts at the Academy of Fine Arts: A Brief History, 1895–1935', in *Defining Russian Graphic Arts*, ed. Alla Rosenfeld, 39–44: 41).
50 See Rosenfeld, 'Search for National Identity'.
51 See Janet Kennedy, 'The *World of Art* and Other Turn-of-the-Century Russian Art Journals, 1898–1910', in *Defining Russian Graphic Arts*, ed. Alla Rosenfeld, 63–78; Alla Rosenfeld, 'The World of Art Group: Book and Poster

Design', in *Defining Russian Graphic Arts*, ed. Alla Rosenfeld, 79–96; Scheijen, *Diaghilev*.

52 For an in-depth discussion of several aspects of this, see Rosenfeld, ed., *Defining Russian Graphic Arts*.

53 Rosenfeld, 'Search for National Identity', 37.

54 Akinsha, 'Second Life', 16, 22–3.

55 On Russian Imperial posters specifically, Douglas Druick and Peter Kort Zegers, 'Introduction', in *Windows on the War*, eds Kort Zegers and Druick, 12–23: 15. See as well Scheijen, *Diaghilev*, and Figes, *Natasha's Dance*.

56 Robert Bird, 'The Functions of Poetry: Tass Windows and the Soviet Media System in Wartime', in *Windows on the War*, eds Kort Zegers and Druick, 92–103: 97.

57 Groys, *Total Art of Stalinism*. See as well Trotsky's inquiry of Mayakovsky in 1922 about what 'futurism' actually meant (L. Maksimenkov, ed., *Bol'shaia tsenzura: Pisately i zhurnalisty v strane sovetov, 1917–1956*, Moscow: Demokratiia-Materik, 2005, 57).

58 Engelstein, *Keys to Happiness*; Pipes, *Russia under the Bolshevik Regime*, 299.

59 Groys, *Total Art*, 5.

60 See Konstantin Akinsha and Adam Jolles, 'Hand-Painted Propaganda: The Tass Poster Studio', in *Windows on the War*, eds Kort Zegers and Druick, 26–51: 49n52.

61 See for some examples Zegers and Druick, eds, *Windows on the War*; the overview of wartime posters available through the University of Nottingham, available at: http://windowsonwar.nottingham.ac.uk/, accessed 19 June 2022; as well as below.

62 See the marvellous digitized collection of Swarthmore College, available at: https://digitalcollections.tricolib.brynmawr.edu/collections/soviet-posters, accessed 21 June 2022.

63 See for example S. I. Ivanov's poster of 1920, which appears similar to expressionist works by artists like Frans Masereel or George Grosz, available at: https://www.posterplakat.com/the-collection/posters/pp-126?src=categories/education-literacy, accessed 24 June 2022.

64 For a study, see Roland Elliott Brown, *Godless Utopia: Soviet Anti-Religious Propaganda*, London: Fuel, 2019.

65 See for the general context Karel Berkhoff, *Motherland in Danger: Soviet Propaganda during World War Two*, Cambridge, MA: Harvard University Press, 2012. This otherwise excellent book has remarkably little to say about posters and their use.

66 On the homefront, see W. Z. Goldman and D. Filtzer, *Fortress Dark and Stern: The Soviet Home Front during World War II*, Oxford: Oxford University Press, 2021.

67 See for a discussion of its genesis https://www.pencioner.ru/news/moya-istoriya/istoriya-plakata-rodina-mat-zovyet, accessed 6 June 2022. See above as a painter Toidze was a derivative dilettante who by the late 1930s made

sycophantic pictures of Stalin in the socialist-realist figurative style (see King, *Commissar Vanishes*, 166).

68 See S. Kotkin, *Magnetic Mountain: Stalinism as a Civilization*, Los Angeles, CA: University of California Press, 1997; Jochen Hellbeck, *Revolution on My Mind: Writing a Diary under Stalin*, Cambridge, MA: Harvard University Press, 2004.

69 Poster image provided by Poster Plakat.com.

Chapter 2

1 Hitler, *Mein Kampf*, 164.
2 N. O'Shaughnessy, *Selling Hitler: Propaganda and the Nazi Brand*, London: Hurst and Company, 2021, vii.
3 Ibid., 26.
4 R. Wistrich, *Weekend in Munich: Art, Propaganda and Terror in the Third Reich*, London: Pavilion, 1995, 14.
5 O'Shaughnessy, *Selling Hitler*, 44.
6 Ibid., 48.
7 H. Heiber, ed., *Goebbels-Reden, Band 1: 1932–1939*, Düsseldorf: Droste Verlag, 1971, 95. It might be noted that Stalin as well appears to have believed in the power of repetition (which has been linked to his studies at an Orthodox seminary as a youth). A clear example of this is the Stalin-edited *Short Course*: see *History of the Communist Party of the Soviet Union (Bolsheviks): Short Course*, New York: International Publishers, 1939.
8 See Welch, 'Propaganda and Indoctrination in the Third Reich', 404–22.
9 Cited in O'Shaughnessy, *Selling Hitler*, 108–9.
10 Clark, *Art and Propaganda in the Twentieth Century*, 61.
11 Ibid.
12 O'Shaughnessy, *Selling Hitler*, 113.
13 S. Wunderlich, *Propaganda des Terrors: Plakate des NS-Staates zwischen 1933 und 1945*, Berlin: Berlin Story Verlag, 2021, 9.
14 M. Poster, ed., *Jean Baudrillard: Selected Writings*, Cambridge: Polity Press, 2001.
15 O'Shaughnessy, *Selling Hitler*, 114.
16 J. Ellul, *Propaganda: The Formation of Men's Attitudes*, New York: Knopf, 1968, 121.
17 Ibid.
18 R. Gellately, *Backing Hitler: Consent and Coercion in Nazi Germany*, Oxford: Oxford UP, 2001, 259.
19 Bytwerk, *Bending Spines*, 6.
20 Ibid., 27.

21 Cited in L. Pine, *Hitler's 'National Community': Society and Culture in Nazi Germany*, London: Bloomsbury, 2017, 41.
22 Bytwerk, *Bending Spines*, 61.
23 Ibid., 141.
24 Ibid., 159.
25 Ellul, *Propaganda*, 11.
26 Wunderlich, *Propaganda des Terrors*, 8.
27 R. Griffin, ed., *Fascism*, Oxford: Oxford University Press, 1995, 4.
28 On this, see J. Herf, *Reactionary Modernism: Technology, Culture and Politics in Weimar and the Third Reich*, Cambridge: Cambridge University Press, 1984.
29 O'Shaughnessy, *Selling Hitler*, 142.
30 Bytwerk, *Bending Spines*, 39.
31 O'Shaughnessy, *Selling Hitler*, 217.
32 Ibid., 225.
33 Ibid., 242.
34 Ibid., 243.
35 Wunderlich, *Propaganda des Terrors*, 10.
36 O'Shaughnessy, *Selling Hitler*, 259.
37 Wunderlich, *Propaganda des Terrors*, 13.
38 Ibid., 13.
39 Ibid., 14.
40 Ibid., 15.
41 S. Luckert and S. Bachrach, *State of Deception: The Power of Nazi Propaganda*, Washington, DC: United States Holocaust Memorial Museum, 2009, 39.
42 Hitler, *Mein Kampf*, 164.
43 Ibid., 169.
44 R. Evans, *The Coming of the Third Reich*, London: Penguin, 2004, 233.
45 Wunderlich, *Propaganda des Terrors*, 18.
46 Ibid., 18.
47 Cited in R. Herzstein, *The War that Hitler Won: The Most Infamous Propaganda Campaign in History*, London: Hamish Hamilton, 1978, 198.
48 Bohrmann, ed., *Politische Plakate*, 611.

Chapter 3

1 Bonnell, *Iconography*, 4, 7–8, 12, 22–3.
2 Norris, *War of Images*, 164–85.
3 Bonnell, *Iconography*, 3–5.

4 Barkhatova, 'Modern Icon', 132. See as well ibid., 134.
5 White, *Bolshevik Poster*, 23–4.
6 The so-called 'Whites' were defeated by the autumn of 1920, but the Red Army was still at war with Poland until the spring of 1921 when it also occupied Georgia.
7 Alla Rosenfeld, 'The World Turned Upside Down: Russian Posters of the First World War, the Bolshevik Revolution, and the Civil War', in *Defining Russian Graphic Arts*, ed. Alla Rosenfeld, 121–32.
8 Rosenfeld, 'World Turned Upside Down', 123.
9 This is Bruce Lincoln's description of early *Rosta* posters: W. Bruce Lincoln, *Red Victory: A History of the Russian Civil War*, New York: Simon & Schuster, 1989, 352. See as well ibid., 353. I do not think Lincoln was entirely correct in stating, 'For the first time, a government on Russian soil had thought it worthwhile to build a base of political support among the masses'; as noted earlier, in the world war the tsarist government had already sought to whip up patriotism in this fashion (see ibid., 353).
10 Barkhatova, 'Modern Icon', 135, 138; White, *Bolshevik Poster*, 25–32.
11 For his work at *Rosta*, see White, *Bolshevik Poster*, 65, 80. Kerzhentsev lost this influential position when criticized by Zhdanov for patronizing Meyerkhol'd's theatre in early 1938, subsequent to which he retired from active political life, but he remained at liberty (see Kees Boterbloem, *Life and Times of Andrei Zhdanov, 1896–1948*, Montréal-Kingston: McGill-Queen's UP, 2004, 169, 401n210). For a short biography, see http://www.hrono.info/biograf/bio_k/kerzencev_pm.php, accessed 9 August 2022.
12 See for example Toland, *Constructing Revolution*, 52. On Cheremnykh, see White, *Bolshevik Poster*, 68–72.
13 See Rosenfeld, 'World Turned Upside Down', 123–5; Barkhatova, 'Modern Icon', 132–3, 151–2.
14 See Sergei N. Povartsov, 'Merezhkovskii, Uells i krasnaia zvezda', *Voprosy Literatury* 6, 2002, 168–86.
15 See White, *Bolshevik Poster*, 25, ill. 2.10. It should be noted, by the way, that especially the French army counted many Africans in the First World War, both from North Africa and from Senegal (Cheremnykh's preceding drawing on this poster appears to indicate that a white French soldier is unwilling to do the capitalists' bidding in Russia). I am not sure how many French colonial troops served in the Entente forces in Russia during its civil war, but Cheremnykh may have referred to news about them.
16 Hergé, *Tintin au Congo*, *Le Petit Vingtième*, June 1930–July 1931, collected into one volume in 1931.
17 Hergé, *Tintin au pays des Soviets*, *Le Petit Vingtième*, January 1929–May 1930.
18 White, *Bolshevik Poster*, 33, ill. 2.21.
19 Poster image provided by Poster Plakat.com.
20 For an elaborate pertinent discussion, see Bonnell, *Iconography of Power*, 65–85.
21 Poster image provided by Poster Plakat.com. Its print-run was 10,000.

22 Poster image provided by Poster Plakat.com. Its price was 2 rubles 50 kopecks, and its print-run 10,000.
23 Poster image provided by Poster Plakat.com. The poster had a relatively small print-run of 7,000 and cost a mere 20 kopecks.
24 Boterbloem, *Life and Death*, 189–192.
25 Rosenfeld, 'World Turned Upside Down', 129–30.
26 Even when he ends his calculation in 1921, White's numbers make evident the trend moving from political-military to cultural-economic themes from 1918 to 1921 (see White, *Bolshevik Poster*, 91 table 1).
27 Barkhatova, 'Modern Icon', 139–40, 158.
28 Barkhatova, 'Modern Icon', 153–4, 156.
29 Rosenfeld, 'World Turned Upside Down', 131.
30 Poster image provided by Poster Plakat.com.
31 See Akinsha, 'Second Life', 45.
32 It is interesting to note that the renowned critic Viktor Shklovsky could not stand the distortion of photographic rendition by the poster-makers, forecasting the Soviet authorities' criticism of the non-representational 'formalism' in the 1930s (see Akinsha, 'Second Life', 13–14).
33 Akinsha, 'Second Life', 23.
34 Akinsha, 'Second Life', 23–4.
35 Rosenfeld, ed., *In the Service of the State*, 11.
36 Akinsha, 'Second Life', 32–5.
37 L. Maksimenkov, 'Vvedenie', in *Bol'shaia tsenzura: Pisately i zhurnalisty v strane sovetov, 1917–1956*, ed. L. Maksimenkov, Moscow: Demokratiia-Materik, 2005, 5–15: 5.
38 See Boterbloem, *The Life and Times*, 116.
39 Matthew E. Lenoe, *Closer to the Masses: Stalinist Culture, Social Revolution, and Soviet Newspapers*, Cambridge, MA: Harvard University Press, 2004, 1–2.
40 Poster image provided by Poster Plakat.com. Made by the anonymous artist Ia. Ch., its print-run was 15,000. It was printed in the very centre of Moscow (near the buildings of the Communist Party's Central Committee) on behalf of the state-labour agency.
41 Still, the select few were remunerated well, as is evident from the comparatively affluent writers' enclave of Peredelkino near Moscow, in which the most celebrated 'engineers of the human soul' had the use of impressive country houses (see K. Vasil'eva and L. Lobov, *Peredelkino, skazanie o pisatel'skom gorodke*, Moscow: Bosplen, 2012). Substantial money prizes and distinctions such as that of 'USSR People's Artist' were given to the most outstanding artists as well.
42 Gough notes how Klutsis's posters were printed in the tens of thousands in 1930 (Gough, 'Back in the USSR', 140). See for further discussion of this Galina Yankovskaya and Rebecca Mitchell, 'The Economic Dimensions of Art in the Stalinist Era: Artists' Cooperatives in the Grip of Ideology and the Plan', *Slavic Review* 4, 2006, 769–91.

43 See Andy Logan and Russel Maloney, 'Pravda (Talk of the Town)', *The New Yorker*, 5 February 1944, 15. For more on *Pravda*, see Jeffrey Brooks, *Thank You, Comrade Stalin! Soviet Public Culture from Revolution to Cold War*, Princeton, NJ: Princeton University Press, 2000. And for more on the importance placed on newspapers in general, see Lenoe, *Closer to the Masses*.

44 As Evgenii Gromov notes, see Evgenii Gromov, *Stalin: Vlast' i iskusstvo*, Moscow: Respublika, 1998, 61. On Stalin's interventions in music Leonid Maksimenkov's work is essential (see for example L. Maksimenkov, *Sumbur vmesto muzyki: Stalinskaia kultur'naia revoliutsiia*, Moscow: Iuridicheskaia kniga, 1997). On Stalin's interest in architecture, see Deyan Sudjic, *Stalin's Architect: Power and Survival in Moscow*, London: Thames & Hudson, 2022.

45 Akinsha, 'Second Life', 199.

46 Ibid., 200.

47 Poster image provided by Poster Plakat.com; 20,000 copies were printed. Kozlinskii had worked together with Mayakovsky on the *Rosta* windows in 1919 and 1920, while Klinch may have been best known for his satirical drawings in magazines.

48 See for example Akinsha, 'Second Life', 58. This has been subject of an in-depth exploration by Anita Pisch (see A. Pisch, *The Personality Cult of Stalin in Soviet Posters: Archetypes, Inventions, and Fabrications*, Canberra: Australian University Press, 2016). This is a useful book, but not always accurate. Neither Stalin nor Zhdanov was ever 'commissar of cultural enlightenment', a post that did not exist – even if the author means 'enlightenment' [education], its people's commissars were Andrei Bubnov and Pyotr Tiurkin in those years. It is true that Zhdanov played a part as the Communist Party's Central Committee [from here: CC] secretary overseeing culture at times before 1941, but besides Stalin and Zhdanov others in this highest Party body and in the Soviet government dealt with culture as well, such as Platon Kerzhentsev, Aleksandr Shcherbakov and various CC *agitprop* department officials. Besides my own biography of Zhdanov, see as well Olesia A. Glotova, 'Andrei Aleksandrovich Zhdanov: Ideologicheskaia deiatel'nost v 1920–1940-e gg.', *kandidat* dissertation, *Rossiiskaia akademiia gosudarstvennoi sluzhby* (Moscow), 2004.

49 See the transformation of a 1929 group photo of Stalin into his famous 1932 photomontaged poster of Stalin overseeing the triumphs of the first Five Year Plan (King, *Commissar Vanishes*, 150–1). For other cultish contributions by Klutsis, see ibid., 188–9, 191.

50 Poster image provided by Poster Plakat.com. As many as 15,000 copies of this poster were printed in 1932.

51 See Gough, 'Back in the USSR', 140; Akinsha, 'Second Life', 57.

52 As is evident from his 1930 poster in support of the secret police (then *GPU*)'s reckoning with 'counterrevolutionary saboteurs' (see King, *Commissar Vanishes*, 147).

53 King, *Commissar Vanishes*, 70.

54 King, *Commissar Vanishes*, 182–3.

55 See, too, Graeme J. Gill, *Symbols and Legitimacy in Soviet Politics*, Cambridge: Cambridge University Press, 2011; the Swarthmore collection illustrates this change of course quite clearly. As a fine example of the transformation of a Russian artist from modernism to socialist realism, the painter Aleksandr Mikhailovich Gerasimov (1881–1963) may serve, who after the war ended up condemning Western art in the most abject terms (see for example Vasiliy Eremin, 'Gerasimov – pridvornyi zhivopisets Stalina', available at: https://historical-fact.livejournal.com/104599.html, accessed 21 June 2022). Gerasimov painted the famous portrait of Lenin speaking to a crowd on Red Square (*Lenin na tribune*) – which was used on many posters – and of Stalin and Voroshilov walking on the Kremlin wall (*I.V. Stalin i K.E. Voroshilov v Kremle*).

56 Gough, 'Back in the USSR', 141–2; Barkhatova, 'Modern Icon', 163–4. The decree was called '*O plakatnoi produktsii*'.

57 See for example the write-up available at: https://tramvaiiskusstv.ru/plakat/articles-plakat/item/742-14-09-2016-obshchestvo-rabotnikov-revolyutsionnogo-plakata-orrp-1931-1932.html, accessed 29 June 2022.

58 Efimov had been involved with the Odesa office of *Rosta* in the early 1920s (see White, *Bolshevik Poster*, 89). See for more on Dolgorukov, Rosenfeld, ed., *In the Service of the State*.

59 See Marilyn Rueschemeyer, Igor Golomshtok and Janet Kennedy, *Soviet Emigre Artists: Life and Work in the USSR and the United States*, New York: M.E. Sharpe, 1985, 37.

60 Rueschemeyer et al., *Soviet Emigre Artists*, 37.

61 Gough, 'Back in the USSR', 152–4.

62 See its description in 'Vystavka "Plakat na sluzhbe piatiletki"'.

63 For more on the short-lived *ORPP*, see the essay available at: https://tramvaiiskusstv.ru/plakat/articles-plakat/item/742-14-09-2016-obshchestvo-rabotnikov-revolyutsionnogo-plakata-orrp-1931-1932.html, accessed 15 August 2022.

64 Our italics. Rosenfeld, ed., *In the Service of the State*, 15.

65 Kowell, 'Agit-Plakat', 32–3; Akinsha, 'Second Life', 67–70; Rosenfeld, ed., *In the Service of the State*, 23–4.

66 As is argued by Evgeny Dobrenko, see, for instance, E. Dobrenko, 'The Disaster of Middlebrow Taste, or, Who "Invented" Socialist Realism', in *Socialist Realism without Shores*, eds Thomas Lahusen and Evgeny Dobrenko, Durham, NC: Duke University Press, 1997, 135–64.

67 See for an illuminating series of documents and commentaries about this development, Katerina Clark and Evgeny Dobrenko, *Soviet Culture and Power: A History in Documents, 1917–1953*, New Haven, CT: Yale University Press, 2007, 229–48.

68 On this trio of artists (who worked together for a while under the name of *KGK*), see Akinsha, 'Second Life', 140–5. Koretskii's work is rendered on two of the figures in this book and his further fate is discussed below.

69 Clark and Dobrenko, *Soviet Culture and Power*, 241–2.

70 Poster image provided by Poster Plakat.com.
71 See S. Sen'kin, 'Lenin v kommune Vkhutemasa', in *Bor'ba za realizm v izobrazitel'nom iskusstve 2-kh godov*, eds V. Perel'man and I. Lebedev, Moscow: Sovetskii khodozhnik, 1962, 90–7.
72 Efimov may have therefore exaggerated about Stalin's personal scrutiny of his work and that of others; what seems clear is that if a dubious poster or cartoon was produced, lower-level *apparatchiks* would bring it to the leaders' attention (either directly passing it on to Stalin or by having it arrive at the desk of one of his lieutenants); see Rees, *Hitler and Stalin*, xv.
73 Its full text in a slightly amended version (for example, the three Baltic republics are mentioned) English is available at: https://www.marxists.org/reference/archive/stalin/works/1936/12/05.htm, accessed 18 August 2022.
74 Ibid.
75 Terry Martin, *The Affirmative Action Empire: Nations and Nationalism in the Soviet Union, 1923–1939*, Ithaca, NY: Cornell University Press, 2001.
76 Poster image provided by Poster Plakat.com. Its print-run was 70,000 and its price 70 kopecks.
77 Poster image provided by Poster Plakat.com. It had a print-run of 100,000.
78 As Platon Kerzhentsev did with Shostakovich's opera *Lady Macbeth of Mtsensk* in 1936 (see for more Maksimenkov, *Sumbur*). Efimov's suggestion that Stalin personally signed off on his caricatures should probably be understood in this sense (see Rees, *Hitler and Stalin*, xv).
79 The 'Trotsky demon' depicted in 1930s Stalinist propaganda meanwhile referred to certain anti-Semitic tropes and may have been based on depictions of White forces anti-Semitic portrayals of him on Russian Civil War posters (see the Ukrainian poster made in Kyiv by an anonymous artist in 1919, available at: https://www.posterplakat.com/the-collection/posters/pp-018?src=categories/civil-war, accessed 24 June 2022). And in its turn, Stalin's demonization inspired Orwell's Goldstein and the two minutes of hate directed at Goldtstein in *Nineteen Eighty-Four*.
80 Akinsha, 'Second Life', 73. This aligns with Groys's argument.

Chapter 4

1 Hitler, *Mein Kampf*, 165.
2 Witamwas, *Geklebte NS-Propaganda*.
3 S. Wunderlich, *Propaganda des Terrors: Plakate des NS-Staates zwischen 1933 und 1945*, Berlin: Berlin Story Verlag, 7.
4 Hitler, *Mein Kampf*, 164.
5 Wunderlich, *Propaganda des Terrors*, 10.
6 E. Schockel, *Das politische Plakat*, Munich, 1938, 5. No publisher?
7 Wunderlich, *Propaganda des Terrors*, 9.

8   Hitler, *Mein Kampf*, 165.
9   Ibid., 169.
10 Ibid., 165.
11 See Welch, 'Nazi Propaganda and the *Volksgmeinschaft*', 213–38. See also D. Welch, *The Third Reich: Politics and Propaganda*, London: Routledge, 2002. Ian Kershaw has also shown the significance of Nazi propaganda upon the popular acceptance of the 'Hitler myth': See I. Kershaw, *The 'Hitler Myth': Image and Reality in the Third Reich*, Oxford: Oxford University Press, 1989, 4–5.
12 Kershaw, *The 'Hitler Myth'*, 3.
13 On 'charismatic authority', see Kershaw, *The 'Hitler Myth'*, 8–9. The model of 'charismatic authority' was proposed by Max Weber (see M. Weber, *Economy and Society*, Berkeley, CA: University of California Press, 1978, 241–2).
14 P. Ayçoberry, *The Social History of the Third Reich, 1933–1945*, New York: New Press, 1999, 68.
15 S. Luckert and S. Bachrach, *State of Deception: The Power of Nazi Propaganda*, Washington, DC: United States Holocaust Memorial Museum, 2009, 74–5.
16 Ibid., 77.
17 A. Barkai, *From Boycott to Annihilation: The Economic Struggle of German Jews, 1933–1943*, Waltham, MA: Brandeis University Press, 1989, 22. See also H. Ahlheim, '*Deutsche, kauft nicht bei Juden!*': *Antisemitismus und politischer Boykott in Deutschland 1924 bis 1935*, Göttingen: Wallstein Verlag, 2011.
18 C. Treitel, *Eating Nature in Modern Germany: Food, Agriculture and Environment, c. 1870–2000*, Cambridge: Cambridge University Press, 2017, 189–90.
19 G. Gerhard, *Nazi Hunger Politics: A History of Food in the Third Reich*, Lanham, MD: Rowman and Littlefield, 2015, 42.
20 R. Proctor, *Racial Hygiene: Medicine under the Nazis*, Cambridge, MA and London: Harvard University Press, 1988, 235.
21 L. Collingham, *The Taste of War: World War Two and the Battle for Food*, London: Allen Lane, 2011, 354.
22 *NS-Frauenwarte*, 1935–6, Issue 16, 525.
23 A historical study comparing the Soviet (Young Pioneers, *Komsomol*) and Nazi youth organizations has not yet been undertaken, which will be especially compelling when placed within the context of the great popularity of youth movements in general in the Interbellum.
24 H. Koch, *The Hitler Youth: Origins and Development, 1922–1945*, New York: Dorset Press, 1975, 101.
25 See P. Stachura, *The German Youth Movement 1900–1945: An Interpretative and Documentary History*, London: Macmillan, 1981.
26 Luckert and Bachrach, *State of Deception*, 81.
27 Ibid., 80.

28 Wunderlich, *Propaganda des Terrors*, 53.
29 Ibid., 45.
30 Ibid., 51.
31 Ibid., 38.
32 Ibid., 73.
33 Ibid., 76.
34 J. Timpe, *Nazi-Organized Recreation and Entertainment in the Third Reich*, London: Palgrave, 2017, 7.
35 Luckert and Bachrach, *State of Deception*, 76.
36 On 'Beauty of Labour', see S. Baranowski, *Strength through Joy: Consumerism and Mass Tourism in the Third Reich*, Cambridge: Cambridge University Press, 2004, 75–117.
37 Timpe, *Nazi-Organized Recreation*, 192.
38 Cited in L. Pine, *Nazi Family Policy, 1933–1945*, Oxford: Berg, 1997, 8.
39 P. Ginsborg, 'The Family Politics of the Great Dictators', in *Family Life in the Twentieth Century*, eds D. Kertzer and M. Barbagli, New Haven, CT, and London: Yale University Press, 2003, 175.
40 J. Chapoutot, *The Law of Blood: Thinking and Acting as a Nazi*, Cambridge, MA: Belknap Press of Harvard University Press, 2018, 19.
41 Wunderlich, *Propaganda des Terrors*, 79.
42 On this, see A. Dümling, 'The Target of Racial Purity: The Degenerate Music Exhibition in Düsseldorf, 1938', in *Art, Culture, and Media under the Third Reich*, ed. R. Etlin, Chicago: Chicago University Press, 2002, 43–72.
43 A parallel with the 1936 Soviet campaign against 'formalist' music such as Shostakovich's *Lady Macbeth of Mstensk* may be recognized. It raises the question of the derivative nature of some Nazi policies, which were ironically borrowed from their hated Bolshevik foes. Kerzhentsev, the instigator of the campaign against the opera, also preferred Rembrandt over experimental art, as we saw in the previous chapter.
44 Cited in E. Levi, *Music in the Third Reich*, London: Palgrave, 1994, 96.
45 M. Turda, *Modernism and Eugenics*, Basingstoke: Palgrave, 2010, 4.
46 M. Grant, *The Passing of the Great Race, or, the Racial Basis of European History*, New York: Charles Scribner's Sons, 1916.
47 Cited in Turda, *Modernism and Eugenics*, 80.
48 Cited in M. Burleigh and W. Wippermann, *The Racial State: Germany 1933–1945*, Cambridge: Cambridge University Press, 1991, 142.
49 S. Kühl, 'The Relationship between Eugenics and the So-Called "Euthanasia Action" in Nazi Germany: A Eugenically Motivated Peace Policy and the Killing of the Mentally Handicapped during the Second World War', in *Science in the Third Reich*, ed. M. Szöllösi-Janze, Oxford: Berg, 2001, 203–4.
50 On this, see G. Aly, P. Chroust and C. Pross, *Cleansing the Fatherland: Nazi Medicine and Racial Hygiene*, Baltimore, MD, and London: Johns Hopkins University Press, 1994, especially 22–98.

51 M. Burleigh, *Death and Deliverance: 'Euthanasia' in Germany 1900–1945*, Cambridge: Cambridge University Press, 1994, 4.
52 See H. Friedlander, 'The T4 Killers: Berlin, Lublin, San Saba', in *The Holocaust and History: The Known, the Unknown, the Disputed, and the Reexamined*, eds M. Berenbaum and A. Peck, Bloomington, IN: Indiana University Press, 1998, 243–52 on the motivations of the T4 practitioners.
53 A. Kallis, *Nazi Propaganda and the Second World War*, Basingstoke and New York: Palgrave Macmillan, 2008, 13.

Chapter 5

1 R. Bessel, *Nazism and War*, London: Weidenfeld & Nicolson, 2004, 49.
2 O. Bartov, 'Soldiers, Nazis and War in the Third Reich', in *The Third Reich*, ed. C. Leitz, Oxford: Blackwell, 1999, 149.
3 S. Wunderlich, *Propaganda des Terrors: Plakate des NS-Staates zwischen 1933 und 1945*, Berlin: Berlin Story Verlag, 2021, 155.
4 Ibid., 152.
5 O'Shaughnessy, *Selling Hitler*, 52.
6 Ibid., 56.
7 O'Shaughnessy, *Selling Hitler*, 73.
8 Wunderlich, *Propaganda des Terrors*, 158.
9 O'Shaughnessy, *Selling Hitler*, 102.
10 Herzstein, *The War that Hitler Won*, 209.
11 O'Shaughnessy, *Selling Hitler*, 73.
12 Ibid., 49.
13 Wunderlich, *Propaganda des Terrors*, 180.
14 Ibid., 180.
15 There was of course a Soviet version (most famously depicting a kerchiefed woman placing a finger against her lips imploring to '*ne boltai*', that is, 'do not blab' of 1941, made by Nina Vatolina and Nikolai Denisov) of this as well.
16 S. Luckert and S. Bachrach, *State of Deception: The Power of Nazi Propaganda*, Washington, DC: United States Holocaust Memorial Museum, 2009, 109.
17 Ibid., 116 and 117.
18 O'Shaughnessy, *Selling Hitler*, 83.
19 Kallis, *Nazi Propaganda and the Second World War*, 12.
20 Luckert and Bachrach, *State of Deception*, 160.
21 Ibid., 160–1.
22 O'Shaughnessy, *Selling Hitler*, 277.

Chapter 6

1. And leaving out the military skirmishes with Japan in Mongolia and Manchuria even before that.
2. The ethnic and socio-economic breakdown of the population there was rather more complex than the crude Soviet differentiation made it out to be. In the cities, for example, the population consisted in considerable numbers of cultural Germans (German speakers who were usually Lutheran in their religious beliefs) and predominantly Yiddish-speaking Jews besides Poles, Ukrainians or Belarusyn. Subsequent collectivization and expropriation of the local bourgeoisie involved massive deportations of alleged anti-Soviet elements (see Gross, *Revolution from Abroad*).
3. Poster image provided by Poster Plakat.com.
4. And, indeed, in 1938 and 1939 the Soviets had also been involved in a sort of defensive military conflict with Japan in the Far East.
5. Poster image provided by Poster Plakat.com; its print-run was 50,000, its price 1 ruble 50 kopecks.
6. Both poster images provided by Poster Plakat.com. The poster rendered on the coloured plate was printed in 14,000 copies, and sold at a price of 60 kopecks. The poster reproduced in image 6.2 had a price of 1 ruble 50 kopecks, with a much larger print-run, of 75,000 copies.
7. Poster image provided by Poster Plakat.com; no fewer than 200,000 copies were printed, each costing 1 ruble.
8. Poster image is provided by Poster Plakat.com. The size of the print-run is unclear, while its price was a fairly hefty 2 rubles and 50 kopecks.
9. Kowell, 'Agit-Plakat', 6. The best overview of them by far is Kort Zegers and Druick, eds, *Windows on the War*. This book renders examples from window posters of almost every week from late June 1941 until the summer of 1945 (see ibid., 165–374).
10. See for example Kort Zegers and Druick, eds, *Windows on the War*, 166.
11. Kowell, 'Agit-Plakat', 28.
12. See for women artists and women poster art in general the exhibition at the Tate Gallery's website, available at: https://www.tate.org.uk/tate-etc/issue-15-spring-2009/short-life-equal-women, accessed 16 June 2022.
13. Akinsha, 'Second Life', 2.
14. Akinsha, 'Second Life', 9. For the post-1953 period, see Kowell, 'Agit-Plakat'.
15. Kowell, 'Agit-Plakat', 4. In 1948, another decree mandated strict adherence to the socialist-realist standard in making posters (ibid., 38). More than two-thirds of posters were rejected by *Isskustvo* in 1952 (ibid., 58).
16. Kowell, 'Agit-Plakat', 4.
17. Kowell, 'Agit-Plakat', 16–17. Her timeline begins in 1956, but the Thaw almost immediately began after Stalin's death in March 1953.

18 Kowell, 'Agit-Plakat', 28–30.
19 For an analysis of Stalin's towering presence, especially in literature, see Leonid Maximenkov, 'An Analysis of the Genesis and Growth of Literary *Staliniana*', unpublished PhD thesis, McGill University, 1992.
20 Poster image provided by Poster Plakat.com.
21 There is of course an on-going scholarly debate about when the Cold War is supposed to have started, whether it was Molotov's icy meeting with Truman in April 1945 or James Byrnes's announcement of an operative a-bomb at Potsdam; at the time of Stalin's election speech or Churchill's speech in Fulton, Missouri, in 1946; with the announcement of the Truman Doctrine and the subsequent rejection of the Marshall Plan by the Soviet Bloc, or the Cominform's founding in 1947; or the Czechoslovak coup of early 1948 and the imposition of the Berlin Blockade (leaving aside George F. Kennan's analyses). For convenience sake, and since we find this most persuasive, we take the spring of 1948 as the point of no return in the break-up between East and West.
22 Poster image provided by Poster Plakat.com.
23 For an insightful and more comprehensive assessment of Soviet culture in the immediate postwar era, see Dobrenko, *Late Stalinism*.
24 See Boterbloem, *Life and Times*, 325–36; Yoram Gorlizki and Oleg Khlevniuk, *Cold Peace: Stalin and the Soviet Ruling Circle, 1945–1952*, Oxford: Oxford UP, 2004; Gennadi Kostyrchenko, *Out of the Red Shadows: Anti-Semitism in Stalin's Russia*, Amherst, NY: Prometheus Books, 1995; Nikolai Krementsov, *The Cure: A Story of Cancer and Politics from the Annals of the Cold War*, Chicago, IL: University of Chicago Press, 2002.
25 Erika Wolf, *Koretsky, The Soviet Photo Poster: 1930–1984*, New York: The New Press, 2012, 7, 9.
26 Perhaps unsurprisingly, Kemenov was an expert on the (conventional albeit skilful) work of the Wanderer Vasily Surikov (1848–1916). A consummate networker and sycophant, his main employment at the time was at the Institute of Art History of the Soviet Academy of Sciences, while, interestingly, he was concomitantly the 'scholarly secretary' (*uchenyi sekretar'*) of the committee that awarded the Stalin Prizes, two of which had been awarded in 1946 and 1949 to Koretskii.
27 Wolf, *Koretsky*, 10.
28 One might suggest that here again Stalin's admitted lack of expertise in visual arts played its role.
29 Edward Cohn, *The High Title of a Communist Postwar Party Discipline and the Values of the Soviet Regime*, DeKalb, IL: Northern Illinois University Press, 2015; Serhy Yekelchyk, *Stalin's Citizens: Everyday Politics in the Wake of Total War*, Oxford: Oxford University Press, 2014.
30 Apart from Dobrenko, *Late Stalinism*, see as well Marina Balina and Evgeny Dobrenko, eds, *Petrified Utopia: Happiness Soviet Style*, London: Anthem Press, 2011.
31 Poster image provided by Poster Plakat.com.

32 Poster image provided by Poster Plakat.com.
33 F. Abramov, *The New Life: A Day on a Collective Farm*, New York: Grove Press, 1963.

Conclusion

1 Jowett and O'Donnell, *Propaganda and Persuasion*, 6.
2 Herf, *Reactionary Modernism*.

BIBLIOGRAPHY

Abramov, F. *The New Life: A Day on a Collective Farm*. New York: Grove Press, 1963.
Ahlheim, H. *'Deutsche, kauft nicht bei Juden!': Antisemitismus und politischer Boykott in Deutschland 1924 bis 1935*. Göttingen: Wallstein Verlag, 2011.
Akinsha, Konstantin. 'The Second Life of Soviet Photomontage, 1935–1980s'. Unpublished PhD dissertation, University of Edinburgh, 2012.
Akinsha, Konstantin and Adam Jolles. 'Hand-Painted Propaganda: The Tass Poster Studio'. In *Windows on the War: Soviet Tass Posters at Home and Abroad*. Eds Peter Kort Zegers and Douglas Druick. New Haven, CT: Yale University Press, 2011: 26–51.
Aly, G., P. Chroust and C. Pross. *Cleansing the Fatherland: Nazi Medicine and Racial Hygiene*. Baltimore and London: Johns Hopkins University Press, 1994.
Anschläge: Politische Plakate in Deutschland 1900–1970. Ed. Friedrich Arnold. Langewiesche-Brandt, 1977.
Anschläge von 'Drüben': DDR-Plakate 1949–1990. Essen: Steidl Verlag, 2015.
Arendt, Hannah. *The Origins of Totalitarianism*. New York: Shocken, 1951.
Ayçoberry, Pierre. *The Social History of the Third Reich, 1933–1945*. New York: New Press, 1999.
Baranowski, Shelley. *Strength through Joy: Consumerism and Mass Tourism in the Third Reich*. Cambridge: Cambridge University Press, 2004.
Barkai, Avraham. *From Boycott to Annihilation: The Economic Struggle of German Jews, 1933–1943*. Waltham, MA: Brandeis University Press, 1989.
Barkhatova, Elena. '"Modern Icon," or "Tool for Mass Propaganda"?: Russian Debate on the Poster'. In *Defining Russian Graphic Arts: From Diaghilev to Stalin, 1898–1934*. Ed. Alla Rosenfeld. New Brunswick, NJ: Rutgers University Press, 1999: 132–65.
Bartov, Omer. 'Soldiers, Nazis and War in the Third Reich'. In *The Third Reich*. Ed. C. Leitz. Oxford: Blackwell, 1999.
Baudrillard, Jean. *Jean Baudrillard: Selected Writings*. Ed. Mark Poster. Cambridge: Polity Press, 2001.
Belodubrovskaya, Maria. *Not according to Plan: Filmmaking under Stalin*. Ithaca, NY: Cornell University Press, 2017.
Belodubrovskaya, Maria. 'Politically Incorrect: Filmmaking under Stalin and the Failure of Power'. Unpublished PhD dissertation, University of Wisconsin in Madison, WI, 2011.
Berkhoff, Karel. *Motherland in Danger: Soviet Propaganda during World War Two*. Cambridge, MA: Harvard University Press, 2012.
Bessel, Richard. *Nazism and War*. London: Weidenfeld & Nicolson, 2004.
Bird, Robert. 'The Functions of Poetry: Tass Windows and the Soviet Media System in Wartime'. In *Windows on the War: Soviet Tass Posters at Home and Abroad*.

Eds Peter Kort Zegers and Douglas Druick. New Haven, CT: Yale University Press, 2011: 92–103.

Bol'shaia tsenzura: Pisately i zhurnalisty v strane sovetov, 1917–1956. Ed. Leonid Maksimenkov. Moscow: Demokratiia-Materik, 2005.

Bonnell, Victoria. *Iconography of Power: Soviet Political Posters under Lenin and Stalin*. Berkeley and Los Angeles, CA: University of California Press, 1999.

Bonnell, Victoria. 'The Leader's Two Bodies: A Study in the Iconography of the "Vozhd"'. *Russian History* 1–4, 1996: 113–40.

Boterbloem, Kees. *Life and Death under Stalin: Kalinin Province, 1945–1953*. Montréal-Kingston: McGill-Queen's University Press, 1999.

Boterbloem, Kees. *The Life and Times of Andrei Zhdanov, 1896–1948*. Montréal-Kingston: McGill-Queen's University Press, 2004.

Brandenberger, David. *Propaganda State in Crisis*. New Haven, CT: Yale University Press, 2012.

Brooks, Jeffrey. *Thank You, Comrade Stalin! Soviet Public Culture from Revolution to Cold War*. Princeton, NJ: Princeton University Press, 2000.

Brown, Roland Elliott. *Godless Utopia: Soviet Anti-Religious Propaganda*. London: Fuel, 2019.

Brzezinski, Zbigniew and Carl J. Friedrich. *Totalitarian Dictatorship and Autocracy*. Cambridge, MA: Harvard University Press, 1956.

Bullock, Alan. *Hitler and Stalin: Parallel Lives*. New York: HarperCollins, 1991.

Burleigh, Michael. *Death and Deliverance: Euthanasia in Germany 1900–1945*. Cambridge: Cambridge University Press, 1994.

Bytwerk, Randall L. *Bending Spines: The Propagandas of Nazi Germany and the German Democratic Republic*. East Lansing, MI: Michigan State University Press, 2004.

Chapoutot, Johann. *The Law of Blood: Thinking and Acting as a Nazi*. Cambridge, MA, 2018.

Clark, Toby. *Art and Propaganda in the Twentieth Century: The Political Image in the Age of Mass Culture*. London: George Weidenfeld and Nicolson, 1997.

Cohn, Edward. *The High Title of a Communist Postwar Party Discipline and the Values of the Soviet Regime*. DeKalb, IL: Northern Illinois University Press, 2015.

Collingham, Lizzie. *The Taste of War: World War Two and the Battle for Food*. London: Allen Lane, 2011.

Davies, Norman. *Europe: A History*. Oxford: Oxford University Press, 1996.

Defining Russian Graphic Arts: From Diaghilev to Stalin, 1898–1934. Ed. Alla Rosenfeld. New Brunswick, NJ: Rutgers University Press, 1999.

Devlin, Judith. 'Visual Channels (1): Posters and Fine Art'. In *Media and Communication in the Soviet Union [1917–1953]: General Perspectives*. Eds Kirill Postoutenko, Alexey Tikhomirov and Dmitri Zakharine. Cham: PalgraveMacMillan, 2021: 21–35.

Dobrenko, E. 'The Disaster of Middlebrow Taste, or, Who "Invented" Socialist Realism'. In *Socialist Realism without Shores*. Eds Thomas Lahusen and Evgeny Dobrenko. Durham, NC: Duke University Press, 1997: 135–64.

Dobrenko, E. *Late Stalinism: The Aesthetics of Politics*. New Haven, CT: Yale University Press, 2020.

Druick, Douglas and Peter Kort Zegers. 'Introduction'. In *Windows on the War: Soviet Tass Posters at Home and Abroad*. Eds Peter Kort Zegers and Douglas Druick. New Haven, CT: Yale University Press, 2011: 12–23.

Dümling, A. 'The Target of Racial Purity: The Degenerate Music Exhibition in Düsseldorf, 1938'. In *Art, Culture, and Media under the Third Reich*. Ed. R. Etlin. Chicago, IL: Universityof Chicago Press, 2002.

Ellul, Jacques. *Propaganda: The Formation of Men's Attitudes*. New York: Knopf, 1968.

Engelstein, Laura. *The Keys to Happiness*. Ithaca, NY: Cornell University Press, 1994.

Eremin, Vasiliy. 'Gerasimov – pridvornyi zhivopisets Stalina'. Available at: https://historical-fact.livejournal.com/104599.html. Accessed 21 June 2022.

Evans, Richard. *The Coming of the Third Reich*. London: Penguin, 2004.

Fascism. Ed. Roger Griffin. Oxford: Oxford University Press, 1995.

Fellows, Erwin W. '"Propaganda": History of a Word'. *American Speech* 3, 1959: 182–9.

Figes, Orlando. *Natasha's Dance: A Cultural History of Russia*. New York: Picador, 2002.

Friedlander, Henry. 'The T4 Killers: Berlin, Lublin, San Saba'. In *The Holocaust and History: The Known, the Unknown, the Disputed, and the Reexamined*. Eds M. Berenbaum and A. Peck. Bloomington: Indiana University Press, 1998.

Für Frieden und Sozialismus: Plakate der Parteien und Massenorganisationen der DDR. Berlin: The Yorck Project, 2006.

Gellately, Robert. *Backing Hitler: Consent and Coercion in Nazi Germany*. Oxford: Oxford University Press, 2001.

Gellately, Robert. *Lenin, Stalin, and Hitler: The Age of Social Catastrophe*. New York: Vintage, 2007.

Gerhard, Gesine. *Nazi Hunger Politics: A History of Food in the Third Reich*. Lanham, MD: Rowman and Littlefield, 2015.

Gill, Graeme J. *Symbols and Legitimacy in Soviet Politics*. Cambridge: Cambridge University Press, 2011.

Ginsborg, Paul. 'The Family Politics of the Great Dictators'. In *Family Life in the Twentieth Century*. Eds D. Kertzer and M. Barbagli. New Haven, CT and London: Yale University Press, 2003.

Gleason, Abbott. *Totalitarianism: The Inner History of the Cold War*. Oxford: Oxford University Press, 1995.

Glotova, Olesia A. 'Andrei Aleksandrovich Zhdanov: Ideologicheskaia deiatel'nost v 1920–1940-e gg'. Unpublished *Kandidat* dissertation *Rossiiskaia akademiia gosudarstvennoi sluzhby* (Moscow), 2004.

Goebbels-Reden. Ed. Helmut Heiber. Band 1: 1932–1939. Düsseldorf: Droste Verlag, 1971.

Goldman, W. Z. and D. Filtzer. *Fortress Dark and Stern: The Soviet Home Front during World War II*. Oxford: Oxford University Press, 2021.

Golomstock, Igor. *Totalitarian Art*. New York: HarperCollins, 1990.

Gorlizki, Yoram and Oleg Khlevniuk. *Cold Peace: Stalin and the Soviet Ruling Circle. 1945–1952*. Oxford: Oxford University Press, 2004.

Gough, Maria. 'Back in the USSR: John Heartfield, Gustavs Klucis, and the Medium of Soviet Propaganda'. *New German Critique*, Summer 2009: 133–83.

Grant, Madison. *The Passing of the Great Race, or, the Racial Basis of European History*. New York: Charles Scribner's Sons, 1916.
Grieve, Victoria. *The Federal Art Project and the Creation of Middlebrow Culture*. Chicago, IL: University of Illinois Press, 2009.
Griffin, Roger. 'In the Shadow of the Megamachine: Reflections on Golomstock's "Iron Law of Totalitarian Art"'. *Third Text* 51, Summer 2000: 29–38.
Grishina, Ekaterina. 'The Graphic Arts at the Academy of Fine Arts: A Brief History, 1895–1935'. In *Defining Russian Graphic Arts: From Diaghilev to Stalin, 1898–1934*. Ed. Alla Rosenfeld. New Brunswick, NJ: Rutgers University Press, 1999: 39–44.
Gromov, Evgenii. *Stalin: Vlast' i iskusstvo*. Moscow: Respublika, 1998.
Gross, Jan T. *Revolution from Abroad: The Soviet Conquest of Poland's Western Ukraine and Western Belorussia*. Princeton, NJ: Princeton University Press, 2002.
Groys, Boris. *The Total Art of Stalinism: Avant-Garde, Aesthetic Dictatorship, and Beyond*. New York: Verso, 2011.
https://www.hagley.org/librarynews/research-national-association-manufacturers-and-visual-propaganda. Accessed 15 March 2024.
Hellbeck, Jochen. *Revolution on My Mind: Writing a Diary under Stalin*. Cambridge, MA: Harvard University Press, 2004.
Heller, Steven. *Iron Fists: Branding the 20th-Century Totalitarian State*. London: Phaidon, 2008.
Herf, Jeffrey. *Reactionary Modernism: Technology, Culture and Politics in Weimar and the Third Reich*. Cambridge: Cambridge University Press, 1984.
Hergé. *Tintin au Congo*. Le Petit Vingtième. June 1930–July 1931.
Hergé. *Tintin au pays des Soviets*. Le Petit Vingtième. January 1929–May 1930.
Herzstein, Robert. *The War That Hitler Won: The Most Infamous Propaganda Campaign in History*. London: Hamish Hamilton, 1978.
Hildermeier, Manfred. *Geschichte der Sowjetunion, 1917–1991. Entstehung und Niedergang des ersten sozialistischen Staates*. Munich: Beck, 1998.
Hitler, Adolf. *Mein Kampf*. London: Pimlico, 1992.
In the Service of the State: Nikolai Dolgorukov and the Art of Persuasion. Ed. Alla Rosenfeld. New York: Merrill C. Berman Collection, 2020.
Jowett, Garth and Victoria O' Donnell. *Propaganda and Persuasion*. London: Sage, 2019.
Kallis, Aristotle. *Nazi Propaganda and the Second World War*. Basingstoke and New York: Palgrave Macmillan, 2008.
Kenez, Peter. *The Birth of the Propaganda State: Soviet Methods of Mass Mobilization, 1917–1929*. Cambridge: Cambridge University Press, 1985.
Kenez, Peter. *Cinema and Soviet Society: From the Revolution to the Death of Stalin, 1917–1953*. London: I.B. Tauris, 2000.
Kennedy, Janet. 'The *World of Art* and Other Turn-of-the-Century Russian Art Journals, 1898–1910'. In *Defining Russian Graphic Arts: From Diaghilev to Stalin, 1898–1934*. Ed. Alla Rosenfeld. New Brunswick, NJ: Rutgers University Press, 1999: 63–78.
Kepley, Jr, Vance. '"Cinefication": Soviet Film Exhibition in the 1920s'. *Film History* 2, 1994: 262–77.
Kershaw, Ian. *The 'Hitler Myth': Image and Reality in the Third Reich*. Oxford: Oxford University Press, 1989.

King, David. *The Commissar Vanishes: The Falsification of Photographs and Art in Stalin's Russia*. New ed. London: Tate, 2014.
Koch, Hanns. *The Hitler Youth: Origins and Development, 1922–1945*. New York: Dorset Press, 1975.
Kopelev, Lev. *The Education of a True Believer*. New York: Harper & Row, 1980.
Kopelev, Lev. *No Jail for Thought*. London: Secker & Warburg, 1977.
Kopelev, Lev. *To Be Preserved Forever*. Philadelphia, PA: Lippincott, 1977.
Kostyrchenko, Gennadi. *Out of the Red Shadows: Anti-Semitism in Stalin's Russia*. Amherst, NY: Prometheus Books, 1995.
Kotkin, S. *Magnetic Mountain: Stalinism as a Civilization*. Los Angeles, CA: University of California Press, 1997.
Kowell, Masha. 'Agit-Plakat: The Destalinization of Soviet Posters (1956–1966)'. Unpublished PhD dissertation, University of Pennsylvania, 2013.
Krementsov, Nikolai. *The Cure: A Story of Cancer and Politics from the Annals of the Cold War*. Chicago, IL: University of Chicago Press, 2002.
Kühl, S. 'The Relationship between Eugenics and the So-Called "Euthanasia Action" in Nazi Germany: A Eugenically Motivated Peace Policy and the Killing of the Mentally Handicapped during the Second World War'. In *Science in the Third Reich*. Ed. M. Szöllösi-Janze. Oxford: Berg, 2001.
Lenin: Sobranie fotografii i kinokadrov. Eds Iu.A. Akhapkin et al. 2 vols. Third rev. ed. Moscow: Panorama, 1990.
Lenin, V.I. [N.] *What Is to Be Done?: Burning Questions of Our Movement*. 1902. Available at: https://www.marxists.org/archive/lenin/works/1901/witbd/iii.htm. Accessed 6 June 2022.
Lenoe, Matthew E. *Closer to the Masses: Stalinist Culture, Social Revolution, and Soviet Newspapers*. Cambridge, MA: Harvard University Press, 2004.
Levi, Erik. *Music in the Third Reich*. London: Macmillan, 1994.
Lincoln, W. Bruce. *Red Victory: A History of the Russian Civil War*. New York: Simon & Schuster, 1989.
Lodder, Christina. *Russian Constructivism*. New Haven, CT: Yale University Press, 1983.
Logan, Andy and Russel Maloney. 'Pravda (Talk of the Town)'. *The New Yorker*, 5 1944: 15.
Lovell, Stephen. *Russia in the Microphone Age: A History of Soviet Radio, 1919–1970*. Oxford: Oxford University Press, 2015.
Luckert, Steven and Susan Bachrach. *State of Deception: The Power of Nazi Propaganda*. Washington, DC: United States Holocaust Memorial Museum, 2009.
Maksimenkov, Leonid. *Sumbur vmesto muzyki: Stalinskaia kultur'naia revoliutsiia*. Moscow: Iuridicheskaia kniga, 1997.
Maksimenkov, Leonid. 'Vvedenie'. In *Bol'shaia tsenzura: Pisately i zhurnalisty v strane sovetov, 1917–1956*. Ed. Leonid Maksimenkov. Moscow: Demokratiia-Materik, 2005: 5–15.
Martin, Terry. *The Affirmative Action Empire: Nations and Nationalism in the Soviet Union, 1923–1939*. Ithaca, NY: Cornell University Press, 2001.
Maximenkov, Leonid. 'An Analysis of the Genesis and Growth of Literary *Staliniana*'. Unpublished PhD thesis, McGill University, 1992.
Nakhimovsky, Alice. 'Efimov, Boris Efimovich'. *The Yivo Encyclopedia of Jews in Eastern Europe*. Available at: https://yivoencyclopedia.org/article.aspx/Efimov_Boris_Efimovich. Accessed 20 July 2022.

'The National Association of Manufacturers and Visual Propaganda'. Available at: https://www.hagley.org/librarynews/research-national-association-manufacturers-and-visual-propaganda. Accessed 15 March 2024.

Nazi Propaganda: The Power and the Limitations. Ed. David Welch. London: Routledge Library Editions, 2015.

Norris, Stephen M. *A War of Images: Russian Popular Prints, Wartime Culture, and National Identity, 1812–1945*. DeKalb, IL: Northern Illinois University Press, 2006.

O'Shaughnessy, Nicholas. *Selling Hitler: Propaganda and the Nazi Brand*. London: Hurst and Company, 2021.

Overy, Richard. *The Dictators: Hitler's Germany, Stalin's Russia*. New York: Norton, 2006.

Petrified Utopia: Happiness Soviet Style. Eds Marina Balina and Evgeny Dobrenko. London: Anthem Press, 2011.

Petrone, Karin. *Life Has Become More Joyous, Comrades: Celebrations in the Time of Stalin*. Bloomington, IN: Indiana University Press, 2000.

Picturing Russian Empire. Eds Valerie Kivelson, Sergei Kozlov and Joan Neuberger. Oxford: Oxford University Press, 2024.

Pine, Lisa. *Hitler's 'National Community': Society and Culture in Nazi Germany*. London: Bloomsbury, 2017.

Pine, Lisa. *Nazi Family Policy, 1933–1945*. Oxford: Berg, 1997.

Pipes, Richard. *Russia under the Bolshevik Regime*. New York: Knopf, 1993.

Pisch, A. *The Personality Cult of Stalin in Soviet Posters: Archetypes, Inventions, and Fabrications*. Canberra: Australian University Press, 2016.

Politische Plakate. Ed. Hans Bohrmann. Dortmund: Harenberg, 1984.

Politische Plakate der Weimarer Republik 1918–1933. Darmstadt: Hessisches Landesmuseum, 1980.

Povartsov, Sergei N. 'Merezhkovskii, Uells i krasnaia zvezda'. *Voprosy Literatury* 6, 2002: 168–86.

Proctor, Robert. *Racial Hygiene: Medicine under the Nazis*. Cambridge, MA and London: Harvard University Press, 1988.

Ree, Erik van. 'Stalinist Ritual and Belief System: Reflections on "Political Religion"'. *Politics, Religion and Ideology* 2–3, 2016: 143–61.

Rees, Laurence. *Hitler and Stalin: The Tyrants and the Second World War*. London: Penguin, 2021.

Rolf, Malte. *Soviet Mass Festivals, 1917–1991*. Pittsburgh, PA: University of Pittsburgh Press, 2013.

Rosenfeld, A. 'The Search for National Identity in Turn-of-the-Century Russian Graphic Design'. In *Defining Russian Graphic Arts: From Diaghilev to Stalin, 1898–1934*. Ed. Alla Rosenfeld. New Brunswick, NJ: Rutgers University Press, 1999: 16–38.

Rosenfeld, A. 'The World of Art Group: Book and Poster Design'. In *Defining Russian Graphic Arts: From Diaghilev to Stalin, 1898–1934*. Ed. Alla Rosenfeld. New Brunswick, NJ: Rutgers University Press, 1999: 79–96.

Rosenfeld, A. 'The World Turned Upside Down: Russian Posters of the First World War, the Bolshevik Revolution, and the Civil War'. In *Defining Russian Graphic Arts: From Diaghilev to Stalin, 1898–1934*. Ed. Alla Rosenfeld. New Brunswick, NJ: Rutgers University Press, 1999: 121–32.

Ross, Corey. *Media and the Making of Modern Germany: Mass Communications, Society, and Politics from the Empire to the Third Reich*. Oxford: Oxford University Press, 2010.

Rueschemeyer, Marilyn, Igor Golomshtok and Janet Kennedy. *Soviet Emigre Artists: Life and Work in the USSR and the United States*. New York: M.E. Sharpe, 1985.

Scheijen, Sjeng. *Diaghilev: A Life*. Oxford: Oxford University Press, 2010.

Schockel, E. *Das politische Plakat: Eine psychologische Betrachtung*. Munich: Zentralverlag der NSDAP, 1938.

Selling Modernity: Advertising in Twentieth-Century Germany. Eds Pamela Swett et al. Durham, NC: Duke University Press, 2007.

Sen'kin, S. 'Lenin v kommune Vkhutemasa'. In *Bor'ba za realizm v izobrazitel'nom iskusstve 2-kh godov*. Eds V. Perel'man and I. Lebedev. Moscow: Sovetskii khodozhnik, 1962: 90–7.

Snyder, Timothy. *Bloodlands: Europe between Hitler and Stalin*. New York: Basic Books, 2010.

Stachura, Peter. *The German Youth Movement 1900–1945: An Interpretative and Documentary History*. London: Macmillan, 1981.

Stalinism and Nazism: Dictatorships in Comparison. Eds Ian Kershaw and Moshe Lewin. Cambridge: Cambridge University Press, 1997.

Stalinism and Nazism: History and Memory Compared. Ed. H. Rousso. Lincoln, NE: University of Nebraska Press, 2004.

Stites, Richard. *Serfdom, Society, and the Arts in Imperial Russia: The Pleasure and the Power*. New Haven, CT: Yale University Press, 2005.

Sudjic, Deyan. *Stalin's Architect: Power and Survival in Moscow*. London: Thames & Hudson, 2022.

Swett, Pamela. *Selling under the Swastika: Advertising and Commercial Culture in Nazi Germany*. Stanford, CA: Stanford University Press, 2013.

Taylor, Richard. *Film Propaganda: Soviet Russia and Nazi Germany*. Second rev. ed. London: I.B. Tauris, 1998.

Timpe, Julia. *Nazi-Organized Recreation and Entertainment in the Third Reich*. London: Palgrave Macmillan, 2017.

Toland, K. *Constructing Revolution: Soviet Propaganda Posters, 1917–1947*. Brunswick, ME: Bowdoin College Museum of Art, 2021.

Treitel, Corinne. *Eating Nature in Modern Germany: Food, Agriculture and Environment, c. 1870–2000*. Cambridge: Cambridge University Press, 2017.

Trostel, Werner. *Schlagwort Brot: Politische Plakate des 20. Jahrhunderts*. Ulm: Vater und Sohn Eiselen Stiftung, 1997.

Turda, Marius. *Modernism and Eugenics*. Basingstoke: Palgrave Macmillan, 2010.

Vashik, K. and N. Baburina. *Real'nost utopii: Iskusstvo russkogo plakata xx veka*. Moscow: Progress-Traditsiia, 2004.

Vasil'eva, K. and L. Lobov. *Peredelkino, skazanie o pisatel'skom gorodke*. Moscow: Bosplen, 2012.

Waschik, K. and N. I. Baburina. *Werben für die Utopie: russische Plakatkunst des 20. Jahrhunderts*. Bietigheim-Bissingen: Tertium, 2003.

Weber, Max. *Economy and Society*. Eds Guenther Roth and Claus Wittich. Berkeley. CA: University of California Press, 1978.

Welch, David. 'Nazi Propaganda and the *Volksgemeinschaft*: Constructing a People's Community'. *Journal of Contemporary History* 2, 2004: 213–38.

Welch, David. 'Propaganda and Indoctrination in the Third Reich: Success or Failure?' *European History Quarterly* 4, 1987: 403–22.
Welch, David. *The Third Reich: Politics and Propaganda*. London and New York: Routledge, 1993.
White, S. *The Bolshevik Poster*. New Haven, CT: Yale University Press, 1988.
Wiesen, S. Jonathan. *Creating the Nazi Marketplace: Commerce and Consumption in the Third Reich*. Cambridge: Cambridge University Press, 2010.
Windows on the War: Soviet Tass Posters at Home and Abroad. Eds Peter Kort Zegers and Douglas Druick. New Haven, CT: Yale University Press, 2011.
Wistrich, Robert. *Weekend in Munich: Art, Propaganda and Terror in the Third Reich*. London: Pavilion, 1995.
Witamwas, Birgit. *Geklebte NS-Propaganda: Verführung und Manipulation durch das Plakat*. Munich: De Gruyter, 2016.
Wolf, Erika. *Koretsky, the Soviet Photo Poster: 1930–1984*. New York: The New Press, 2012.
Wolf, Erika. 'When Photographs Speak, to Whom Do They Talk? The Origins and Audience of *SSSR na stroike* (*USSR in Construction*)'. *Left History* 6.2, 1999: 53–82.
Wunderlich, Sylke. *Propaganda des Terrors: Plakate des NS-Staates zwischen 1933 und 1945 – Propaganda Posters of the Nazi Terror Regime*. Berlin: Berlin Story Verlag, 2020.
Yankovskaya, Galina and Rebecca Mitchell. 'The Economic Dimensions of Art in the Stalinist Era: Artists' Cooperatives in the Grip of Ideology and the Plan'. *Slavic Review* 4, 2006: 769–91.
Yekelchyk, Serhy. *Stalin's Citizens: Everyday Politics in the Wake of Total War*. Oxford: Oxford University Press, 2014.
Zimmermann, Clemens. 'From Propaganda to Modernization: Media Policy and Media Audiences under National Socialism'. *German History* 3, 2006: 431–54.

INDEX

Abramov, Fyodor 133
'*Adolf Hitler ist der Sieg!*' ('Adolf Hitler is Victory!') 10, 95, 106, 137
aesthetics 61
   Bolshevik 7
   proletarian vanguard 9
   of Soviet posters 9, 19–23, 47
Agit-Plakat movement 126, 130, 132–3
agitprop 11, 15–16, 23–5, 49, 59, 117, 119, 124
   *apparatchik*s 56
agriculture, poster 55–6, 75, 133
Albrecht, Felix 41
'*Alle Kraft gespannt! Totaler Krieg – Kürzester Krieg!*' ('All Power Ahead! Total War – Shortest War!') 107
'All Germany listens to the *Führer* with the People's Radio' 86
Allied bombings 102–3, 114
All Life Is a Struggle 92
All-(Soviet) Union poster exhibition, Moscow 5, 62
Anschluß (union) 81, 99
anti-Semitic posters 10, 31, 43, 73, 90, 104, 157 n.79
   during wartime period 110–14
anti-Semitism 31, 129, 147 n.12
   and eugenics 89–93
Anton, Ottomar 98
Apsitis, Aleksandrs 49–50
'*Arbeiter der Stirn der Faust Wählt den Frontsoldaten Hitler!*' ('Workers of the Mind, of the Fist: Vote for Front Soldier: Hitler!') 8, 40

'*Arbeit Freiheit und Brot!*' ('Work, Freedom and Bread!') 41
Artists' Association of Revolutionary Russia (*AKhRR*) 55–6
Aryanization of the economy 90
'*Auch Du*' ('You too') 98
'*Auch Du gehörst dem Führer*' ('You too, belong to the *Führer*') 77
'*Auch Du zur Leibstandarte-SS Adolf Hitler*' ('You too can be one of Adolf Hitler's Personal Bodyguards') 98
Ausmerze (eradication) 88
autarky 72, 75–6, 137
Axster-Heudtlass, Maria von 107
Axster-Heudtlass, Werner von 83, 107

Baiuskin, V. S. 127
Bakst, Leon 22
Ballets Russes 7, 22
Battle of Berlin 102, 103
Battle of Kursk 101, 119
Battle of Moscow 119
Battle of Stalingrad 54, 101, 119
Bauer, Friedrich Franz 81
Bauer, Karl Ferdinand 81
'Beat the Whites with the Red Wedge' 22
'Beautiful Workplaces' 85
Belarussian (Belarusyns) and Ukrainian 66, 117–19
Belgium 50
Belopol'skii, Boris Naumovich 128
Berlin Blockade 162 n.21
Berlin Olympic Games, poster 80
Bespalov, Nikolai N. 130

'Beware of Typhus – Avoid Jews' 112
The Birth of a Nation 24
black listening 109
Blank, Richard 109–10
Blut und Boden (Blood and Soil) 34, 75, 141
Bogoroditsa (Mother of God) 51
Bol'shakov, I. G. 16
Bolsheviks (Communists) 11–13, 15–16, 20, 106
  aesthetics 7
  free-market economy 20
  propaganda 48
  and Soviet posters 23–7, 47–8
Bolshevism 14–15, 23, 106
Book of Revelation, Whore of Babylon 50
Brik, Lilya 49
Briullov, Karl 21
Bubnov, Andrei 154 n.48
Budyonny, S. M. 61, 138
Bund deutscher Mädel (BDM) 77–9
  '*Bund Deutscher Mädel in der Hitler Jugend*' ('League of German Girls in the Hitler Youth') 9, 72, 79, 137
  Reichssporttag (National Sport Day) 79
  Sport Day of the BDM 79
Byrnes, James 162 n.21

Cahill, Holger 4
Campbell-Ewald Company 4
captioned cartoons 49
Caxton, William 2
Central Committee of the Communist Party 17, 59, 61–2, 128, 155 n.48
Chagall, Marc 21
Chamberlain, Neville 99
charismatic authority 74, 158 n.13
Cheremnykh, Mikhail 49–50, 61, 125, 153 n.15
Chéret, Jules 2
Christianity 16
Churchill 103, 162 n.21
cinematography 19

civil war 8, 13–15, 21, 24, 48–50, 57, 61, 125, 127, 135–6
  and famine 52
  poster art 55
Cold War 23, 128, 162 n.21
colour lithograph posters 2
colour picture poster 2
communications 2–3, 47–8
  interpenetration of conflict with 106
  mass 2–3, 10–11, 45, 57, 71, 86
Constructivists 2, 19, 65, 126, 138
Council of Trent (1545–63) 143 n.2
cultural life, Nazi posters and 73, 88–9
cultural revolution 58
cultural-technological centre (agronomical corner) 55

Dada artists 22
'*Darum Deine Stimme dem Führer!*' ('Thus, Your Vote for the Leader!') 74
'*Das Volk wählt Liste 1 – Nationalsozialisten*' ('The People Vote for List 1 – National Socialists') 43
Degenerate Art Exhibition 73, 88
Degenerate Art poster 89
Degenerate Music Exhibition 73, 89
Denikin, Anton 1, 146 n.9
Deni, Victor 60–1, 121–3
'*Der Ewige Jude*' ('The Eternal Jew') 10, 73, 90, 111–12
'*Der Führerversprach: Motorisierung Deutschlands*' 83–4
'*Der ist Schuld am Kriege!*' ('He is Responsible for the War!') 112–13
'*Der Schlag muss sitzen!*' ('The Blow must Hit Home!') 43
Der Stürmer 43, 90, 115
'*Deutsche Frauen Denkt an Eure Kinder*' ('German Women Think of your Children') 43
Deutsches Jungvolk (DJ) 77
Die Rothschilds (*The Rothschilds*) 111
'Dig for Victory' 4
Diktat 96

Dlugach, Mikhail 61
Dneprostroi 60, 62
Dolgorukov, Nikolai 61
Dovzhenko, Oleksandr 147 n.19
Dzhambul 67

Efimov, Boris 61, 124, 126, 132, 134, 141, 147 n.12, 149 n.38, 156 n.58, 157 n.72, 157 n.78
'*Ein Kampf, Ein Sieg!*' ('One Struggle, One Victory!') 105
Eintopf (one-pot dish) 9, 72, 76, 137
'*Ein Volk, Ein Reich, Ein Führer*' ('One People, One Empire, One Leader') 9, 72–4, 99, 136
Eisenstein, Sergei 16, 24, 55
   typage and montage 56
election posters 8, 39, 42–3, 53
'*Elend u. Hunger*' ('Misery and Hunger') 39
'The Endless Steppe Woke Up from Its Dream, and Happiness Is Brought to Us by the Spring of Communism!' 67
Engelhard, Wilhelm Jakob 43
Engels, Friedrich 65, 127
enlightenment 61, 71, 154 n.48
Entartete Kunst (degenerate art) 88–9
equality 50, 53–4, 65–6, 126, 138–9
Ersatz 19
Eschle, Max 108
ethnic equality 53, 66, 139
ethnic harmony 66
euthanasia campaign 73, 92–3
events posters 80–2
   Bayreuth Festival 82
   Gau (regional) Days and Festivals 81
   Memorial Day of the Movement 81
   Olympic Games 80–1
   Party Rally 81
   Police and Day of the Armed Forces 81
Ezhov, Nikolai 16

Fall, Leo 89
famine, civil war and 14, 52–3, 55, 67

'Female Proletarians Toward New Triumphs! For Technology, Culture, For a New Existence!' 52–3
filmmaking 16, 92
First World War 1–3, 10, 12, 19, 21, 37, 40, 48, 96, 100, 101, 111, 113, 153 n.15
Fischer, Eugen 92
Five Year Plans 59–61, 63, 127–8, 130, 155 n.49
Flagg, James Montgomery 3
foreign policy 9, 95
   SA, SS and *Wehrmacht* 95–8
   total war 105–10
   and war 93
formalism 27, 63, 129, 154 n.32
'For Peace in the Entire World!' 17
'Forward toward Communism!' 17
Franke, Heinz 40
'*Frau im Luftschutz!*' ('Women in air-raid protection!') 108
'*Freiheit, Recht und Brot unserer Volk*' ('Freedom, Justice and Bread for our *Volk*') 107
French Revolution 22
Frick, Wilhelm 87
'Friendship of the Peoples' (*Druzhba Narodov*) 65–9, 119, 139
Fritzsche, Hans 115
'*Frontstadt Frankfurt wird gehalten!*' ('Front City Frankfurt will be held!') 114
Führer, cult of 33, 74, 77, 99, 106, 137
Futurism 22–3, 150 n.57

Gau (regional) Days and Festivals 81
Gauleiter (regional leader) 43, 45, 102
'*Gegen Hunger und Verzweiflung! Wählt Hitler!*' ('Against Hunger and Despair! Vote Hitler!') 40
gender equality 52–4, 126, 139
Gerasimov, Aleksandr Mikhailovich 130, 156 n.55
German Communist Party (KPD) 36, 40, 63, 82
German Democratic Republic 7–8
German Propaganda Studio (DPA) 101

German Socialist Party (SPD) 36, 40, 82
'Germany's Future and Our Movement' 36
Gitsevich, Vera 63
Glavlit 62, 130
Gleichschaltung 35, 48, 77
Glory to the Mother Heroine 131–2
Goebbels, Joseph 30–2, 44–5, 71, 74–5, 99–103, 106, 115, 136, 141, 149 n.38
   dazzling campaign poster 30
   twelve-year propaganda campaign 141
Goering, Hermann 102
Golden Age 21, 149 n.44
Goncharova, Natalia 22
Gordon, M. A. 124
Gorky, Maksim 59, 68
gramophones 18
Grant, Madison 91
Great Depression 4
Great German Art Exhibition 88–9
Great Patriotic War 10, 25, 121, 123–4, 126–7, 136, 138
Great Terror (1937–8) 14, 17, 53, 61, 130, 132, 135
   collectivization and 61, 134
   posters in 63–5
Great Turn 55, 135, 137
   posters after 56–63
'Greetings to the Great Stalin' 66
Griffith, D. W. 24
'The Growth of Soviet Agriculture after a Decade' 55
Guevara, Che 1
GULag (*Glavnoe Upravlenie Lagerei*) 14
Gulag Archipelago 14

Hague Convention on Land Warfare (1907) 100
'Hail to the Great Stalin!' 17
Hanich, Bruno 112
Harlan, Veit 111
'*Hass und Vernichtung unserer Feinden*' ('Hate and Destruction of our Enemies') 107

'Having All Rights, Soviet Women Vote for a Socialist Motherland, for a Happy Life!' 53–4
Hearst, W. R. 24
Heartfield, John 17, 27, 126
Hergé, *Tintin au Congo* 50
Herrenvolk (master race) 35
High Stalinism 128
'*Hilf auch Du mit!*' ('You help out too!') 108
Himmler, Heinrich 97–8
Hindemith 89
'*Hinter den Feindmächten: der Jude*' ('Behind the Enemy Powers: the Jew') 112
Hippler, Fritz 111
historical materialism 12
historiographical survey 6–8
Hitler, Adolf 2, 15, 25, 31–2, 35–6, 39, 43–5, 71, 73, 81–2, 86, 95–6, 99, 105, 115, 119, 136, 149 n.38
   Mein Kampf 8, 29, 38
   national unity and cult of 73–6
   poster 40–1
'*Hitler baut auf, helft mit. Kauft Deutsche Ware*' ('Hitler is building. Help out. Buy German goods') 75
'*Hitler baut auf – Wählt Liste 1*' ('Hitler is making progress – Vote for List 1') 43
Hitler myth 74, 114, 158 n.11
'Hitler: Our Last Hope' 8
Hitler Youth (*Hitler Jugend, HJ*) 9, 72, 76–7, 98, 107, 114, 137
'Hitler Youth: Germany's Future' 78
'Hoarder, you should be ashamed of yourself!' 108
Hoffmann, Heinrich 40
Hogarth, William 19
Hohlwein, Ludwig 43, 79–80, 98, 108
Holocaust 120

Impressionism 21
'*In der Staub mit allen Feinden Grossdeutschlands*' ('Into the Dust with all Enemies of Greater Germany!') 9, 95, 100, 137

industrialization 13, 57–8, 62
Industrial Revolution 140
International Women's Day, poster 132–3
Internatsional 50
Italy 2
　Futurist movement 7, 23
'It Is Our Sacred Obligation to Extend a Helping Hand to the Fraternal Peoples of Western Ukraine and Western Belarus' 118–19
Ivanov, S. I., poster 150 n.63
Ivanov, Viktor S. 17–18, 118–19
Ivan the Terrible 16

'*Ja! Führer wir folgen Dir!*' ('Yes! Führer, we will follow you!') 74
'*Jeder Volksgenosse Rundfunkhörer*' ('Every National Comrade a Radio Listener') 85
Jewish-British plutocracy 111
Jews 95, 110–11, 113, 115, 137
Judas-Trotsky 63
Judeo-Bolshevik enemy 35
Judeo-Bolsheviks 88, 106
Jud Süss (*Jew Süss*) 90, 111
'*Jugend dient dem Führer: Alle zehnjährigen in die HJ*' ('Youth serves the *Führer*: All ten-year-olds in the *HJ*') 77–8
Jungmädelschaft (JM) 77

Kampfgemeinschaft (fighting community) 97
Kandinsky, Vasilii 21
'*Kannst Du das verantworten?*' ('Do you want to be responsible for this?') 108
Karanchentsov, Pyotr Ia. 53–4
Kazak culture 67
'Keep Mum She's Not So Dumb! Careless Talk Costs Lives' 4
Kerzhentsev, Platon 49, 63, 130, 153 n.11, 157 n.78, 159 n.43
Khrapchenko, M. B. 130
Khrushchev, Nikita 130, 134, 141, 146 n.6
　cult of personality 128

Khudsovet 62
'Kill him! He Killed Your Loved Ones, Burned Your House Down, Destroyed Your Workplace!' 120
kinderreich (rich in children) 87
Kirov, Sergei 62–3
Kitchener, Horatio 1, 3
Klein, Richard 80–1, 89
Klinch, Boris G. 59, 154 n.47
Klotz 79
Klutsis, Gustav Gustavovich 17, 27, 56, 59–65, 68, 126, 141, 148 n.29, 154 n.42
Knoblok, Boris 63
Kokorekin, Aleksei A. 120
Kopelev, Lev 121, 146 n.7
Koretskii, Viktor Borisovich 27, 61, 63, 124, 129–30, 141, 156 n.68
Kozlinskii, Vladimir I. 59, 155 n.47
Kraft durch Freude/KdF (Strength through Joy) organization 9, 72, 82–3, 137
　joy production 85
　propaganda poster for 84
　Schönheit der Arbeit ('Beauty of Labour') 85
　travel poster 83
Krokodil 24, 126
kulaks 53, 60, 68, 139
Kulik, Marshal Grigorii 129
Kutuzov, Marshal 126
Kuznetsov, Nikolai 129
KWHW (*Kriegswinterhilfswerk*, War Winter Relief Agency) 76

land of the soviets 16
Law on the Hitler Youth 77
League of German Girls. *See Bund deutscher Mädel* (BDM)
Lebedev, Polikarp I. 130
Le Bon, Gustave 35
　The Crowd: A Study of the Popular Mind 32
Leete, Alfred 3
Leningrad 119–20, 125
Leningrad Affair 129

Lenin, V. I. N. 11–13, 16, 23–4, 65, 128
  Mausoleum 66
  What Is to Be Done? 11
Lenz, Fritz 92
Ley, Robert 107
Lincoln, Bruce 153 n.9
Lissitzky, El 22
lithographic presses/posters 2, 19, 21, 47
'Long Live the Brotherly Union and Great Friendship of the USSR Peoples!' 66
'Long Live the Great, Invincible Banner of Marx, Engels, Lenin, and Stalin! Long Live Leninism!' 64
lubki 20–2, 47–9, 138
Luftwaffe 102

Machtergreifung (seizure of power) 29, 36, 74, 82
Machtübernahme 63
macro-historical development 3
Maksimenkov, Leonid 56–7, 67, 155 n.44
Malevich, Kazimir 20–2, 48
Maliutin, Ivan 49
Marize-Krasnokutskaia, Mariia Alekseevna 66–7
Marshall Plan 162 n.21
Marxism-Leninism 9, 59, 136
Marx, Karl 11, 13, 65, 127
mass communication 2–3, 10–11, 57, 71
  modern methods and 45
mass media 3, 10, 23–4, 57
mass politics 140
Matejko, Theo 103
Mayakovsky, Vladimir 20, 22–3, 48–9, 55–6, 126–7, 141, 155 n.47
Memorial Day of the Movement 81
Mensheviks 12
Mikoyan, Anastas 129
Minin, Kuz'ma 124, 126, 139
Minzlaff, Christian 85
Mir Isskustva 7, 21
Mjölnir (Hans Schweitzer) 40–1, 89–90, 100, 106–7, 109, 112, 115

Molotov, Vyacheslav 129, 162 n.21
Moor, Dmitrii 1, 20, 50, 54, 60–2, 64–5
  'Did You Sign up as a Volunteer?' 1
Motto of the NSDAP 107
Moulin Rouge, posters 19

Nagel, Gunther 75
National Air Raid Protection League 108
National Boycott of Jewish Businesses 75
National Socialism 33, 35, 39, 41, 71–2, 75, 107
National Socialist German Workers' Party (NSDAP) 8, 29, 31, 33–4, 36, 38–41, 43–4, 71–3, 80–1, 87, 96, 115, 136
National Socialist ideology 71, 87
Nazi Germany 1, 4, 15, 48, 105, 107, 110, 120, 139, 142
Nazi posters 4, 6, 8, 29, 31, 136–7, 139, 141
  before 1933 36–45
  aesthetic language of 72
  anti-Semitism and eugenics 89–93
  artists 71, 115
  and cultural life 88–9
  early Nazi poster 37
  election posters 39, 42–3
  events posters 80–2
  family 87–8, 140
  foreign policy (*see* foreign policy)
  mass politics 140–1
  national community (*see* *Volksgemeinschaft* (national community))
  people's car and radio 82–7
  propaganda 7–8, 45, 71–3, 87, 93, 99, 103, 116, 137, 158 n.11
    history and historiography 29–36
    as political advertising 31
  typography 35
  wartime 10, 95, 137
  youth 76–80
Nazism/Nazis 6, 30–6, 38–9, 44, 60, 62, 73, 79, 85, 89, 93, 100–1, 110
  genocidal policy 112

posters against the 117–21
reactionary modernism 141
'*Ne Boltai!*' ('Do not Blab!') 132
Neuner, Hein 77–8
Nevsky, Alexander 16, 126
New Economic Policy (NEP) 8, 14, 55, 57, 135
The New Life 132–4
Non-Aggression Pact (Molotov-Ribbentrop Pact) 117
Novikov, Aleksandr 129
'Nowhere Can the Monster Hide! It Will Receive its Just Desserts!' 122
Nuremberg Rallies 32, 80–1, 96

October Revolution 124, 130
Olympia: Fest der Völker (Olympia: Festival of Nations) 80
Olympic Games, poster 80
Operation Bagration 120
Operation Barbarossa 119
ORPP 62
Orthodox Church 50
Orwell, George 121
    Animal Farm 121
    Goldstein 157 n.79
    Nineteen-Eighty Four 26, 121, 157 n.79
'Our Forces Are Countless!' 123–4
'Out with the Jewish Haggling Mind' 89

Party's Central Propaganda Office 72
'Passionate Greetings to Our Leader and Teacher the Great Stalin!' 64
patriotism 126, 153 n.9
    patriotic posters 20, 48
people-beast (*narod-zver*) 49
persuasion 3, 30, 32, 37
Peter the Great 134
Petzold, Willy 80
photographs in posters 16–17, 19, 22, 77, 129, 131, 148 n.20
photomontage technique 2, 16–17, 21–2, 27, 36, 56, 60–1, 63–4, 68, 74, 81, 123, 126, 129, 138, 155 n.49
photo-story 17, 148 n.25

Pointillism 21
Police and Day of the Armed Forces 81
political cartoons 20, 24
political poster 5, 13, 20–1, 23, 48, 72, 129, 132, 136
Popova, Liubov 22
'*Populations abandonnées, faites confiance au soldat allemand*' ('Abandoned populations, place your trust in German soldiers') 103, 104
poster artists 47, 60, 65, 71, 115, 121, 123–4, 129, 133
poster-child 60
'The Poster in the Service of the Five Year Plan' 62
poster-makers 9–10, 15, 22, 49, 61, 66, 68, 117, 123, 127, 129–30, 133, 136, 138, 141, 154 n.32
posters 1–2, 4–5, 45, 135, 140. *See also specific posters*
    anti-Semitic 10, 31, 43, 73, 90, 104, 110–14, 157 n.79
    as propaganda media 9, 29, 106
    workers, soldiers and women 142
postwar posters 15, 67, 121, 127
    character of 127–32
    cultural crackdown 129
postwar reconstruction 60, 135
Pozharskii, Dmitrii 124, 126, 139
Pravda 17, 59, 128–9
propaganda 2–4, 16, 47, 71, 75, 103, 142. *See also* Nazi posters, propaganda
    agitation and 11, 24
    and education 25
    visual 4–5, 20, 42
The Protocols of the Elders of Zion 113
public spaces 31, 115–16, 141–2
Pudovkin, Vsevolod 16
Pulitzer, Joseph 24
Putin, Vladimir 132

radio broadcasting 18, 19, 85–6, 109
Rally of Greater Germany 81
'The Rally of Labour' 81
Red Army 1, 13–14, 22, 101, 114, 121, 127, 153 n.6

Rehak, Bruno 90, 111
Reich 11, 16
'*Reichsberufs-Wettkampf der deutschen Jugend*' ('Reich Vocational Competition for German Youth') 79
Reichskulturkammer (RKK) 31
Reichstag 38
Reiter, Hans 76
Rembrandt 63, 159 n.43
Repin, Ilya 63
Riefenstahl, Leni 16, 80
Rodchenko, Aleksandr 17, 55–6, 61, 138, 148 n.25
Roehm, Ernst 97
Roerich, Nicholas 21
Romanov, Mikhail 124
Roosevelt, Franklin Delano 103
Rosenfeld, Alla 7, 21, 55, 62
Rosta 10, 20, 49, 55, 125–7, 153 n.11, 155 n.47
Rozanova, Olga 22
Rüdin, Ernst 92
Rueschemeyer, Marilyn 61
Rupprecht, Philipp 43, 115
Russia 50
    capitalism's weakest link 12
    déclassé petit-bourgeoisie and *lumpenproletariat* 56
    Imperial posters 150 n.55
    October coup (1917) 5, 9, 49
Russian Civil War 1, 14, 17, 47–8, 147 n.9, 153 n.15
Russian Civil War posters 157 n.79
Russian Marxist party 12
Russian Socialist Federative Socialist Republic (RSFSR) 50

Schafft uns Jugendherbergen ('Build us Youth Hostels') 79
Schirach, Baldur von 77
'*Schluss jetzt!*' ('Enough is enough!') 41
Schlüter, Horst 90
Schockel, Erwin, *Das politische Plakat* 72
Schoenberg 89
'*Schönheit der Arbeit*' ('Beauty of Labour') 85
Schreck, Julius 98

Schutzstaffel (SS) 34, 71, 95, 99
    recruitment poster in the Netherlands 105
    SA and 96–8
Schweitzer, Hans. *See* Mjölnir (Hans Schweitzer)
Schwitters, Kurt 68
Second World War 1, 3, 9–11, 13–14, 17–18, 22, 25, 27, 48, 53–4, 95, 97, 111, 132–3, 137, 139
    Blitzkrieg successes 99
    Soviet posters in 117, 135
        against the Nazis 117–21
        postwar poster 127–32
        rallying behind the flag 121–7
    Third *Reich* and 99–102
Semar, Sepp 98
Sen'kin, Sergei 64–5
Short Course of the History of the All-Union Communist Party (Bolsheviks) 128
Shostakovich, Dmitrii 49, 63
    Lady Macbeth of Mtsensk 49, 157 n.78, 159 n.43
Shpir, A. F. 127
'*Sieg oder Bolschewismus*' ('Victory or Bolshevism') 106
'*Sieg über Versailles*' ('Victory over Versailles') 99
Sins of the Father 92
Slavs 66, 120
Soborova, Aleksandra S. 51–2
socialist realism 9, 56, 61, 156 n.55
socialist transformation 57
Solovyov, Mikhail Mikhailovich 132–3
Soviet-Finnish War 119
Soviet intelligentsia 128
Soviet *lubok* 56
Soviet photo-novella 139
Soviet posters 4–11, 59–60, 137–9, 141–2
    aesthetics 19–23, 47
    after Stalin 132–4
    after the Great Turn 56–63
    birth of 47–51
    Bolsheviks and 23–7, 47–8
    colour 22
    culture 7, 10, 20, 147 n.10

experimentation with form (1920s) 51–6
farmers 140
friendship of the peoples 65–9
Great Patriotic War 10, 121, 123, 136
    in the Great Terror 63–5
    ideology 11–15, 140
    Orthodox tradition in 47
    political poster art 136
    in Russian language 5, 7
    in Second World War 117
        against the Nazis 117–21
        postwar poster 127–32
        rallying behind the flag 121–7
    technology 15–19
    Western artistic tradition 47
'Soviet Radio Earnestly Serves the Cause of Peace!' 17
Soviet Union 1, 5, 20, 23, 37, 50, 59, 62–3, 65–7, 93, 100, 106, 113, 135, 139–40
    capitalists 59–60
    economic transformation 57, 63
    human rights and freedoms 65
    nationalities and Friendship of the Peoples 66
    Nazi invasion of 117
    Poland and the 117–18
    radiofication 130
Spain 2
Spanish-American War 24
Speer, Albert 81, 108
Spießbürger 57
Spindel 77
Spring, Blasius 96
SS Einsatzgruppen 112
Stalin 2, 6, 9, 16–17, 23, 26–7, 37, 49, 54, 57, 60–1, 63, 65, 67, 119, 127–9, 136, 138, 151 n.7, 155 n.48, 156 n.55, 157 n.72, 162 n.19
    autocracy 15, 25, 59
    Great Turn 55, 58
    photomontaged poster 154 n.49
    poster after 132–4
Stalinism 6, 56, 148 n.21
State Publishing House of Art (IZOGIZ) 61–2, 127
sterilization 9, 73, 90–2

stormtroopers (*Sturmabteilung, SA*) 44, 71, 75, 81, 95–8, 105
Strasser, Gregor 36
Straus, Oscar 89
Stravinsky 89
Streicher, Julius 43, 115
'*Studenten: Seit Propagandisten des Führers*' ('Students: Be Propagandists for the Leader') 43
'Study the Great Path of the Party of Lenin-Stalin!' 128
Sturm-und-Drang 14
Style Moderne period 21
'Sun and Green for All Workers' 85
Surikov, Vasily 63, 162 n.26
Suvorov, Aleksandr 126

TASS poster windows 10, 53, 125–6
Tatlin, Vladimir 22
Thaw 126
themes, posters 8, 10, 13, 57, 62, 68, 95, 137, 141
Third *Reich* 7–8, 33–5, 72, 80, 82, 87, 89, 93, 107, 115–16, 135
    and Second World War 99–103
    USSR and 100
Tiurkin, Pyotr 154 n.48
Toidze, Irakli Moisevich 1, 150 n.67
    poster 4, 10, 126, 139
    '*Rodina-Mat' zovyet*' ('The Motherland Calls') 1, 25
'To Love Thy Neighbour as Thyself' 60
totalitarianism 6–7, 68
total war 105–10, 115, 140
Toulouse-Lautrec, Henri de 19–20
trade posters 20
Tramvai iskusstv 7
Treaty of Versailles 33, 95–6, 99
Tretyakov's Gallery, Moscow 62–3
Trotsky demon 157 n.79
Trotsky, Lev 12–13, 15–16, 22
Truman Doctrine 162 n.21
Trump, Donald J. 2

Uhlen 85
Ukraine 133
    collectivization in 53
    famine 14, 62

Uncle Sam poster 1, 3
'Under Lenin's Banner Go Forward toward the Destruction of the German-Fascist Aggressors!' 127
unemployment 38, 74
Union of Socialist Soviet Republics (USSR). *See* Soviet Union
Union of USSR Artists 61
'*Unsere letzte Hoffnung: Hitler*' ('Our Last Hope: Hitler') 40
US Army recruitment poster 3
US National Association of Manufacturers (NAM) 4
'The USSR Is the Shock Brigade of the Global Proletariat' 64

Vatolina, Nina Nikolaevicha 132
Verkerke, Engel 144 n.20
Verräter (Traitor) 109
Verschuer, Otmar von 92
Vierthaler, Hans 88
visual propaganda 4–5, 20, 42, 58, 72, 111, 141, 148 n.29
VKhUTEIN (Higher Artistic-Technological Institute) 56
VKhUTEMAS (Higher Artistic-Technological Workshop) 56
Volk 32, 76, 80, 87, 93, 107–9, 112
Völkischer Beobachter (*People's Observer*) 36
Volkova, Mariia Isaevna 53
Volksbrot (people's bread) 76
Volksempfänger (people's receiver) 85–6
Volksgemeinschaft (national community) 9, 33, 35, 71–3, 82, 99, 107, 115, 135–7
  Eintopf (one-pot dish) 76
  national unity and cult of Hitler 73–6
Volksgenossen (national comrades) 76, 81, 136
Volkssturm (people's army) 109–10, 114, 139
Volkswagen (people's car) 9, 72, 82–7, 137, 140

Vollkornbrot (whole-grain bread) campaign 75–6
Voroshilov, K. E. 61, 138, 156 n.55
Vrubel, Mikhail 21

Waffen-SS 98, 104
Wagner, Gerhard 75, 92
Wagner, Richard 82
Wählt Hitler ('Vote Hitler') 41
Wall Street Crash 38
war-guilt clause 96
wartime posters 53, 95, 127, 137, 139, 150 n.61
  anti-Semitic 110–14
  total war 105–10
'The Week of the Protection of Motherhood and Youth, of the Orphaned and Ill Child' 51
Wehrmacht 95, 100–1, 105, 107, 109, 112
  SA and SS 96–8
  Tag der Wehrmacht (Day of the Armed Forces) 96
Weimar Republic 33, 35, 38, 41, 44, 87, 92
Weltanschauung (worldview) 32
Whites 1, 127, 153 n.6
White Sea-Baltic Canal project 148 n.25
'Why Are You Not in the Army?' ('*Otchego vy ne v armii?*') 1
Wiertz, Jupp 82
Wilhelm, Kaiser 99
Windows on the War 7
Winterhilfswerk (*WHW*)/Winter Relief Agency 76, 79
'*Wir sind die Garanten der Zukunft*' ('We are the guarantors of the future') 79
Witte, Hermann 78
Wittig-Friesen, Hans 39
'Women of Britain Come into the Factories' 4
women, posters 54–5, 126, 132–3, 161 n.12
  in air raid protection 108
  as child carers 20, 52, 139

Women's Labour Service 109
working class 11–13, 39–40, 82
Works Progress Administration (WPA)
    Federal Art Project 4
Würbel, Franz Theodor 80

youth, German 72, 76–80, 137
    Gleichschaltung (co-ordination) 77

Zeitgeist 140
Zeppelinfeld 81

Zhdanov, Andrei 56, 68, 129, 138, 153 n.11, 155 n.48
    poster 124–5
Zhukov, Georgy 129
Zhukovsky, Vasily 134
Ziegler, Hans Severus 88–9
Zill, R. Gerhard 106
Zinoviev, Grigorii 16
'*Zug um Zug zerriß Adolf Hitler das Diktat von Versailles!*' ('Step by Step Adolf Hitler Tore Up the Treaty of Versailles!') 99